T0375644

EVERLASTING COVENANTS

Understanding the Bible by Examining God's Permanent
Relationships with Individuals and Groups

JAMES R. WARD

WESTBOW
PRESS®
A DIVISION OF THOMAS NELSON
& ZONDERVAN

WestBow Press books may be ordered through booksellers or by contacting:

WestBow Press
A Division of Thomas Nelson & Zondervan
1663 Liberty Drive
Bloomington, IN 47403
www.westbowpress.com
844-714-3454

All scripture passages are taken from the New International Version (NIV) except where otherwise indicated.

Scripture quotations marked NIV are taken from the Holy Bible, New International Version®, NIV®. Copyright © 1973, 1978, 1984 by Biblica, Inc.™ Used by permission of Zondervan. All rights reserved worldwide.

ISBN: 979-8-3850-0973-2 (sc)
ISBN: 979-8-3850-0974-9 (hc)
ISBN: 979-8-3850-0975-6 (e)

Library of Congress Control Number: 2023919271

Print information available on the last page.

WestBow Press rev. date: 3/20/2024

To my grandson, James Jesse Ward

From the very conception of this book, I knew that I would be dedicating this to him. He is the joy of our lives. I sincerely hope that he will one day understand what God has done for him and how much God loves him. It is also my hope that we, all his family, will prove to be good stewards in demonstrating that love to him. Maybe one day, as he grows in the grace and knowledge of our Lord Jesus Christ, this book might be of some benefit to him.

CONTENTS

Preface ix

Acknowledgments xi

Abbreviations of the Books of the Bible xiii

Glossary xv

The Covenant with Noah 1

The Covenant with Abraham 23

The Covenant with Israel: At Sinai 53

The Covenant with Israel: At Moab and Shechem 79

The Covenant with Israel's Royal Line 89

The Covenant with Israel's Priestly Line 119

The Covenant with Israel: In the Future 140

The Mediator of the Covenants 153

A Light for the Gentiles 191

Questions and Answers 221

Bibliography 245

Biblical and Extrabiblical Index 249

PREFACE

A covenant is a bond or agreement between individuals that defines the relationship between the involved parties and their responsibilities to each other. The agreement might be unconditional, in which the responsibilities of one or both parties remain intact regardless of the other party's fidelity. Or, if conditional or obligatory, one's responsibilities might change depending on the other's compliance with the terms of the agreement. The covenant could also be promissory, in that one party has simply committed themselves to an action relative to the other.

The study of God's covenants is one of the essential keys to unlocking scripture. It serves as a road map to help sojourning Bible students know where they are with respect to God's overall plan regardless of where they might have opened the scriptures in their quest to understand sacred history. For many people these days, the Bible is irrelevant. For others, it contains meaningful stories, poetry, prophecy, and directives that enlighten us and guide us back to our Creator. However, without a road map, we sometimes misinterpret the signs and directives along the way if we are unsure of exactly where we are on the journey.

Understanding God's everlasting covenants helps the Bible student to know what God is doing at a particular time in history and with whom he is interacting. Without such, it is easy to misapply or misinterpret God's statements, commands, or promises and rob ourselves of the plain and simple understanding of the text at hand. It can also cause us to take knowledge from later portions of scripture and read them back into earlier ones, ultimately skewing our interpretation of something that would otherwise be relatively simple.

This book will focus on the perpetuity of God's covenants. I have specifically referenced passages that contain the phrase "everlasting covenant" (ברית עולם—*brit olam*). Such a covenant is permanent. This simple understanding of the word עולם (*olam*—"everlasting") can have a profound effect on the way we understand scripture and the way we segregate the commands and promises of God with respect to his relationships with different covenant partners.

God is sovereign over all, and yet he has chosen to interact with us via promises and covenants in which he obligates not only us but also himself. It is intriguing that the Creator of heaven and earth would deal with the human race in such a manner. It is as though he is respecting the image of himself that he has placed within humanity, seeking not only his rightful place as Lord of all but also seeking to establish and maintain a relationship with those who embrace that image.

ACKNOWLEDGMENTS

I am very grateful for my wife, Anita, and my daughter, Camille, who were my primary assistants in editing this book. As in life in general, they helped to point out my habitual errors (in this case, the literary ones) and painstakingly verified as many of the footnotes as possible. I am especially grateful to Anita for understanding how important this work was to me and allowing me to spend some of "our" time to complete it.

Many thanks to my pastor, Dean Monkemeier, for reviewing the manuscript.

I will forever be grateful to Dr. Rabbi Bernard Grossfeld, who passed away in 2013. I had the privilege of sitting under his tutelage for over ten years. He led me and my fellow students through the translation of numerous books and selected passages of the Old Testament. He taught me to appreciate and utilize the great ancient Jewish literature. He forever changed the way I study Tanakh. May his memory be for a blessing. זכרונו לברכה

ABBREVIATIONS OF THE BOOKS OF THE BIBLE

OLD TESTAMENT BOOKS

Gen.—Genesis

Exod.—Exodus

Lev.—Leviticus

Num.—Numbers

Deut.—Deuteronomy

Josh.—Joshua

Judg.—Judges

Ruth—Ruth

1 Sam.—1 Samuel

2 Sam.—2 Samuel

1 Kings—1 Kings

2 Kings—2 Kings

1 Chron.—1 Chronicles

2 Chron.—2 Chronicles

Ezra—Ezra

Neh.—Nehemiah

Esther—Esther

Job—Job

Ps.—Psalms

Prov.—Proverbs

Eccles.—Ecclesiastes

Song of Sol.—Song of Solomon

Isa.—Isaiah

Jer.—Jeremiah

Lam.—Lamentations

Ezek.—Ezekiel

Dan.—Daniel

Hos.—Hosea

Joel—Joel

Amos—Amos

Obad.—Obadiah

Jon.—Jonah

Mic.—Micah

Nah.—Nahum

Hab.—Habakkuk

Zeph.—Zephaniah

Hag.—Haggai

Zech.—Zechariah

Mal.—Malachi

NEW TESTAMENT BOOKS

Matt.—Matthew

Mark—Mark

Luke—Luke

John—John

Acts—Acts

Rom.—Romans

1 Cor.—1 Corinthians

2 Cor.—2 Corinthians

Gal.—Galatians

Eph.—Ephesians

Phil.—Philippians

Col.—Colossians

1 Thess.—1 Thessalonians

2 Thess.—2 Thessalonians

1 Tim.—1 Timothy

2 Tim.—2 Timothy

Titus—Titus

Philem.—Philemon

Heb.—Hebrews

James—James

1 Pet.—1 Peter

2 Pet.—2 Peter

1 John—1 John

2 John—2 John

3 John—3 John

Jude—Jude

Rev.—Revelation

GLOSSARY

Abodah Zarah. A tractate of the Talmud, part of the Nezikin order, that addresses the topic of idolatry.

AM (Anno Mundi). A calendar era based on the number of years since creation.

Bava Kamma. The first of a series of three Talmudic tractates in the order Nezikin ("Damages") that deals with civil matters such as damages and torts.

BBE. The Bible in Basic English.

BCE. Before Common Era (comparable to BC).

CE. Common Era (comparable to AD).

Enoch (1 Enoch). The first of three ancient Hebrew apocalyptic religious texts, ascribed by tradition to Enoch, the great-grandfather of Noah.

Gemarah. The component of the Talmud comprising rabbinical analysis of and commentary on the Mishnah.

Genesis Rabbah. A midrash comprising a collection of ancient rabbinical homiletical interpretations of the Book of Genesis.

Jasher (Jash). A Hebrew Midrash covering the period between creation and the conquest of Canaan.

JPS. Jewish Publication Society.

Jubilees (Jub.). An ancient Jewish religious work covering the same period as the book of Genesis.

LXX. The Septuagint, a Greek translation of the Hebrew scriptures from the second and third centuries BCE.

Messianic Jews. Torah-observant Jews who believe Jesus/Yeshua to be the Messiah.

Mishnah. The first major written collection of the Jewish oral traditions that are known as the Oral Torah.

MSG. *The Message: The Bible in Contemporary Language.*

Nedarim (b. Ned.). Nedarim tractate of the Babylonian Talmud containing laws relating to vows and oaths.

NET. *New English Translation of the Bible.*

New Covenant. The renewed covenant between God and Israel/Judah specifically announced through the prophet Jeremiah.

New Testament. A collection of ancient religious Jewish writings recognized as inspired and authoritative by both Messianic Judaism and Christianity.

NIV. *New International Version of the Bible.*

NKJV. *New King James Version of the Bible.*

NLT. *New Living Translation of the Bible.*

NRSV. *New Revised Standard Version of the Bible.*

Old Testament. A collection of ancient religious Jewish writings sometimes classified as the Law, the Prophets, and the Writings recognized as inspired and authoritative by both Judaism and Christianity.

Talmud. The central text of Rabbinic Judaism and the primary source of Jewish religious law and theology.

Targum. An Aramaic translation of the Hebrew Bible.

Testament of the Twelve Patriarchs (T12P). A constituent of the apocryphal scriptures connected with the Bible. It is believed to be a pseudepigraphic work of the dying commands of the twelve sons of Jacob.

Tosefta. A compilation of the Jewish oral law from the late second century, acting as a supplement to the Mishnah.

ברית עולם לא תשכח

An everlasting covenant will not be forgotten (Jer. 50:5).

THE COVENANT WITH NOAH

God's covenant with Noah and his family is really a covenant with the entire world. At the time, there were only eight people on earth. However, God's intended recipients were Noah's family and all their future descendants, making the covenant transgenerational. It is an obligatory covenant. All parties involved have responsibilities. Since God initiated this covenant, his obligations equate to promises. The obligations for humanity are the commands that he has included.

The story is a familiar one to most Bible students. Based on a literal reading of the genealogies in Genesis chapter 5, the story begins a little over sixteen centuries after the creation story. God saw the wickedness on earth and was grieved that he had made man. God chose a righteous man, Noah, to preserve humanity. In Genesis chapter 6, God informed Noah about what he has planned, why he is doing it, and how Noah is to build an ark according to certain specifications. Immediately after informing Noah that "Everything on earth will perish,"[1] God said, "But I will establish my covenant [ברית] with you."[2] This is the first occurrence of the Hebrew word *brit* in the Bible. The story continues with the forty-day flood and their time on the ark, which lasted for over a year. The earth was completely dry by the twenty-seventh day of the second month.[3] According to the Book of Jubilees, the events described in Genesis 8:20–9:17 took place in the third month.[4]

---

[1] Genesis 6:17.
[2] Genesis 6:18.
[3] Genesis 8:14.
[4] Jubilees 6:1.

The text in Genesis chapter 9 reads very much like a legal document. The obligations of the party of the first part, Noah and his sons and the generations to follow, are listed in section 1 (verses 1–7). The obligations of the party of the second part, God, are listed in section 2 (verses 8–17).

The Details of the Covenant for Humanity

God began with the human obligations in this covenant. The specifics are listed in Genesis 9:1–7. His first and last statements in this section are reiterations of a previous command.

> Be fruitful and increase in number and fill the earth (Gen. 9:1).

> As for you, be fruitful and increase in number; multiply on the earth and increase upon it (Gen. 9:7).

This was first stated to Adam and Eve.[5] His second statement also reflects a previous command but now includes a modification.

> The fear and dread of you will fall upon all the beasts of the earth and all the birds of the air, upon every creature that moves along the ground, and upon all the fish of the sea; they are given into your hands. Everything that lives and moves will be food for you. Just as I gave you the green plant, I now give you everything. But you must not eat meat that has its lifeblood still in it (Gen. 9:2–4).

The previous command to Adam and Eve regarding food was that they could eat "every seed-bearing plant and every tree that has fruit with seed in it."[6] And then to all living creatures, he said, "I give every green plant for food."[7] Originally, God created humans to be vegetarian. At

---

[5] Genesis 1:28.
[6] Genesis 1:29.
[7] Genesis 1:30.

this point in history, such a diet was likely impractical. It would be a while before planting and harvesting would yield a new crop for them. The new protein in their diet, along with whatever remained from their stored rations on the ark, would sustain them until harvest time.

The addition of a new food item brings with it an additional restriction. Life must be respected, even animal life. So when using animals for food, one is required to ensure that it is dead. Nahum M. Sarna states:

> Partaking of the flesh of a living animal is prohibited. It must first be slaughtered. This prohibition is known in rabbinic parlance as *'ever min he-hai*, "a limb [cut off] from a living animal." ... This means that the flesh may not be eaten unless the life-blood has first been drained. These laws are incumbent on all humanity. In rabbinic theology they, together with those of the succeeding verses, form part of what are known as the "Noahide Laws."[8]

This prohibition is carried over to the Sinai Covenant, where God states, "For the life of a creature is in the blood."[9] Also, Sarna's comment about the Noahide Laws is noteworthy and will be discussed at length later.

God's third statement, not surprisingly, demonstrated his respect for human life and his willingness to enforce such respect on humans and animals alike. This statement (command) is so important that God uses a simple literary form to make it easier to remember. Chiastic structure is a literary form that is especially useful in oral traditions. The Bible has many examples of it. Essentially, if you can remember half of the passage or phrase, you can remember all of it. Words or phrases might be ordered, for example, in an ABCCBA format. Let's look at Genesis 9:6 (remember to read from right to left):

---

[8] Nahum M. Sarna, *The JPS Torah Commentary: Genesis* (Philadelphia: the Jewish Publication Society, 1989), 60–61.

[9] Leviticus 17:11, 17:14.

יִשָּׁפֵךְ	דָּמוֹ	בָּאָדָם	הָאָדָם	דַּם	שֹׁפֵךְ
will-be-shed	his-blood	by-man	(of) man	blood	the-one-who-sheds

Here is the Hebrew text with just the root words:

שׁפך	דמ	אדם	אדם	דם	שׁפך
(A)	(B)	(C)	(C)	(B)	(A)

The chiastic form is evident in both languages.

The simplicity of the text and the severity of the crime work together to convey a very simple message. God has instituted capital punishment for the crime of murder, and he does not want this order to be forgotten. He has not presented it as optional legislation; it is a divine decree. Later, in the Sinai covenant, God will say more about this subject. Specifically, he will address second-degree murder[10] and the punishment for animals that kill people.[11]

Before leaving this topic, it would be beneficial to use some deductive reasoning to understand the broader importance of this historic moment. God has essentially instituted a human government. He has given humanity the authority to exercise the ultimate penalty for the ultimate crime. It follows, then, that he has also given humanity authority over lessor crimes and the right to issue rulings with lessor penalties. After destroying a world that "was corrupt in God's sight and was full of violence,"[12] God was now including future generations to be part of the solution. It certainly will not eliminate evil from the world, but it will provide a means to remediate damages and hold evildoers accountable. No doubt, this event is what the apostle Paul had in mind when he said:

---

[10] Exodus 21:12–13; Numbers 35:9–28.
[11] Exodus 21:28–32.
[12] Genesis 6:11.

Everyone must submit himself to the governing authorities, for there is no authority except that which God has established. The authorities that exist have been established by God. Consequently, he who rebels against the authority is rebelling against what God has instituted, and those who do so will bring judgment upon themselves. For rulers hold no terror for those who do right, but for those who do wrong. Do you want to be free from fear of the one in authority? Then do what is right and he will commend you. For he is God's servant to do you good. But if you do wrong, be afraid, for he does not bear the sword for nothing. He is God's servant, an agent of wrath to bring punishment on the wrong doer. Therefore, it is necessary to submit to the authorities, not only because of possible punishment but also because of conscience (Rom. 13:1–5).

The Details of the Covenant for God

Humanity's obligations regarding this covenant (ברית—*brit*) have been officially documented. Now, God will state the details of his own covenantal obligations. These details are listed in Genesis 9:8–17. This section has three parts:

God states that he is "establishing" his covenant and the relevant details in verses 9–11.

God states that he is "setting/putting" the sign of the covenant and the relevant details in verses 12–16.

God states that his covenant is officially "established" in verse 17.

Part 1

> Then God blessed Noah and his sons, saying to them,
> "I now establish my covenant with you and your
> descendants after you and with every living creature
> that was with you—the birds, the livestock, and the
> wild animals, all those that came out of the ark with
> you—every living creature of the earth. I establish my
> covenant with you: Never again [לא ... עוד] will all life be
> cut off by the waters of a flood; never again [לא ... עוד]
> will there be a flood to destroy the earth" (Gen. 9:8–11,
> *Hebrew text added*).

The Hebrew verb for "establish" in verse 9 (קום—*qum*) is in participle
(-*ing*) form. It is preceded by a word denoting immediacy (הנה—*hinneh*),
often translated as "behold" in older English translations. Thus, a better
translation would be, "I am now establishing my covenant." It is as
though we are witnessing God giving testimony of his commitment in
real time. He lists the benefactors of his commitment, ultimately "every
living creature of the earth." He states what he is committing to do, or
more specifically, to "never again" do. The phrase in verse 11, "I establish
my covenant with you," should be translated in the future tense,[13] "I will
establish." It anticipates his final covenant ratification in verse 17.

Part 2

> And God said, "This is the sign of the covenant I am
> making with you and every living creature with you, a
> covenant for all generations to come [לדרת עולם]: I have
> set my rainbow in the clouds, and it will be the sign of
> the covenant between me and the earth" (Gen. 9:12–13,
> *Hebrew text added*).

---

[13] *Waw* consecutive perfect.

Our focus here is the sign of the covenant. A sign is a reminder of the special relationship between the parties of a covenant. For the Abrahamic Covenant, the sign was circumcision.[14] For the Israelites and the Sinai Covenant, the sign was the Sabbath.[15]

The phrase in verse 12, "This is the sign of the covenant I am making," is not quite accurate. It seems to imply that God is "making" a covenant. In reality, he is "putting/setting" the sign of his covenant in place. The Hebrew verb here, which is incorrectly translated as "making," is the same word found in verse 13 and is translated as "I have set." The Jewish Publication Society more accurately translates it as follows:

> "This is the sign that I set for the covenant between Me and you."[16]

This word for "set" in verse 12 (נתן—*natan*), like the word for "establish" (קום—*qum*) in verse 9, is a participle and could be translated as "I am setting." Consequently, it is as though we are witnessing God giving testimony of his action in real time.

God continued with an explanation of the sign's purpose.

> Whenever I bring clouds over the earth and the rainbow appears in the clouds, I will remember my covenant between me and you and all living creatures of every kind. Never again [לא ...עוד] will the waters become a flood to destroy all life. Whenever the rainbow is in the clouds, I will see it and remember the everlasting covenant [עולם ברית] between God and all living creatures of every kind on the earth" (Gen. 9:14–16, *Hebrew text added*).

---

14 Genesis 17:1–27.
15 Exodus 31:12–17; Ezekiel 20:12.
16 Sarna, *JPS Torah Commentary*, 62.

It is difficult to comprehend why God would need to provide a reminder for himself. Nonetheless, he twice states that when he sees it, he will remember his covenant. No doubt, it also will serve as a reminder to humanity that God has not forgotten his covenant. It is important to note that God uses the phrase "never again" (לא... עוד) three times, twice in verse 11 and once in verse 15. This helps to reinforce our understanding of the key phrase in verse 16, "everlasting covenant" (ברית עולם—*brit olam*). God will never again flood the earth because this covenant is everlasting. Likewise, the requirements for humanity in verses 1–7 are also part of the "everlasting covenant" (ברית עולם—*brit olam*). It will not be superseded by future covenants or dispensations. It is permanent and remains in force to this day.

Part 3

> So God said to Noah, "This is the sign of the covenant
> that I have established between me and all life on the
> earth" (Gen. 9:17).

In verse 9, the word "establish" (קום—*qum*) is in participle (-*ing*) form. The suggested translation therefore was, "I am now establishing my covenant." Here, the verb is in the perfect tense, denoting completed action—"I have established"—referring to the covenant. God is no longer stating the terms of the covenant, what he is doing, or man's responsibilities. It is done. The covenant is established. This verse essentially represents God's signature on the dotted line.

The Ratification of the Covenant

As covenants are written and the responsibilities are delineated, the parties involved must ratify the final form of the agreement. In Holy Scripture, this is often done with a ceremony.

The Sinai Covenant was offered to Israel in the third month of the year they left Egypt.[17] The elders were summoned, and Moses presented God's offer to them. They agreed "to do everything the LORD has said."[18] First, they received the Ten Commandments audibly. Then Moses returned to the mountain for the details of the covenant. He presented those details to the people upon returning. The people ratified the covenant by responding with one voice, "Everything the LORD has said we will do,"[19] and by offering burnt and fellowship offerings. Normally, all the blood of a sacrifice would be sprinkled on the altar. However, on this occasion, half was sprinkled on the altar and half was sprinkled on the people.[20] [21] This distinction likely represented the binding responsibilities of each party in the covenant. The people then reiterated their commitment by stating, "We will do everything the LORD has said; we will obey."[22] These offerings are part of the ceremony that finalized the covenant between God and Israel.

Later, in the book of Deuteronomy, the generation that survived forty years in the wilderness found themselves in a similar situation. Before crossing the Jordan River to begin the conquest of the promised land, they needed to ratify the covenant again. The terms of the covenant included the ordinances and judgments recorded by Moses in Deuteronomy chapters 12–26 and everything decreed previously on Mount Sinai.[23] Although there was an admonition, possibly a ceremony, by Moses to ratify the covenant[24] and an actual record of that commitment by both parties,[25] there is no record of a ceremony involving sacrifices. However, in Deuteronomy 27, Moses gave specific instructions about

---

[17] Exodus 19:1-6.

[18] Exodus 19:7–8.

[19] Exodus 24:3.

[20] Exodus 24:4–6.

[21] Most likely, the blood that was sprinkled on the people was sprinkled on the twelve stone pillars that Moses had erected to represent the people.

[22] Exodus 24:7.

[23] Deuteronomy 29:1.

[24] Deuteronomy 29:2-15.

[25] Deuteronomy 26:16–19.

the covenant renewal that was to take place after they crossed the Jordan. The ceremony included both burnt offerings and fellowship offerings.[26]

Considering these later examples, we can make similar observations regarding the Noahic Covenant. The end of Genesis 8 depicts such a ceremony.

> Then Noah built an altar to the LORD and, taking some of all the clean animals and clean birds, he sacrificed burnt offerings on it. The LORD smelled the pleasing aroma and said in his heart: "Never again will I curse the ground because of man, even though every inclination of his heart is evil from childhood. And never again will I destroy all living creatures, as I have done. As long as the earth endures, seedtime and harvest, cold and heat, summer and winter, day and night will never cease" (Gen. 8:20–22).

At first, this might appear simply as an offering of dedication (the primary purpose of a burnt offering), especially after the long ordeal of the flood. However, what God said "in his heart" indicates that it was not spoken at this ceremony but was reminiscent of the time he stated it forthright in chapter 9. The pleasing aroma reminded him of the obligation he placed on himself. Thus, God's response indicates that the offering ceremony is related to the covenant. This observation helps us to better understand the chronology of these events. At some point, probably after Noah obeyed God's command to leave the ark,[27] God presented him the terms of the covenant—both his and humanity's obligations as they are listed in Genesis 9:1–17. The offerings in Genesis 8:20 are part of the covenant ratification ceremony. Just as God was reminded at that time of his part of the agreement, no doubt Noah and his family were reminded of their part of the agreement. The eight people involved in this covenant represented not only a family but the entire population of the earth at that time. In the story of the Garden of

---

[26] Deuteronomy 27:6–7; Joshua 8:30–31.
[27] Genesis 8:15–19.

Eden, the decision of two people affected the generations that followed them. Likewise, the decision of eight people regarding their covenant relationship with God is binding upon their descendants. God called it "the everlasting covenant (עולם ברית—*brit olam*)."[28] It is binding, it is permanent, and it is still in effect.

The Noahide Laws

We discussed humanity's obligations as they are listed in Genesis 9:1–7. I mentioned that God was essentially instituting a human government. He gave humanity the authority to exercise the ultimate penalty for the ultimate crime. It seems reasonable to assume that he had also given humanity authority over lessor crimes and the right to issue rulings with lessor penalties. The Noahide Laws, as they are known in Judaism, include those other crimes and, in doing so, help to bring clarity to the Scriptures, including the New Testament.

Christendom has frequently been at a disadvantage because it has not always aligned itself with ancient Jewish literature. Two examples of such documents are Genesis Rabbah and the Tosefta. These documents demonstrate an early understanding of all the laws God gave to Noah, an understanding that was contemporary with, and even predated, the early Church. Genesis Rabbah is Midrashic literature that provides an interpretation of the biblical texts. Regarding these Noahide Laws, it states:

> The children of Noah were enjoined concerning seven things: Idolatry, incest, murder, cursing the Divine Name [blasphemy], civil law, and a limb torn from a living animal.[29]

---

[28] Genesis 9:16

[29] *Midrash Rabbah Volume I.* Translated by Rabbi Dr. H. Freedman and Maurice Simon (London: the Soncino Press, 1961), 272.

This document was probably written between 300 CE and 500 CE,[30] but it reflects a long-held tradition. You might have noticed that this list contains only six items. Various rabbinic opinions follow the above citation and provide a possible seventh law.

The Tosefta, a supplement to the Mishnah (the oral law), is much older than Genesis Rabbah. Both the Tosefta and Mishnah were compiled in written form by the second century CE.[31] However, as an oral tradition first, their origins are centuries older. Regarding the Noahide Laws, the Tosefta states in Abodah Zarah 8:4:

> Concerning seven religious requirements were the children of Noah admonished: setting up courts of justice, idolatry, blasphemy [cursing the name of God], fornication, bloodshed, and thievery.[32]

Again, this list contains six laws. Abodah Zarah 8:6 adds a seventh law regarding the act of cutting a limb from a living animal, reminiscent of the command in Genesis 9:4.

Finally, much later in the Gemara portion of Talmud, it states in Sanhedrin 56a:

> Our Rabbis taught: seven precepts were the sons of Noah commanded: social laws; to refrain from blasphemy, idolatry; adultery; bloodshed; robbery; and eating flesh cut from a living animal.[33]

In each case, the references to "civil law," "setting up courts of justice," and "social laws" relate to the responsibility of the Gentile nations to set up judicial systems that respect the other six laws.

---

[30] Wikipedia, s.v. "Genesis Rabbah," https://en.wikipedia.org/wiki/Genesis_Rabbah.

[31] Wikipedia, s.v. "Tosefta," https://en.wikipedia.org/wiki/Tosefta.

[32] *The Tosefta Volume II.* Translated by Jacob Neusner (Peabody: Hendrickson Publishers, 2002), 1291–1292.

[33] Tzvee Zahavy, *Halakhah.com* (based on the classic Soncino translation), https://www.halakhah.com.

There is one mention of these laws in modern times that might be of interest to Americans. Although it might be only a political statement, George W. Bush signed Proclamation 5956, which in part, states:

> Ethical values are the foundation for civilized society. A society that fails to recognize or adhere to them cannot endure.

The principles of moral and ethical conduct that have formed the basis for all civilizations come to us, in part, from the centuries-old Seven Noahide Laws. The Noahide Laws are actually seven commandments given to man by God, as recorded in the Old Testament. These commandments include prohibitions against murder, robbery, adultery, blasphemy, and greed, as well as the positive order to establish courts of justice.

Through the leadership of Rabbi Menachem Schneerson and the worldwide Lubavitch movement, the Noahide Laws—and standards of conduct duly derived from them—have been promulgated around the globe.[34]

The Jerusalem Council

The early church was Jewish. Its center of operation was in Jerusalem, and its reputed leaders were James, Peter, and John.[35] Various Jewish missionaries had already begun presenting the Messiah Jesus to the Gentiles, of whom Paul is the most well-known. Around 50 CE, after the apostle Paul's first missionary journey, the early church was forced to address a developing issue. As Gentiles began turning to Jesus, there arose a disagreement regarding their responsibilities and rules for conduct.

---

[34] Proclamation 5956—Education Day, USA, 1989 and 1990, The American Presidency Project, https://www.presidency.ucsb.edu/documents/proclamation-5956-education-day-usa-1989-and-1990.
[35] Galatians 2:9.

The point of disagreement was first stated in Antioch by some believers who had arrived from Judea.

> Unless you are circumcised, according to the custom taught by Moses, you cannot be saved (Acts 15:1).

This view goes so far as to tie the act of circumcision to one's salvation. The issue had to be settled so that there would be consistency among those bringing the Good News to the Gentiles. The council meeting took place in Jerusalem. Paul and Barnabas were appointed by their synagogue in Antioch to attend.[36] During the meeting, some Pharisees[37] stated:

> The Gentiles must be circumcised and required to obey the law of Moses (Acts 15:5).

This view seems to focus more on the issue at hand. Now that many of the Gentiles believed in the Jewish Messiah, how were they to conduct themselves going forward? When we examine both parts of the Pharisees' statement, it becomes clear that they were proposing more than just a circumcision requirement. To be circumcised means to place oneself physically under the Abrahamic Covenant.[38] Obeying the law of Moses means to place oneself under the Sinai Covenant. Ultimately, they were saying that the Gentile believers must convert to Judaism.

> Again, I declare to every man who lets himself be circumcised that he is obligated to obey the whole law (Gal. 5:3).

So, then, are the Gentile believers required to convert?

---

[36] Acts 15:2.

[37] Pharisees are often viewed critically by Christians. It should be noted that the presence of these Pharisees at the council indicates that they were Messianic, Jewish believers in Jesus. Paul was a Pharisee (Phil. 3:5).

[38] Paul addresses this issue as it applies to Gentile believers in Romans 4.

Unfortunately, Luke did not include the minutes from this meeting when he wrote the book of Acts. We are told only that there was much discussion.[39] At some point, Peter testified to the group about his encounter at the house of a God-fearing Gentile, a Roman centurion named Cornelius. The entire story is found in Acts 10:1–11:18. In the end, the Holy Spirit came upon this group of Gentiles. It left a lasting impression on Peter regarding God's acceptance of non-Jewish believers. To the council, he said:

> Brothers, you know that some time ago God made a choice among you that the Gentiles might hear from my lips the message of the gospel and believe. God, who knows the heart showed that he accepted them by giving the Holy Spirit to them, just as he did to us. He made no distinction between us and them, for he purified their hearts by faith. Now then, why do you try to test God by putting on the necks of the disciples a yoke[40] that neither we nor our fathers have been able to bear? No! We believe that it is through the grace of our Lord Jesus that we are saved, just as they are (Acts 15:7–11).

Later, Paul and Barnabas provided evidence of God's acceptance of the Gentile believers: they testified about the miracles and wonders he performed through them during their journeys.

Finally, James, the half brother of Jesus and leader of the council, quoted one of the many examples from the prophets who speak about the inclusion of Gentiles among the faithful.[41] Afterward, he rendered his decision on the matter. First, he states, "It is my judgement, therefore, that we should not make it difficult for the Gentiles who are turning to God."[42] Then he continues with a grammatical disjunctive. He no doubt

---

[39] Acts 15:7.

[40] This "yoke" is not to be understood as a burden but as a guide, and a difficult one at that. He is referring to Torah and the Sinai Covenant.

[41] Acts 15:16–18; Amos 9:11–12.

[42] Acts 15:19.

addressed the council in Hebrew or Aramaic, but Luke records it in Greek and uses the word αλλα (but, rather, instead). In other words, we will *not* require Gentile believers to be circumcised and obey the law of Moses (they are not participants in the Sinai Covenant), *but rather*, we will write to them and tell them to follow these rules:

> Abstain from food polluted by idols, from sexual immorality, from the meat of strangled animals and from blood (Acts 15:20).

At first, this short list of rules may appear confusing. Why these? From where did James, or the council, acquire them? We might be tempted to simply continue reading and not attempt to answer these questions. However, our earlier discussion about the Noahide Laws might lead us to the answers. Do you remember the list from Talmud?

> Social laws; to refrain from blasphemy, idolatry; adultery; bloodshed; robbery; and eating flesh cut from a living animal.[43]

Obviously, there is no one-for-one correlation between this list and the one given by James. Let's examine them both and see where there is agreement.

Noahide Laws	Jerusalem Council Laws
Social laws	—
Blasphemy	—
Idolatry	Abstain from food polluted by idols
Adultery	Sexual immorality
Bloodshed	Blood
Robbery	—
Eating flesh cut from a living animal	Meat of strangled animals

---

[43] Tzvee Zahavy, Halakhah.com (based on the classic Soncino translation), https://www.halakhah.com.

Unmatched items

Social laws. Talmud Sanhedrin 56b seems to indicate that the rabbis understood that this was not a directive from God to Noah. They recognized this law by way of reasoning. The Noahide Laws are directed at all humankind. Therefore, the governments of the world are obliged to enforce them just as Israel was instructed to set up courts to litigate the laws God gave to them. It may have been omitted from the council's list because their intended audience were individual believers and not their respective governments.[44]

Blasphemy. It is difficult to explain why this prohibition was excluded. However, it may be fair to assume a general cognizance of such a prohibition. Now that the Gentiles were turning to the one true God, it would seem reasonable that they would know not to speak irreverently about him.

Robbery/theft. The omission of this item is most difficult to explain.

Matched items

Idolatry. The admonition to abstain from food polluted by idols addressed a form of idolatry applicable to the first century. As in ancient Judaism, pagan religions also offered animal sacrifices, which were consumed by their priests and temple guests. If believers in Jesus were to participate in such an event, even in ignorance, it would appear that they participated in the worship of the particular deity. The prohibition of the council is simply addressing a contemporary example of the broader category of idolatry. The apostle Paul addresses the nuances of this restriction in 1 Corinthians 8:1–13 and 10:14–33.

Adultery. The council's restriction uses the broader term of "sexual immorality," of which adultery is the worst violation. This is the reason

---

[44] The first recipients of the council's written decision were "the Gentile believers in Antioch, Syria and Cilicia" (Acts 15:23).

it is specifically addressed in the Ten Commandments and is considered a capital offense.

Bloodshed. The council uses the term "blood." Both terms refer to murder.[45]

Eating flesh cut from a living animal. This also appears to be a contemporary application of the Noahide law. The original command given to Noah (Gen. 9:4) was in conjunction with the new directive about eating meat. Its purpose was to avoid animal cruelty, specifically the eating of a live animal. One can deduce from the council's prohibition that, for whatever reason, strangling an animal instead of slaughtering it was a common practice. Since the animal certainly suffered during this process, it violated the spirit of the Noahide law.

To summarize, the line-by-line comparison of the Noahide laws and the decision of the Jerusalem Council are not conclusive. However, the similarities are undeniable. We must remember that the traditional Jewish understanding of the Noahide laws predates the first century. The council was called to order only because there was an alternate opinion developing and the issue needed to be settled to maintain a consistent message. The council's decision brought clarity by reaffirming the long-held view that the Gentiles were obligated to obey only the Noahide laws. The accuracy of their decision is obvious to those who remember that the Noahide laws are part of the Noahic Covenant, which is an everlasting covenant (ברית עולם—*brit olam*).[46]

---

[45] The first occurrence of the word "bloodshed" is in Genesis 4:10–11. The Hebrew word is דמים (*damim*), the plural form of דם (*dam*), and it literally means "bloods." The rabbis of the Talmud noticed this and argued that "for in the case of Cain, who killed his brother, that it is written: The bloods of thy brother cry unto me ... his blood and the blood of his [potential] descendants," (Sanhedrin 4:5). The singular form "blood," דם (*dam*), is also used to refer to murder. In Numbers 35:27, the phrase "without being guilty of murder" is אין לו דם (*ein lo dam*), or literally, "there is not to him blood."

[46] Genesis 9:16.

A Final Observation

The casual Bible reader often overlooks the significance of the post-flood events that happened on Mount Ararat. For many, the most important points of interest are how God saved Noah and his family and why there is a rainbow after a storm. A few concern themselves with the meaning of a covenant, the stated commandments, the related Jewish traditional understanding, or even the institution of a human government. Sometimes if we compare the events from one story with those from another, one we consider very significant, it helps us to appreciate the importance of both. Consider the following areas of comparison:

	Flood Story	Exodus Story
Mountain	Ararat	Sinai
Month	Third	Third
Covenant	Noahic	Mosaic/Sinaitic
Covenant Ceremony	Gen. 8:20	Exod. 24:3–8
Laws	2 (Gen.) 7 (Jewish tradition)	10 (initially) 613 (total)
Survivors	8	2 million (600,000 men)
תבה	Ark	Basket

Mountain

Twice in human history, God dispensed his laws and established a covenant from a mountain.[47]

Month

According to the biblical narrative, the earth was completely dry on the twenty-seventh day of the second month.[48] At that time, or shortly after, God issued the order to disembark. Noah and his family and all the animals departed from the ark. We demonstrated earlier that the details

---

[47] Also, the final confirmation of the Abrahamic Covenant happened on a mountain in the area of Moriah (Gen. 22:2, 15–18).

[48] Genesis 8:14.

of the Noahic Covenant found in Genesis 9 were probably expressed before the covenant ratification ceremony in Genesis 8:20–22. Also, for that ceremony, Noah took the time to build an altar. It is conceivable that all of this could have easily taken more than three days putting the ceremony well into the third month. The book of Jubilees puts all these events in the following month.

> And on the new moon of the third month, he went forth from the ark, and built an altar on that mountain.[49]

Regarding the timing of the Sinai Covenant:

> In the third month after Israel left Egypt—on the very day—they came to the desert of Sinai (Exod. 19:1).

Jubilees 6:11 seems to indicate that the timing of the Sinai Covenant was intended to match that of the Noahic Covenant. Jubilees 6:18 states that Noah celebrated this day every year until his death. Thus, Noah commemorated the giving of the Noahic Covenant and related laws in much the same way that the Jewish people have celebrated Shavuoth (Feast of Weeks, Pentecost) in the third month of every year to commemorate the giving of the Sinai Covenant and the Torah.

Covenant

Both the flood story and the Exodus story end with their respective covenants. Both covenants are obligatory, containing the responsibilities of both parties. Both covenants are transgenerational. Noah was told that the covenant was "with you and all of your descendants"[50] and "a covenant for all generations to come."[51] During the covenant ratification ceremony on the Plains of Moab, Moses (speaking for the Lord) told the surviving generation of Israelites,

---

[49] R. H. Charles, *The Apocrypha and Pseudepigrapha of the Old Testament* (Oxford: Clarendon Press, 1913), Jubilees 6:1.

[50] Genesis 9:8.

[51] Genesis 9:12.

I am making this covenant, with its oath, not only with you who are standing here with us today in the presence of the LORD our God but also with those who are not here today (Deut. 29:14).

Covenant Ceremony

This was discussed previously in the section called "The Ratification of the Covenant." The Noahic Covenant ceremony is briefly mentioned in Genesis 8:20–22. The Sinai Covenant ceremony is found in Exodus 24:3–8. There is another ceremony on the Plains of Moab prior to the conquest of Canaan in Deuteronomy 29 and 30 and another after entering Canaan in Joshua 8:30–35.

Laws

The Noahide laws were discussed earlier. Two are listed in Genesis 9:1–7. Jewish tradition recognizes six, with a seventh being implied. These are most likely the source of the laws recognized by the Jerusalem Council as being applicable to Gentile believers. The laws of the Sinai Covenant are expressed throughout the books of Exodus, Leviticus, Numbers, and Deuteronomy.

Survivors

This comparison is often overlooked. In the flood story, eight people survived a worldwide cataclysm. In the Exodus story, about 2 million (600,000 men) survived a four-hundred-year ordeal that began with their ancestor wandering in a country not his own and their ultimate enslavement.[52]

---

[52] Genesis 15:13.

תבה

As odd as it may seem, the only place the Hebrew word תבה (*tebah*) is found in the whole Bible is in these two stories. It occurs twenty-three times in Genesis 6–9 and twice in Exodus 2. In the flood story, it is translated as "ark." In the Exodus story, it is translated as "basket." In both stories, the תבה (*tebah*) is a flotation device that carries people. It is interesting that the lead characters in both stories were in life-threatening situations. Noah was facing a worldwide flood. Moses was facing the decree from Pharaoh that all newborn boys were to be thrown into the Nile. Without divine intervention, both would have died from drowning. Ultimately, both survived their ordeals by being carried away in a תבה (*tebah*).

The final observation: In both the flood story and the Exodus story, the main character is used by God to rescue a group of people. He brings the survivors to a mountain and, in the third month, mediates a transgenerational covenant between them and God. The covenant comes with a set of laws. It concludes with a covenant ratification ceremony that involves animal sacrifices. None of this could have been possible had not the main character been saved from a watery death by way of a תבה (*tebah*).

Hopefully, this comparison helps to illuminate the importance of the everlasting covenant (ברית עולם—*brit olam*) made on Mount Ararat so long ago.

THE COVENANT
WITH ABRAHAM

Genesis presents the Abrahamic Covenant in multiple stages. It begins with a promise and then continues with a covenantal ceremony, a sign, and an oath. After Abraham's death, it was ratified by his son Isaac and his grandson Jacob. Commentators often begin their exposition of the Abrahamic Covenant with the Abrahamic promise found in Genesis 12. However, we must understand the historical context of God's interactions with Abraham. To do that, we must examine three historical events: the allotment of the nations, the judgment of the nations, and the divine appointments over the nations.

The Allotment of the Nations

Moses records an interesting note in the genealogy of Shem.

> Two sons were born to Eber:
>
> One was named Peleg, because in his time the earth was divided (Gen. 10:25).

The phrase "the earth was divided" refers to the time when the sons of Noah allotted various portions of the earth as inheritance for their descendants. With a divine representative in attendance to sanction the agreement, the brothers drew lots to determine which third of the earth they would receive. The entire story is found in the eighth and ninth chapters of the book of Jubilees. It begins as follows:

> And it came to pass in the beginning of the thirty-third jubilee then they divided the earth into three parts, for Shem and Ham and Japheth, according to the inheritance of each, in the first year of the first week when one of us who had been sent[53] was with them. And he called his sons, and they drew nigh to him, they and their children, and he divided the earth into the lots, which his three sons were to take in possession, and they reached forth their hands, and took the writing out of the bosom of Noah, their father.[54]

> And there came forth on the writing as Shem's lot the middle of the earth which he should take as an inheritance for himself and for his sons for the generations of eternity.[55]

Jubilees goes on to describe the allotments of Ham and Japheth using somewhat familiar landmarks and place-names. Ultimately, Shem received the center third of the earth, Ham received the southern third, and Japheth the northern third. Later, in Jubilees chapter 9, Noah's sons allot portions of their inheritance to their sons.[56]

All of this took place under the angelic supervision of "one of us who had been sent."

This event might sound very familiar to Bible students. In Numbers 34, God defines the boundaries of the promised land. He also instructs Moses

---

[53] The book of Jubilees claims to be information given to Moses by an angel. The phrase "one of us who had been sent" refers to one of the angels who had been sent to assist Noah and his sons after the flood.

[54] Charles, *Apocrypha and Pseudepigrapha of the Old Testament*, Jubilees 8:10–11.

[55] Charles, Jubilees 8:12.

[56] It is interesting that after the Tower of Babel dispersion (in the thirty-fourth jubilee), everyone went to their allotted inheritances except Canaan. His allotment was in northwest Africa (Jub. 9:1). However, he settled in the land from Lebanon to the river of Egypt (Jub. 10:29), which belonged to Shem. "For this reason, that land is named Canaan" (Jub. 10:34).

to tell Joshua and Eleazar to "assign this land by lot as an inheritance" and to appoint "one leader from each tribe to help assign the land." All of this was accomplished after the conquest and is documented in Joshua 13–21. In much the same way, Ham, Shem, and Japheth received their inheritance by lot and, as the leaders of their family groups, divided the earth for their descendants.

The Judgment of the Nations

According to the book of Jubilees, seventy-six years[57] after the earth was divided, the world's population rose in rebellion against God. They said to each other:

> "Come, let's make bricks and bake them thoroughly."
> They used brick instead of stone, and tar for mortar.
> Then they said, "Come, let us build ourselves a city, with
> a tower that reaches to the heavens, so that we may make
> a name for ourselves and not be scattered over the earth"
> (Gen. 11:3–4).

Unfortunately, the brevity of the biblical narrative can sometimes obscure the magnitude of such a major event. This was much more than a community development project. In these two verses, there are two major acts of rebellion. The first one was the building project itself and its choice of technology, "brick instead of stone, and tar for mortar." This was nothing short of a complete dismissal of the Noahic Covenant, specifically, God's promise to never again destroy the earth with a flood. They were essentially making plans to protect themselves from God's judgment should he ever effect such an event again.[58] The second act of

---

[57] The earth was divided by Noah's sons in the 1,569th year after creation. Seventy-six years later, the building of the city and the tower on the plain in Shinar began and lasted forty-three years. The confusion of the languages and dispersion took place in the 1688th year (Jub. 8:10, 10:21, 10:27).

[58] This was evidently part of the building efforts of Nimrod (Gen. 10:8–10). After his work ended abruptly in Shinar (Gen. 10:10–11, 11:2, 11:8), he continued building in Assyria. Flavius Josephus (37–c.100 CE) claims that Nimrod said, "He

rebellion is the blatant refusal to follow God's directive to replenish the earth.[59] Instead, they sought self-aggrandizement, to "make a name for ourselves," and to urbanize and "not be scattered over the earth."[60]

The earthly consequence of this rebellion is clear from the text. The LORD came down to see the city and the tower.[61] It appears that he was making a visual confirmation of what had been reported to him. At first, this idea might be difficult for some Bible students, especially with respect to their understanding of divine omniscience. However, the angels[62] of God perform reconnaissance work[63] and routinely present themselves before the LORD.[64] This concept is evident later when the LORD is speaking to Abraham about the cities of Sodom and Gomorrah.

> The outcry against Sodom and Gomorrah is so great and their sin so grievous that I will go down and see if what they have done is as bad as the outcry that has reached me. If not, I will know (Gen. 18:20–21).

---

would be revenged on God, if he should have a mind to drown the world again: for that he would build a tower too high for the waters to be able to reach! And that he would avenge himself on God for destroying their forefathers!". Josephus goes on to say, "It was built of burnt brick cemented together with mortar, made of bitumen, that it might not be liable to admit water." See Ant. book 1 chapter 4 in *The Works of Josephus*, (Peabody: Hendrickson Publishers, 1988), 35.

[59] Genesis 9:1, 9:7.

[60] Josephus suggests that they questioned God's motives regarding his directive. "God admonished them to send out colonies: but they, imagining the prosperity they enjoyed was not derived from the favor of God, but supposing that their own power was the proper cause of the plentiful condition they were in, did not obey him. Nay, they added to this their disobedience to the divine will, the suspicion that they were therefore ordered to send out separate colonies, that, being divided asunder, they might be oppressed." See *Works of Josephus*, 35.

[61] Genesis 11:5.

[62] The word "angel" comes from the Hebrew word מלאך (*malakh*) and simply means "messenger." Interestingly, the Bible translators seem to prefer "angel" or "messenger," depending on who sent them. The same word is translated both ways in proximate verses (Gen. 32:1, 32:3).

[63] In 1 Enoch, angels are called "watchers." In the Bible, they are sometimes called "the eyes of the LORD" (2 Chron. 16:9; Prov. 15:3; Zech. 4:10; Rev. 4:5, 5:6).

[64] Job 1:6, 2:1.

Then the LORD caused the work to stop and forced them to scatter over the face of the earth by confusing their languages. Now they could interact only with their respective family groups (based on Genesis 10, there were seventy in total). Previously, there had been only one language used by everyone.[65]

The heavenly consequence for this worldwide rebellion, which follows, is not mentioned in Genesis 11. We must consult other passages of scripture for details, of which there are not many. However, the information is consistent and helps to provide a backdrop for the Abrahamic Covenant.

The Divine Appointments over the Nations

Deuteronomy 32 is known as the Song of Moses. It was given to him by God for a specific purpose, "to teach it to the Israelites … that it may be a witness for me against them."[66] In it, God speaks of their future rebelliousness and his continued commitment to them. However, there is a section of it that is relevant to our topic.

> Remember the days of old;
> consider the generations long past.
> Ask your father and he will tell you,
> your elders, and they will explain to you.
> When the Most High gave the nations their inheritance,
> when he divided all mankind,
> he set up boundaries for the peoples
> according to the number of the sons of Israel.
> For the LORD's portion is his people,
> Jacob his allotted inheritance (Deut. 32:7–9).

Considering what has already been explained in the previous section, "The Allotment of the Nations," the phrases "gave the nations their inheritance," "divided all mankind," and "set up boundaries for the

---

[65] Genesis 11:1.
[66] Deuteronomy 31:19–22.

people" refer to the time when Noah's sons divided the earth among their descendants, overseen by a heaven-sent messenger/witness. What the verse above says about Israel and Jacob in the final stanzas must be examined. The Israelite people were not one of the seventy nations that received an inheritance, for they simply did not exist yet. Their creation and inheritance will be addressed in the Abraham story. And so, the phrase, "according to the number of the sons of Israel," is awkward. We need to consult other ancient biblical manuscripts in order to understand that there are variant readings.

The phrase "the sons of Israel" (בני ישראל—*bnei yisra'el*) is from the Masoretic text. However, a fragment from the Dead Sea Scrolls text says, "the sons of God." Also, the Septuagint, which is translated from Hebrew manuscripts older than the Masoretic text says, "the angels of God" or "the sons of God," depending on the manuscript.[67] One other Greek text and a Latin text says, "the sons of God." Most likely, the original reading was "the sons of God" (בני אלהים—*bnei elohim*).[68]

If "the LORD's portion is his people, Jacob his allotted inheritance," it implies that the other nations are not (or are no longer) his portion nor his allotted inheritance. His relationship with Jacob, the Israelites, as stated in Deuteronomy 32:9, implies a disassociation from the other nations. The rebellion on the plain of Shinar, with the building of the city and Tower of Babel, was a rejection of God himself. The judgment of God via the confusion of languages was God's rejection of them. Dividing the nations according to the number of the sons of God is understood by many to mean that, as a heavenly consequence, God delegated the oversight of the rebellious nations to subordinate heavenly beings.[69] We must remember

---

[67] See footnote 2 in Excursus 31 in Jeffery H. Tigay, *The JPS Torah Commentary: Deuteronomy* (Philadelphia: the Jewish Publication Society, 1996), 546.

[68] For a more detailed explanation, see Tigay, 513–515. Also, the same term is used in Genesis 6:2 and Job 1:6, 2:1.

[69] Rambam (c.1176–c.1178), in his Mishneh Torah, lists ten classifications of heavenly beings: חיות הקדש (*hayoth hakodesh*), אופנים (*ophanim*), אראלים (*erelim*), חשמלים (*hashmalim*), שרפים (*seraphim*), מלאכים (*malachim*), אלהים (*elohim*), בני אלהים (*bene elohim*), כרובים (*cherubim*), and אישים (*ishim*). See Foundations of the Torah 2:7 in The Sefaria Library, https://www.sefaria.org/

that the everlasting covenant (עולם ברית—*brit olam*) he made with Noah and his family[70] was still in effect. His faithfulness to the covenant restricted him from destroying the world again. And so the nations would now be governed indirectly by God via delegated heavenly overseers.[71] In a very real sense, the nations would now be in exile from God.

Michael Heiser's comments on this subject provide a good segue for our next topic.

> Deuteronomy 32:8–9 describes how Yahweh's dispersal of the nations at Babel resulted in his *disinheriting* those nations as his people. This is the Old Testament equivalent of Romans 1:18–25, a familiar passage wherein God "gave [humankind] over" to their persistent rebellion. The statement in Deuteronomy 32:9 that "the LORD's [i.e., Yahweh's] portion is his people, Jacob his allotted heritage" tips us off that a contrast in affection and ownership is intended. Yahweh in effect decided that the people of the world's nations were no longer going to be in relationship to him. He would begin anew. He would enter into covenant relationship with a new people that did not yet exist: Israel. The implications of this decision and this passage are crucial to understanding much of what's in the Old Testament.[72]

Mishneh_Torah,_Foundations_of_the_TorMishneh_Torah,_Foundations_of_the_Torah?tab=contents. The apostle Paul suggests a divine hierarchy using terms such as "rule," "authority," "power," and "dominion" referring to the "heavenly realm" (Eph. 1:21, 6:12; 1 Cor. 15:24; Col. 2:10).

[70] Genesis 9:16.

[71] This understanding helps us to interpret Psalm 82. In verse 1, God stands in the divine assembly and judges the "gods" (אלהים—*elohim*). In verse 6, he calls them "gods" (אלהים—*elohim*) and "sons of the Most High" (עליון בני—*bnei elyon*). He chastises them for defending the unjust and showing partiality (v. 2) and admonishes them to defend the weak and maintain the rights of the poor (vv. 3–4). Although he has delegated his authority to them to rule over the nations, he is also prepared to deal with their incompetence (v. 7).

[72] Michael S. Heiser, *The Unseen Realm: Recovering the Supernatural Worldview of the Bible* (Bellingham: Lexham Press, 2015), 113.

God would indeed "begin anew" and "enter into a covenant relationship with new people." However, the previous agreement made on Mount Ararat, the covenant and its laws, had not been terminated. His desire for the nations of the world to return to him is clearly seen in his statements to Abraham. From the promise ("and all peoples on earth will be blessed through you"[73]) to the oath ("and through your offspring, all nations on earth will be blessed"[74]), God's love and redemptive agenda for all humankind is revealed.

The Abrahamic Covenant: The Promises (Genesis 12 and 13)

According to the book of Jubilees, Abraham (or Abram as he was named by his mother) was born in Ur of the Chaldeans 1876 years after creation. That would be approximately 188 years after the confusion of languages at Babel in 1688 AM. He began to question the idolatry of his day early in life. It seems his father played a role in the service of idols; however, he was merely feigning worship for fear of the people. Abraham had conversations with him about it, exhorting him to worship the God of Heaven. Abraham reached a breaking point in his disgust of the practice and, at about sixty years of age, set fire to the house of idols. Unfortunately, in an effort to salvage what remained, his brother Haran ran into the building but was overcome by the flames. Obviously, Abraham's actions greatly upset the idol worshipers. So he became a fugitive. He and his family fled Ur to go to Canaan. However, they settled in a city named Haran.[75, 76]

---

[73] Genesis 12:3.

[74] Genesis 22:18.

[75] Jubilees 11:13–12:15.

[76] This is an interesting turn of events because prior to this moment, Abraham was probably well known and appreciated for his contributions to the agricultural industry (Jub. 11:17–23). This reference specifically credits him with the invention of the seeder plow.

The book of Jubilees's version of the story continues with Abraham residing in Haran for about fourteen years. One evening, he was contemplating whether to remain there or simply to return to Ur.

And he prayed that night and said,

"My God, God Most High, Thou alone art my God, And Thee and Thy dominion have I chosen. And thou hast created all things, and all things that are the work of Thy hands. Deliver me from the hands of evil spirits who have dominion over the thoughts of men's hearts, and let them not lead me astray from thee, my God. And stablish Thou me and my seed forever that we go not astray from henceforth and forevermore."

And he said,

"Shall I return to Ur of the Chaldees who seek my face that I may return to them, am I to remain here in this place? The right path before Thee prosper it in the hands of Thy servant that he may fulfill it and that I may not walk in the deceitfulness of my heart, Oh my God."[77]

A heavenly messenger brought God's reply to Abraham.[78]

Leave your country, your people and your father's household and go to the land I will show you.
I will make you into a great nation
and I will bless you;
I will make your name great,
and you will be a blessing.
I will bless those who bless you,
and whoever curses you I will curse;
and all peoples of the earth
will be blessed through you (Gen. 12:1–3).

---

[77] Charles, *Apocrypha and Pseudepigrapha of the Old Testament*, Jubilees 12:19–21.
[78] Jubilees 12:22.

This is the first of three promises that God made to Abraham prior to the covenant ceremony in Genesis 15. At a time in Abraham's life when he needed guidance, God gave him direction and revealed his plan for his life. He would grant him posterity, prosperity, prominence, and protection. However, the last stanza of the promise reveals God's motivation. He would use Abraham to bless "all peoples of the earth." The previous covenant with "all the peoples of the earth" had not been revoked. It was everlasting. It appeared that God's rejection of the nations and the delegation of their oversight to the "sons of God"[79] was not permanent. God had a plan, and Abraham was a major piece of the puzzle.

The next promise was given to Abraham after he arrived in Canaan, having traveled as far as Shechem.[80] Here, he added to the first promise the very important land provision.

To your offspring I will give this land (Gen. 12:7).

There are three important requirements when creating a great nation. Obviously, one needs many, many people. Next, laws are needed to govern them, to provide justice and security. Finally, they will need a place to call their own. This passage is God's official decree that this area was to be the homeland of Abraham's offspring. The importance of this provision cannot be understated. There have been many disagreements about this very issue throughout history, and many battles have been fought to gain control of this portion of the Middle East. It is a contentious issue to this very day.

The third promise occurred during another difficult time in Abraham's life. Both he and his nephew Lot had acquired much livestock and people

---

[79] Deuteronomy 32:8.

[80] Shechem is located about midway between the Sea of Galilee and the Dead Sea, approximately thirty-five miles west of the Jordan River. It is located in the valley between Mount Ebal and Mount Gerizim. The intricacies of God's plan are demonstrated when, about 495 years later, his descendants gathered at this very place to recite the blessings and the curses of the covenant God made with them (Deut. 27:1–26; Josh. 8:30–35).

to tend them. The quarrel that arose was not between the two of them but, rather, between their herdsmen. They came to a mutual agreement that it was in everyone's best interest to part company. Obviously, Abraham was feeling the pain of separation from his only blood relative in a strange land. It is unclear whether Abraham had ever considered what Lot's role might be regarding the promises of God and how this separation might affect it. Whatever the reason, God chose this moment to reiterate and elaborate on his promises saying,

> Lift up your eyes from where you are and look north and south, east and west. All the land that you see I will give to you and your offspring forever. I will make your offspring like the dust of the earth so that if anyone could count the dust, then your offspring could be counted. Go, walk through the length and the breadth of the land, for I am giving it to you (Gen. 13:14–17).

Here, God's promises to Abraham of many descendants and to provide a homeland for them are repeated[81] and forever linked together.

The Abrahamic Covenant: The Melchizedekian Blessing (Genesis 14)

Genesis 14 contains an interesting story about an ancient military encounter between four Eastern kings and the five kings of the Dead Sea area. In their victory, the four kings of the East carried off goods, food, and people from Sodom and Gomorrah. One of their captives was Abraham's nephew Lot and his family. Abraham was able to muster 318 trained men who were able to rescue them and others.

The story serves as a precursor to what will happen in chapter 15. Upon Abraham's return, Melchizedek, the king of Salem (ancient Jerusalem)

---

[81] Joseph, when interpreting Pharaoh's two-part dream, said that prophetic duplication indicates that "the matter has been firmly established by God" (Gen. 41:32).

meets with Abraham to bless him. Melchizedek was an intriguing character. He was both king and priest and, oddly, a priest of "the Most High God" in Canaanite territory. His role in the Abrahamic Covenant should not go unnoticed. In fact, his office of king/priest illuminates our understanding of the role of Israel's Messiah.[82] It is not an accident that this event occurs between the final form of God's promise in Genesis chapter 13 and the covenant ceremony in chapter 15.

And so Melchizedek blessed Abraham saying:

> Blessed be Abram by God Most High,
> Creator of heaven and earth.
> And blessed be God Most High,
> who delivered your enemies into your hand (Gen. 14:19–20).

The statement in Genesis 12:2—"I will bless you"—is a promise. This statement from the priest of the Most High God is an official decree. In fact, it would be more accurate to translate the blessing above as "blessed is" instead of "blessed be." God had given Abraham wealth and prestige. He had fulfilled his promise. In a manner like the Exodus, God acted first, demonstrating his ability to prosper and protect. Then he offered a covenant relationship between himself and the people. Likewise, God promised to bless Abraham. He blessed him greatly during his time in Egypt, so much so that he and Lot had to part ways because "the land could not support them while they stayed together."[83] And now, he is declared "blessed" by God's spokesperson. The next order of business would be the covenant ceremony.

The significance of this blessing might be even greater when we consider that there are many who believe that Melchizedek was Noah's son Shem.[84]

---

[82] Psalm 110:4, Hebrew 4:14–5:10, 7:1–9:28.

[83] Genesis 13:6.

[84] I.e., b. Nedarim 32, Jasher 16:11. The Jewish sages generally cite the Talmud reference. This claim is conceivable if one uses the genealogies found in Genesis 11 to calculate the relative ages of Shem and Abraham. By this account, Abraham

If so, then this event relates to the blessing Shem received from his father in Genesis 9:26 and would imply that by blessing Abraham, he was "passing the torch."

The Abrahamic Covenant: The Ceremony (Genesis 15)

The Abrahamic Covenant, unlike its predecessor, is a promissory covenant. God is the only obligated party in this agreement by virtue of the promises he has made. Indeed, Abraham was required to leave his country and, later, required to maintain the sign of the covenant—circumcision. However, unlike the Noahic and Sinaitic covenants, he was not given a body of laws as part of the agreement.[85] Abraham's part in all of this was simply to believe God.

In the opening verses of Genesis 15, we see God speaking to Abraham in a vision. Abraham recognized that he and his wife, Sara, were already past the age of having children. And so God reassured him that he would have a son who would be his heir and directed his attention to the number of stars in the sky and told him, "So shall your offspring be."[86] He also restated his promise about possessing the land. These two promises are mentioned together just as they were in Genesis 13:14–17.

---

was 150 when Shem died. However, the chronology provided in Jubilees calculates Shem's death as preceding Abraham's birth.

[85] It can be argued that Abraham did receive laws from God. In Genesis 26:5, God tells Isaac, "Abraham obeyed me and kept my requirements (מִשְׁמֶרֶת—mishmeroth), my commandments (מִצְוֹת—mitsvoth), my decrees (חֻקּוֹת—khuqqoth), and my laws (תּוֹרָה—torah)." This list is comparable to one given by Moses in Deuteronomy 11:1, "Love the LORD your God and keep his requirements (מִשְׁמֶרֶת—mishmeroth), his decrees (חֻקּוֹת—khuqqoth), his judgments (מִשְׁפָּטִים—mishpatim), and his commands (מִצְוֹת—mitsvoth) always." Also, in Jubilees 21, there is a list of practices that Abraham passed on to his son Isaac just before his death that are comparable to those found in Leviticus. Nonetheless, none of the aforementioned items was included in the Abrahamic Covenant.

[86] Genesis 15:5.

What happened next is best understood after reading ahead, where it says, "On that day the LORD made a covenant with Abram."[87] God told Abraham to bring him a heifer, a goat, a ram, a dove, and a young pigeon. He was told to cut the animals in half and to arrange the halves opposite one another, except for the birds. All of this was preparation for the covenant ceremony. Once Abraham had fallen into a deep sleep, God gave him a timeline for when his descendants would return to possess the land. Then as he was performing the ceremony, he stated the terms of the covenant.

> Then the Lord said to him, "Know for certain that your descendants will be strangers in a country not their own, and they will be enslaved and mistreated four hundred years. But I will punish the nation they serve as slaves, and afterward they will come out with great possessions. You, however, will go to your fathers in peace and be buried at a good old age. In the fourth generation your descendants will come back here, for the sin of the Amorites has not yet reached its full measure" (Gen. 15:13–16).

> On that day the LORD made a covenant with Abram and said, "To your descendants I give this land, from the river of Egypt to the great river, the Euphrates—the land of the Kenites, Kenezzites, Kadmonites, Hittites, Perizzites, Rephaites, Amorites, Canaanites, Girgashites and Jebusites" (Gen 15:18–19).

There is much that can be said about the historical use of this type of covenant ceremony, the timeline, the imagery of the smoking firepot and animal pieces, and the specific people groups in the list. However, for our purposes, we must understand that this was the moment when "the LORD made a covenant with Abram." This is the first time in the Abraham story that the word "covenant" (ברית—brit), is used. The timing of this event is also significant. The word of the LORD came to Abraham in a vision and

---

[87] Genesis 15:18.

told him to bring the animals for the covenant ceremony[88] on the "new moon of the third month."[89] However, for a reason not stated in text, he waited until the middle of the month to do it.[90] We can now add the Abrahamic Covenant to those everlasting covenants that were initiated in the third month (Noahic, Sinaitic). But now, it aligns more precisely with the timing of the Sinaitic Covenant[91] and the birth of Isaac.[92]

The promises had been made, and the blessing had been given; but now, God had stated the terms of his covenant and ratified it. Once again, as with Noah, the LORD had signed on the dotted line.

The Abrahamic Covenant: The Sign (Genesis 17)

There are two topics discussed in Genesis 17. They are intrinsic to one another. The secondary topic is Abraham's many descendants and how God was going to establish his covenant promise to make that happen. However, the primary topic is the covenantal sign. Abraham and his descendants would be responsible for the application of this sign.

When Abraham was ninety-nine years old,

> The LORD appeared to him and said,
> "I am God Almighty; walk before me and be blameless. I
> will confirm my covenant between me and you and will
> greatly increase your numbers" (Gen. 17:1–2).

---

[88] Genesis 15:1–9.

[89] Jubilees 14:1–9.

[90] Jubilees 14:10.

[91] "In the third month after the Israelites left Egypt—on the very day—they came to the Desert of Sinai" (Exod. 19:1). "On the very day" corresponds to the day of the first month when they left Egypt, which was the fifteenth. Also, the Feast of Weeks (Pentecost) is fifty days after the First Fruits celebration in the first month, which would also place it in the middle of the third month.

[92] "And she bare a son in the third month, and in the middle of the month, at the time of which the Lord had spoken to Abraham ... Isaac was born" (Jub. 16:13).

The two topics are mentioned in verse 2. The details of God's statement—"I will greatly increase your numbers"—are presented in verses 3–8. The details of the statement–"I will confirm my covenant"–are presented in verses 9–14. It may be noted that the topic in verses 9–14 is the sign of the covenant and, at first glance, not about confirming the covenant. So before proceeding, we need to discuss some technical details.

The understanding of certain Hebrew words will help bring clarity to this portion of chapter 17. The first word, כרת (karat), means "to cut." The word קום (qum) means "to arise, stand," or, in the Hiphil aspect, "to cause to stand, establish." The word נתן (natan) means "to give, put, set."

The word כרת (karat) is used throughout the Old Testament when discussing the initiation of a covenant. The literal Hebrew phrase is "cut a covenant," although it is never translated that way. There is an example of this in the covenant ceremony with Abraham.

> On that day, the LORD made [כרת] a covenant with Abram (Gen. 15:18).

When God speaks of establishing or fulfilling his part of a covenant, the word קום (qum) is usually used. There are three examples of this in Genesis 17.

> I will establish [קום] my covenant (Gen. 17:7).

> I will establish [קום] my covenant with him (Gen. 17:19).

> But my covenant I will establish [קום] with Isaac (Gen. 17:21).

When God provides a sign for the covenant in question, the word נתן (natan) is used.

> For the Noahic Covenant:

> "This is the sign that I set [נתן] for the covenant between Me and you" (Gen. 9:12, JPS).[93]

---

[93] Sarna, *JPS Torah Commentary: Genesis*, 62.

For the Sinaitic Covenant:

> "Also I gave [נתן] them my Sabbaths as a sign between
> us" (Ezek. 20:12).

Equipped with this information, we can now locate an awkward translation in Genesis 17, correct it, and, hopefully, provide better continuity and understanding. Below is the verse in question:

> "I will confirm my covenant between me and you and
> will greatly increase your numbers" (Gen. 17:2).

The Hebrew word translated as "confirm" by the NIV is our word נתן (*natan*), "to give, put, set." Other translations also use the word "confirm." The NLT, MSG, BBE, NRSV, and NKJV all translate it as "make." The NASB translates it as "establish," as if the original word were קום (*qum*). Although a literal translation might be uncomfortable, it will help point us in the right direction. The verse "I will give/put/set my covenant between you and me" seems to imply that God is not speaking so much about the covenant directly but, rather, about the sign of the covenant. And so, we understand this verse to mean that he will "give" him the sign of the covenant (discussed in verses 9–14) and greatly increase Abraham's numbers (discussed in verses 3–8). The two topics will be addressed in reverse order.

Now let us examine these two portions of the text.

In a manner similar to the previous covenant, God lists the responsibilities of each party. The first section begins with "As for me." The second one begins with "As for you." The second section contains the main idea of the chapter and is, therefore, the primary topic. The first section contains important information about what God will do regarding the covenant and makes the topic in the second section, the sign of the covenant, possible.

> Abraham fell face down, and God said to him, "As for
> me, this is my covenant with you: you will be the father

of many nations. No longer will you be called Abram: your name will be Abraham, for I have made you a father of many nations. I will make you very fruitful: I will make nations of you, and kings will come from you. I will establish my covenant as an everlasting covenant [ברית עולם—*brit olam*] between me and you and your descendants after you for the generations to come, to be your God and the God of your descendants after you. The whole land of Canaan, where you are now an alien, I will give as an everlasting possession to you and your descendants after you; And I will be their God" (Gen. 17:3–8, *Hebrew text added*).

The reference above to "father of many nations" harkens back to the original promise in Genesis 12:2. However, God said that he would make Abraham "into a great nation." The change from singular to plural might be related to the events in Genesis 16 when, thirteen years earlier, Hagar was instructed by the angel of the Lord to return to her mistress, evidently, so that Ishmael would be born in Abraham's household. In doing so, Ishmael would inherit a portion of the Abrahamic Covenant, specifically that God would bless him and make him into a great nation.[94] Also, after Sarah's death, Abraham married Keturah and fathered children through her. In the end, Abraham was the father not only of the Israelites but also of the Ishmaelites (early Arab tribes),[95] as well as of others such as the Midianites (i.e., Jethro, Moses's father-in-law).[96]

The timing of the phrase "I will establish my covenant as an everlasting covenant" is notable. The covenant was ratified in Genesis 15. There, the covenant was "cut" (כרת—*karat*). Here, God tells Abraham that he will establish (קום—*qum*) his covenant. As stated earlier, קום (*qum*) means "to arise, stand." Even though God spoke about Abraham's descendants during the ratification ceremony, Abraham and Sarah did not have any children at that point. God's declaration to establish his covenant

---

[94] Genesis 17:18, 20–21, 24–25.

[95] Genesis 25:12–18.

[96] Genesis 25:1–4; Exodus 2:15–16, 3:1.

essentially means that the time had come for him to "make good" on his commitment. Either he had done something or was about to do something that would enable Abraham and Sarah to have children. We must understand these statements in the context of the overall chronology, for in about one year, Sarah would give birth to Isaac.[97]

If Abraham had died without having children, the covenant would have died with him. But since God established the covenant with him and his descendants, his lineage and the covenant will continue in perpetuity. This is the first time God refers to his covenant with Abraham as an everlasting covenant (ברית עולם—*brit olam*). As was the previous covenant with Noah, and ultimately with the whole world, this covenant is also permanent. Verses 7 and 8 above clearly state that this includes both the promises of progeny and property. For the land, "I will give as an everlasting possession" (אחזת עולם—*akhuzat olam*).

In the next section, God introduces the covenantal sign.

> The presence of signs in many of the biblical covenants also emphasizes that the divine covenants bind people together. The token of the rainbow, the seal of circumcision, the sign of the Sabbath—these covenantal signs enforce the binding character of the covenant. An interpersonal commitment which may be guaranteed has come into effect by way of the covenantal bond. Just as a bride and groom interchange rings as "token and pledge" of their "constant faith and abiding love," so the signs of the covenant symbolized the permanence of the bond between God and his people.[98]

It should be noted that this sign was not mentioned during the covenant ratification ceremony over thirteen years earlier. It is being added now in the same way an addendum or rider is attached to a pre-existing

---

[97] Genesis 17:1, 18:14, 21:5.

[98] O. Palmer Robertson, *The Christ of the Covenants* (Phillipsburg: Presbyterian and Reformed Publishing, 1980), 7.

contract. This sign has no effect on the perpetuity of the covenant, rather it demonstrates one's participation in it.

> Then God said to Abraham, "As for you, you must keep my covenant, you and your descendants after you for the generations to come. This is my covenant with you and your descendants after you, the covenant you are to keep: every male among you shall be circumcised. You are to undergo circumcision, and it will be the sign of the covenant between me and you. For the generations to come every male among you who is eight days old must be circumcised, including those born in your household or bought with money from a foreigner—those who are not your offspring. Whether born in your household or bought with your money, they must be circumcised. My covenant in your flesh is to be an everlasting covenant. Any uncircumcised male, who has not been circumcised in the flesh, will be cut off from his people; he has broken my covenant" (Gen. 17:9–14).

The sign is intended for Abraham, his (male) descendants, as well as their servants. Initially, the responsibility to circumcise falls upon the father. When an uncircumcised son comes of age, the responsibility is upon the individual. The decision to not be circumcised is a decision to not participate in the covenant. Ideally, this physical act is an outward sign of an inward reality. In light of the many admonitions from God to the Israelites to "circumcise their hearts," faith and action must accompany the sign of circumcision to effect its validity. The apostle Paul (Rabbi Sha'ul) stated it quite succinctly:

> Circumcision has value if you observe the law, but if you break the law, you have become as though you had not been circumcised. If those who are not circumcised keep the law's requirements, will they not be regarded as though they were circumcised? The one who is not circumcised physically and yet obeys the law will

condemn you who, even though you have the written
code and circumcision, are a law breaker.

A man is not a Jew if he is only one outwardly, nor
is circumcision merely outward and physical. No, a
man is a Jew if he is one inwardly; and circumcision
is circumcision of the heart, by the spirit, not by the
written code. Such a man's praise is not from men, but
from God (Rom. 2:25–29).

Abraham, the man of faith, did not hesitate to obey God's instructions.
For on that very day,

Abraham took his son Ishmael and all those in his
household or bought with his money, every male in
his household, and circumcised them. Abraham was
ninety-nine years old when he was circumcised, and
his son Ishmael was thirteen; Abraham and his son
Ishmael were both circumcised on that same day. And
every male in Abraham's household, including those
born in his household or bought from a foreigner, was
circumcised with him (Gen. 17:23–27).

The Abrahamic Covenant: The Oath (Genesis 22)

The events of Genesis 22 relate to the final phase of the Abrahamic
Covenant. The focal point of the story is found in verses 15–18, where
God commits himself by an oath to all that he has said to date. It has
been decades since he first called Abraham from Ur of the Chaldeans.
It is easy to view the events of Abraham's life as a series of successive
stories that happened in less than one-third of his 175 years on earth.
However, if we evaluate the major events together, we can see a common
legal procedure unfolding: a promise is presented, a contract is written,
possibly a token is passed between the parties, and an oath is taken. As
a result, Abraham became a willing participant in God's project to build

his own nation after the nations of the world rejected him centuries earlier at the Tower of Babel.

The events that precede the oath paragraph are described by the text as a time when "God tested Abraham."[99] It is a well-known story to most Bible students. God instructed Abraham to take Isaac to one of the mountains in the region of Moriah and to offer him there as a sacrifice. Abraham complied and left the very next morning, taking with him Isaac, two servants, and enough wood to perform the offering. The biblical narrative is completely void of any description of the anguish and confusion that he was undoubtedly suffering. We are told only that he obeyed.[100] The pain of this ordeal was compounded by the fact that

---

[99] Genesis 22:1. The book of Jubilees tells a story about a heavenly conversation much like the one in Job 1:6–11 and, 2:1–5 that factors in this test. "And it came to pass in the seventh week, in the first year thereof, in the first month in this jubilee, on the twelfth of this month, there were voices in heaven regarding Abraham, that he was faithful in all that He told him, and that he loved the Lord, and that in every affliction he was faithful. and the prince Mastema came and said before God, 'behold, Abraham loves Isaac his son, and he delights in him above all things else; bid him offer him as a burnt offering on the altar, and thou wilt see if he will do this command, and thou wilt know if he is faithful in everything wherein thou dost try him.'" See Charles, *Apocrypha and Pseudepigrapha of the Old Testament*, Jubilees 17:15–16.

[100] Isaac's role in this story is often overlooked. To appreciate it, we must attempt to assess his age. In the very next chapter, his mother, Sarah, dies at age 127. She was ninety years old when he was born, making Isaac's age thirty-seven. So we can ascertain that he is younger than that in Genesis 22. The book of Jubilees provides a chronology for the book of Genesis using the creation of the earth as a starting point. Jubilees 15:1 designates 1979 AM as the year that God gave Abraham the covenant sign of circumcision. Therefore, Isaac would have been born in 1980 AM, one year later. Jubilees 17:15 designates 2003 AM as the year when Abraham was told to offer his son. Using these two latter dates, we can calculate Isaac's age at this time to be twenty-three years.

And so, Isaac was not a young boy when God told Abraham to offer him at Moriah. He was a young man, stronger and healthier than his 123-year-old father. Abraham would have been unable to bind him and place him on the altar without his consent, once he became aware that he was to be the burnt offering. The fact that he was bound and placed on the altar demonstrates that Isaac was a willing participant. Evidently, he trusted his father and was willing to offer himself to God.

his son questioned him about the missing component: "The fire and the wood are here, but where is the lamb for the burnt offering?"[101] Nonetheless, Abraham passed the test: After binding his son and laying him on the altar, he raised his knife to slay him. But God intervened:

> Do not lay a hand on the boy ... Now I know that you fear God, because you have not withheld from me your son, your only son (Gen. 22:12).

Instead of sacrificing his son, Abraham sacrificed a ram that had been caught in a thicket. Then Abraham was told,

> I swear by myself, declares the LORD, that because you have done this and have not withheld your son, your only son, I will surely bless you and make your descendants as numerous as the stars in the sky and as the sand on the seashore. Your descendants will take possession of the cities of their enemies, and through your offspring all nations of the earth will be blessed, because you have obeyed me (Gen. 22:16–18).

The oath was concise. It included every responsibility that God had placed upon himself regarding Abraham's descendants, the land, and the goal of blessing the nations of the earth. The importance of the oath to the Abrahamic Covenant is stated by the writer of the book of Hebrews.

> When God made his promise to Abraham, since there was no one greater for him to swear by, he swore by himself, saying, "I will surely bless you and give you many descendants." And so after waiting patiently, Abraham received what was promised.

> Men swear by someone greater than themselves, and the oath confirms what is said and puts an end to all argument. Because God wanted to make the unchanging

---

[101] Genesis 22:7.

nature of his purpose very clear to the heirs of what was promised, he confirmed it with an oath (Heb. 6:13–17).

One might inquire as to why God would need to take an oath. Or why God would rely on the obedience of a mere human being to leave his country to create a new nation and bless all nations. Or why God would bother to announce his plans to the prophets, sometimes centuries in advance of their fulfillment. I suggest that it has everything to do with God's understanding of human nature and our shortcomings. In his compassion, he does these things to provide us with hope. Regarding prophecy, he provides insight to its recipients about the future to help them interpret or survive the present. Regarding covenants and oaths, he provides an anchor in the past to help us establish a foundation for our faith. God did not need to take an oath to fulfill his promises to Abraham. However, he did it anyway. And here we are, thousands of years later, still discussing it. His descendants survive to this day despite opposition throughout the centuries. And many of us who are of "the nations of the earth" have been blessed by them, especially by one in particular.[102]

The Abrahamic Covenant: Passes to Isaac (Genesis 25)

In the time of the patriarchs, Canaan was part of Egypt.[103] When famine struck the land, people would travel to Egypt to purchase grain to supplement their diminished harvests. Such a famine happened in the lifetime of both Abraham and Isaac, and both made their way to Egypt. However, when Isaac had traveled as far as the land of the Philistines, the LORD appeared to him and said,

> Do not go down to Egypt; live in the land where I tell you
> to live. Stay in this land for a while, and I will be with you

---

[102] Galatians 3:16.

[103] This was true until twenty-one years after the death of Joseph when the king of Egypt went to war with the king of Canaan. The king of Canaan was victorious and subsequently closed the routes to Egypt (Jub. 46:8–11).

and will bless you. For to you and your descendants I will give all these lands and will confirm the oath I swore to your father Abraham. I will make your descendants as numerous as the stars in the sky and will give them all these lands, and through your offspring all nations on earth will be blessed, because Abraham obeyed me and kept my requirements, my commands, my decrees, and my laws (Gen. 26:2–5).

This statement from God confirms what he had said to Abraham after giving him the sign of circumcision before Isaac was born. Although he would also bless Ishmael with many descendants, the full benefits of the covenant would be passed to Isaac. "But my covenant I will establish with Isaac ..."[104] Here, he includes both components of the covenant, progeny, and property, along with the promise of blessing all nations.

It should be noted that the Bible does not record a covenant ratification ceremony. Nor does it record Abraham's blessing of Isaac as it does Isaac's and Jacob's blessing of their children. However, the book of Jubilees does record such a blessing.

> And observe the ordinance of the Most High God,
> And do his will and be upright in all things.
> And he will bless thee in all thy deeds,
> And will raise up from thee a plant of righteousness through all the earth, throughout all generations of the earth,
> And my name and thy name shall not be forgotten under heaven forever.
> Go, my son in peace.
> May the Most High God, my God and thy God, strengthen thee to do his will
> And may he bless all thy seed and the residue of thy seed for the generations forever, with all righteous blessings,

---

[104] Genesis 17:21.

That thou mayest be a blessing on all the earth (Jub. 21:23–25).

The Abrahamic Covenant: Passes to Jacob (Genesis 35)

The story of Jacob's involvement with the Abrahamic Covenant begins while he was still in his mother's womb. His and his twin brother Esau's birth was, like their father's, a miraculous event. Isaac married Rebekah when he was forty years old.[105] Rebekah was barren for many years, prompting Isaac to pray on her behalf. Finally, when he was about sixty, she conceived twin boys.[106] The pregnancy was very difficult to the point that she "went to inquire of the LORD."[107]

The LORD said to her,

"Two nations are in your womb,
and two peoples from within you will be separated;
one people will be stronger than the other,
and the older will serve the younger" (Gen. 25:23).

When the boys were born, Esau came into the world first, followed by Jacob, who was grasping his brother's heel. Jacob, the younger twin, had already been set apart by God. As their lives progress, we begin to see certain character traits in each of them that God obviously noticed when they were still in the womb, for example, Esau's disregard for his responsibilities as the firstborn. The right of the firstborn carries with it a

---

[105] Genesis 25:20.

[106] Genesis 25:26.

[107] Genesis 25:22. The phrase "she went" implies that she did not "pray," as Isaac had done in verse 21, but actually traveled somewhere. This could indicate the existence of prophets of the LORD at this time who would have inquired on her behalf. Another explanation is based on the fact that she and Isaac were living in Beer Lahai Roi at the time (Gen. 24:62). This was where the LORD met with Hagar at a well when she fled from Sarai (Gen. 16). She named this well at that time to commemorate her encounter with God. It is possible that Rebekah went to this nearby well and had a similar encounter.

double portion of the father's inheritance. However, in this case, it would also include the divine covenant that Isaac received from his father. Apparently, Esau did not appreciate the value of either and sold it to his brother Jacob for a meal.[108] When the time came for Isaac to give the blessing, Jacob took advantage of his acquired rights and, unfortunately, his father's poor eyesight. His mother, apparently remembering the prophecy she had received earlier, aided him in this endeavor.[109] Upon hearing that Jacob has received his father's blessing, Esau made plans to kill his brother once their father had passed away.[110] Such was the character of Esau.

His brother's hatred for him prompted Jacob to flee the land of Canaan to go live with his mother's relatives in Paddan Aram. He left Beersheba and camped near a city called Luz (Bethel). There, God spoke to him in a dream regarding the covenant.

> I am the LORD, the God of your father Abraham and the God of Isaac. I will give you and your descendants the land on which you are lying. Your descendants will be like the dust of the earth, and you will spread out to the west and to the east, to the north and to the south. All peoples on earth will be blessed through you and your offspring. I am with you and will watch over you wherever you go, and I will bring you back to this land. I will not leave you until I have done what I have promised you (Gen. 28:13–15).

As with his father and his grandfather, God offered Jacob many descendants and the very land on which he was lying to be their home. He also included the clause about using them to bless all the peoples

---

[108] Genesis 25:27–34.

[109] There is a substantial passage in Jubilees 19:15–30 that describes how Abraham noticed a difference in the boys. He took Rebekah aside and advised her to watch over Jacob because he would be the recipient of the covenant. If this conversation really happened, it would further explain Rebekah's boldness in helping Jacob deceive his father to receive the blessing.

[110] Genesis 27:41.

of the earth. There are other important items in this passage that must be noted. Firstly, God addressed himself as the "God of your father Abraham and the God of Isaac," not as Jacob's God. That relationship had not yet been established. Secondly, God knew that he was fleeing the land of Canaan. He did not stop him from leaving but, instead, stated his intentions to make his journey successful and to bring him back home. With this understanding, we can see that God was offering the covenant to Jacob and promising to protect him. The actual ratification of the Abrahamic Covenant between God and Jacob would not happen for at least twenty years. Whether or not it would pass to Jacob would depend on how he responded to God's offer.[111] However, we are given an indication of what that response might be.

> Then Jacob made a vow, saying, "If God will be with me and will watch over me on this journey I am taking and will give me food to eat and clothes to wear so that I returned safely to my father's house, then the LORD will be my God" (Gen. 28:20–21).

God would make good on his promise, and Jacob would make good on his vow.

Jacob eventually arrived in Paddan Aram, specifically in a place called Haran, where his mother's family lived. Interestingly, it was where Abraham lived when God first spoke to him, telling him to leave his country and making the promises to him that have now been made to Jacob.[112] He married and had many children. He had many negative encounters with Laban, who was both his father-in-law and employer. When the time was right, God spoke to him once again in a dream:

> Go back to the land of your fathers and to your relatives, and I will be with you (Gen. 31:3).

---

[111] The scriptures are ripe with stories that demonstrate the interplay between divine sovereignty and human free will. How these two things work together has been the subject of *many* discussions in our family.

[112] Genesis 11:31–12:3.

> I am the God of Bethel, where you anointed a pillar and
> where you made a vow to me. Now leave this land at
> once and go back to your native land (Gen. 31:13).

Bethel is the name Jacob gave to the place where God first spoke his promises to him.[113] God was reminding him of the encounter, of the pillar he erected to mark the place, and of the vow he made. God had given him "food to eat and clothes to wear" since that day. It was now time for Jacob to fulfill his vow.

Jacob obeyed God's command to return to Canaan. Many events transpired prior to his arrival at Bethel, including an encounter with his brother Esau, and even the angel of the LORD. But once he arrived, his first task was to build an altar.[114] The biblical text offers no other details about the altar, nor the offerings made upon it.[115] However, it is undoubtedly a component of what would be the covenant ratification ceremony. What was promised twenty years earlier would now become official. Although the Hebrew word is not used specifically, this ceremony was the "cutting" (כרת—*karat*) of a covenant (ברית—*brit*) between God and Jacob. God stated it officially when he told Jacob,

> I am God almighty; Be fruitful and increase in number. A
> nation and a community of nations will come from you,
> and kings will come from your body. The land I gave to
> Abraham and Isaac I also give to you, and I will give this
> land to your descendants after you (Gen. 35:11–12).

Jacob had been faithful to his vow. The LORD protected him and brought him back to the land of Canaan. And now, the LORD was Jacob's God. In

---

[113] Genesis 28:16–19.

[114] Genesis 35:3, 35:7.

[115] Jubilees 32:4 states that Jacob offered as burnt offerings fourteen oxen, twenty-eight rams, forty-nine sheep, seven lambs, and twenty-one goat kids. The burnt offerings would have represented his dedication to the LORD, denoting that the LORD was now his God. Then Jubilees 32:5 says he offered two oxen, four rams, four sheep, four he-goats, two yearling sheep, and two goat kids daily for seven days as offerings of thanksgiving in fulfillment of his vow.

the future, God would repeatedly refer to himself with this self-imposed appellation. When Moses asked God regarding his name and who he should say sent him, God's answer was

> The LORD, the God of your fathers—the God of Abraham, the God of Isaac, and the God of Jacob—has sent me to you (Exod. 3:15 [3:16, 4:5]).

This was how God identified himself to the Israelites in Egypt just before he delivered them from Pharaoh to bring them back to the land of Canaan. It is a very appropriate title indeed. After all, he was simply fulfilling a four-hundred-year-old promise.[116]

---

[116] Exodus 3:17, 6:4, 6:8.

THE COVENANT
WITH ISRAEL:
AT SINAI

We need to understand the geopolitical environment during this period. Until the death of Joseph, Canaan was considered part of Egypt, or at least a protectorate with its own leader.[117] This would explain the practice of the patriarchs to journey to Egypt for grain when there was a famine in Canaan. However, twenty-one years after the death of Joseph,[118] there was a war between the kings of Egypt and Canaan, and Canaan was victorious.[119] This created a problem for the king of Egypt. He had a very large and growing population within his borders who identified themselves with the land of the king who had just defeated him. In fact, some of these Israelites would travel to Canaan to bury their dead.[120] After the war, this practice was stopped because the border between the two countries was closed.[121] Egypt's concern about Israel's identification with the land of Canaan prompted its king to come to a conclusion:

> "Look," he said to his people, "the Israelites have become much too numerous for us. Come, we must deal shrewdly with them or they will become even more numerous and, if war breaks out, will join our enemies, fight against us and leave the country" (Exod. 1:8–9).

---

[117] This may be the reason why the Septuagint and the Samaritan Pentateuch specify "Egypt and Canaan" in Exodus 12:40.

[118] Jubilees 46:8.

[119] Jubilees 46:9, 11.

[120] Genesis 50:4–14.

[121] Jubilees 46:7.

It was at this time that the king issued a decree that they be placed under forced labor.[122] And thus their oppression began. However, this did not reduce the Israelite population. Sixty-seven years later,[123] another king issued this infamous decree:

> Every boy that is born you must throw into the Nile, but
> let every girl live (Exod. 1:22).

These geopolitical events happened between the time of Joseph and the Exodus and are relevant factors in our attempt to calculate the overall time frame.

It is also important to understand some of the specifics of the prophecy given to Abraham during the covenant ceremony. What are the details of the prophecy? When will the prophecy begin? When will it be fulfilled?

> Know for certain that your descendants will be strangers
> in a country not their own, and they will be enslaved and
> mistreated four hundred years (Gen. 15:13).

> In the fourth generation your descendants will come
> back here, for the sin of the Amorites has not yet reached
> its full measure (Gen. 15:16).

The first reference contains two specific phases. Both phases involve Abraham's descendants being "strangers in a country not their own." We know from subsequent Bible stories that this will happen in two countries, Canaan and Egypt. Abraham is already a stranger in a country not his own but the starting point for this prophecy will be when a descendant is also one. And so the first phase of the four-hundred-year time range will begin with the birth of Isaac, his first descendant. It will also include the time when Jacob resides in Canaan. The second phase will be the time when his descendants reside in Egypt, during which they will endure enslavement and mistreatment. We must understand

---

[122] Exodus 1:11–14.
[123] c.f. Jubilees 46:9, 47:1–2.

that this prophecy does not imply that they would be in Egypt for four hundred years. The second reference above helps to support this. They would reside in a country that would enslave them for only four generations.

Finally, we must examine the time frame between the Abrahamic and Sinaitic Covenants. The latter is based on the former, and the chronological details between them are often overlooked. There are numerous explanations of these details, and many of them have merit. Each one requires its own interpretations, presuppositions if you will, about when a number is to be understood with exactness or generality, or even rounded. I have chosen to use the age references for certain people from Genesis and Exodus to calculate the time frame. I will also use similar references from Jubilees to support those values and to supply the missing chronology between the two books of the Bible. We must remember that numerical precision will be difficult using this method because the ages of the people involved are given in full-year increments. We do not know if the additional months of one's age caused the author to round up or down. Therefore, numerical proximity will be our goal.

And so let us begin the chronology.

Years	Description	Sources
60	From Isaac's birth to Jacob's birth	Genesis 25:26
147	Jacob's life span	Genesis 47:9, 28

54	From Jacob's death to Joseph's death	Joseph was 30 when the seven years of plenty began (Gen. 41:46).
		Jacob was 130 in the second year of the famine (Gen. 47:9),
		    thus, Joseph was 39 (91-year difference).
		Jacob died at age 147 (Gen. 47:28),
		    thus, Joseph was 56.
		Joseph died at age 110 (Gen. 50:26),
		    thus, Joseph died 54 years after Jacob.
		
		Additional support:
		Jubilees 46:8 2242 AM[124] Death of Joseph
		Jubilees 45:13 -2188 AM[125] Death of Jacob
		               54 years

21	From the death of Joseph to the decree to close the Egyptian/Canaanite border and to subject the Israelites to forced labor	Jubilees 46:9 2263 AM[126] War/decree Jubilees 46:8 -2242 AM Death of Joseph 21 years
67	From the decree to Moses's birth (years of slavery)	Jubilees 47:1 2330 AM[127] Birth of Moses Jubilees 46:8 -2263 AM War/decree 67 years
80	Moses's age in Exodus (years of slavery)	Exodus 7:7

---

[124] Lit. "in the forty-sixth jubilee, in the sixth week, in the second year."

[125] Jubilees 19:1, 19:12, Using both verses, Jacob was born in the forty-second Jubilee, in the sixth week, in the second year.

[126] Lit. "in the forty-seventh jubilee, in the second week, in the second year."

[127] Lit. "in the fourth week, in the sixth year thereof, in the forty-eighth jubilee."

429	Total	Genesis 15:13, Exodus 12:40
		Additional support:
		Jubilees 15:1 1979 AM Announcement of Isaac's birth, one year in advance
		Genesis 17:21
		... thus 1980 AM Birth of Isaac
		Jubilees 48:1 2410 AM[127] Moses's return to Egypt
		... thus 2410 AM Moses's return
		-1980 AM Isaac's birth
		430 years

We can make some additional observations using the above chronology. We can calculate the time the Israelites spent in Egypt by adding the years from Jacob's death to the Exodus (54 + 21 + 67 + 80 = 222) and then adding the years Jacob spent there after arriving in the second year of the famine until his death (147 – 130 = 17). Thus the Israelites were in Egypt 239 years.[129] The duration of Israelite servitude can be determined by calculating the time from the decree to enslave them to the time of the Exodus (67 + 80), or 147 years. Finally, we can confirm the statement that God made to Abraham: "In the fourth generation your descendants will come back here."[130] We simply need to identify the family line of just one person who entered Egypt with Jacob and whose great-grandson left Egypt with Moses. Exodus 6:14–20 might have been included in the Exodus story for this very reason. It is a partial genealogy of the Israelites. Oddly, it lists the sons of Jacob in birth order but includes only the first three, stopping at Levi. The purpose of the shortened list is made evident in verses 26–27, to support the legitimacy of the leadership of Moses and Aaron. However, it serves our purpose quite well, for Moses and Aaron

---

[128] Lit. "in the second week in the second year in the fiftieth jubilee."

[129] Exodus 12 of Targum Jonathon says, "And the days of the dwelling of the sons of Israel in Mizraim" (Egypt) "were thirty weeks of years (thirty times seven years), which is the sum of 210 years." See *The Targums of Onkelos and Jonathan Ben Uzziel On the Pentateuch*, http://www.targum.info/pj/psjon.htm.

[130] Genesis 15:16.

were the fourth generation from Levi. They were the sons of Amram (who lived 137 years), the son of Kohath (who lived 133 years), and the son of Levi (who lived 137 years). Obviously, their life spans overlapped. Nonetheless, it is not difficult to comprehend how the lives of three men, each of whom lived over 130 years, and the eighty-year-old Moses could have easily spanned the 239 years that Israel spent in Egypt. It is precisely details like these that should give us confidence in the biblical record. Simple storytellers are not always concerned about such details, but for chroniclers, they are indispensable. When you add divine inspiration to the equation, it becomes clear that God wanted the accuracy of his statements documented.

There is one final observation. The 430-year total from Exodus 12:40 is matched by the calculation derived from the dates found in Jubilees 15:1 and 48:1. This would seem to indicate that the four-hundred-year prophecy given to Abraham in Genesis 15:13 is to be understood as a general or rounded number.

The Covenant with Israel: Overview

The covenant that God made with the Israelites at Mount Sinai was an obligatory one: both parties had responsibilities. It was a covenant that was national and transgenerational. The Ten Commandments, and the judgments and statutes that followed, were documented by Moses in the Book of the Covenant and subsequently ratified by the people. Additional covenantal stipulations are given progressively throughout the books of Exodus, Leviticus, and Numbers. In Deuteronomy, while the Israelites were encamped on the Plains of Moab, they were given specific terms in preparation for their settlement of the land of Canaan. There, the terms given at Sinai and Moab were merged and ratified by the second generation of those who left Egypt.

After the conquest of Canaan, Israel would vacillate between faithfulness and apostasy over the centuries. Ultimately, they were removed from the land and exiled to other countries. All of this was anticipated by

God and prophetically documented by Moses. At no time was the covenant between God and Israel nullified. Israel's compliance with the covenant permitted them entrance to and residence in the promised land. Noncompliance inhibited their entrance to the land, removed God's protection while in the land, and caused their expulsion. God's blessings and his punishments were documented in the Torah. Israel's reception of either blessing or punishment[131] demonstrated that God was being faithful to the covenant.

In the end of days, there will be one final ratification of this covenant with Israel. It will require more than just faithful Jewish individuals. There needs to be a faithful generation and belief on a national level. The covenant with Israel has previously been renewed. First, it happened after the incident with the golden calf, only after Moses interceded for the people. Then, it happened after the spies returned from Canaan with a bad report that led to an uprising. Once again, Moses interceded. The last renewal will conclude with the final form of the Israelite covenant—a permanent Davidic kingship, a permanent Levitical priesthood, and a permanent temple. These truths are attested to by the prophets.

As we approach the Sinai component of God's covenant with Israel, we must keep this overview in mind. It is the beginning of another everlasting covenant (ברית עולם—*brit olam*).

The Covenant with Israel: The Preliminaries

Moses first encountered God's messenger while tending the flock of his father-in-law in the land of Midian. He was born in Egypt, and although he was an Israelite, he was raised in Pharaoh's court. He left Egypt as a fugitive because he killed an Egyptian to prevent him from fatally beating an Israelite.[132] He stayed in Midian for about forty years. The scriptures tell us that about the time that Moses was eighty years old,[133]

---

[131] Amos 3:2.
[132] Exodus 2:11–15.
[133] Exodus 7:7.

the Israelites groaned in their slavery and cried out, and their cry for help because of their slavery went up to God. God heard their groaning and he remembered his covenant with Abraham, with Isaac and with Jacob (Exod. 2:23–24).

The four-hundred-year prophecy regarding Abraham's descendants had expired, and it was now time for God to act upon it. One day, Moses was tending the flocks on Mount Horeb when the messenger of the LORD spoke to him from the burning bush. The way he introduced himself is noteworthy:

> "I am the God of your father, the God of Abraham, the God of Isaac and the God of Jacob" (Exod. 3:6).

He identified himself as the God of the men with whom he has a made a covenant. The first part of the covenant had already been fulfilled. Abraham's descendants had become a massive group of people numbering around 2 million.[134] Now he announced his intention to fulfill the second part:

> The LORD said, "I have indeed seen the misery of my people in Egypt. I have heard them crying out because of their slave drivers, and I am concerned about their suffering. So I have come down to rescue them from the hand of the Egyptians and to bring them up out of that land into a good and spacious land, a land flowing with milk and honey—the home of the Canaanites, Hittites, Amorites, Perizzites, Hivites, and Jebusites" (Exod. 3:7–8).

After Moses and Aaron's first encounter with Pharaoh, God spoke to Moses again:

---

[134] Exodus 12:37, Numbers 2:32–33. This number accounts only for the men over the age of twenty (Num. 1:3). It does not include the women and children, nor the Levites.

"I am the LORD. I appeared to Abraham, to Isaac and to Jacob ... I also established my covenant with them to give them the land of Canaan, where they lived as aliens ... I have remembered my covenant" (Exod. 6:2–5).

Then, as with previous covenants, God prefaced the one he was about to make with Israel with many promises:

"Therefore, say to the Israelites: 'I am the LORD, and *I will bring you* out from under the yoke of the Egyptians. *I will free you* from being slave to them, and *I will redeem you* with an outstretched arm and with mighty acts of judgment. *I will take you* as my own people, and I will be your God. Then you will know that I am the LORD your God, who brought you out from under the yoke of the Egyptians. And *I will bring you* to the land I swore with uplifted hand to give to Abraham, to Isaac and to Jacob. *I will give it to you* as a possession. I am the LORD'" (Exod. 6:6–8, *italics added*).

The covenant that God was about to make with the Israelites was intricately woven into the fabric of the Abrahamic Covenant. He was acting on compassion and faithfulness. For he said, "I am concerned about their suffering" and "I have remembered my covenant."

The Covenant with Israel: The Offer

In the third month[135] after the Exodus, the Israelites arrived at Mount Sinai.[136] At that time, Moses ascended the mountain and received these words from God.

---

[135] The importance of this time of the year was developed in earlier chapters. It corresponds to the timing of the Noahic Covenant, the Abrahamic Covenant, and the birth of Isaac.
[136] Exodus 19:1.

"This is what you are to say to the house of Jacob and what you are to tell the people of Israel: 'You yourselves have seen what I did to Egypt, and how I carried you on eagles' wings and brought you to myself. Now if you obey me fully and keep my covenant, then out of all the nations you will be my treasured possession. Although the whole earth is mine, you will be for me a kingdom of priests and a holy nation.' These are the words you are to speak to the Israelites" (Exod. 19:3–6).

The terms of the covenant are quite simple. The Israelites are to keep the covenant by obeying God fully and God will treasure them above all other nations. The use of the word "nation" is important. The first occurrence of the word in "out of all the nations" is the plural form of עַם (am), which would be better translated as "peoples." However, the second occurrence in "a holy nation" is the word more commonly translated as "nation," גּוֹי (goy). God's offer of a covenant was not solely to the people currently camped at the base of the mountain. Rather, his covenant would be with the nation of which they were citizens. The covenant was transgenerational. Later, when the second generation ratified the covenant on the Plains of Moab, Moses made this point abundantly clear:

> I am making this covenant, with its oath, not only with you who are standing here with us today in the presence of the LORD our God but also with those who are not here today (Deut. 29:14).

Tigay explains:

> That is, future generations … According to Midrash Tanhuma, the phrase refers to those who were spiritually present: the souls of all future generations of Jews (and, adds Bekhor Shor, of proselytes) were present and bound themselves to God by this covenant. In any case, the point of the text is that the mutual commitments made here

by God and Israel are binding for all future generations. Ancient Near Eastern treaties likewise stipulate that they are binding on the parties' descendants.[137]

This important detail explains why, throughout biblical history, punishments were meted out to individuals and to entire generations that had broken the covenant through disobedience, and yet the covenant itself remains intact. Once the covenant was ratified, whether the Israelites were settled in the promised land or in exile, they were a nation in the eyes of God and set apart for him.

Moses took this message back to the people. He summoned the elders and told them the words that God had commanded him to speak.

> The people all responded together, "We will do everything the LORD has said." So Moses brought their answer back to the Lord (Exod. 19:8).

Although they agreed to the terms of the covenant, this appears to be a preliminary agreement with the details to follow. In Exodus 20–23, God will reveal the specifics. Later, in chapter 24, they will be presented with an actual document containing the details and an opportunity to confirm their decision to "do everything the LORD has said."

The Covenant with Israel: The Details

On the third day[138] after their preliminary agreement to obey the LORD, Moses led the people to the foot of the mountain. At that time, God began to relay the details of his covenant. The first part was announced directly to the people. The remaining parts were delivered to Moses privately. All the information was eventually transcribed by Moses into a document

---

[137] Jeffery H. Tigay, *The JPS Torah Commentary: Deuteronomy* (Philadelphia: the Jewish Publication Society, 1996), 278.
[138] Exodus 19:11, 19:16.

that would later be known as the Book of the Covenant.[139] The subject matter can be divided into three parts: the Ten Commandments,[140] the Judgments, and the Decrees.[141]

The Ten Commandments

The commandments listed in Exodus 20:3–17 constitute the very heart of the Torah. These are the commandments that were written in stone.

> He declared to you his covenant, the Ten Commandments, which he commanded you to follow and then wrote them on two stone tablets. And the LORD directed me at that time to teach you the decrees and laws[142] you are to follow in the land that you are crossing the Jordan to possess (Deut. 4:13–14).

It is not coincidental that these verses conveniently list the three divisions of the Book of the Covenant.

The preeminence of these commandments is clearly understood in that, having been written in stone, the media itself is called "the tablets of the covenant."[143] These commandments are the starting point for everything that follows. The subsequent decrees and judgments both here and in the rest of the Torah expound upon and delineate what is contained

---

[139] Exodus 24:4, 24:7.

[140] The actual phrase used in Exodus 34:28 and Deuteronomy 4:13 and 10:4 is "the ten words" (עשרת הדברים—*asheret hadevarim*)

[141] These two categories are most often paired together. The decrees/statutes/ordinances (חקים—*khuqqim*) and the judgments (מפטים—*mishpatim*) constitute the major section of Deuteronomy. Chapters 12–26 are introduced by these terms in Deuteronomy 12:1. For a complete list of terms that can be used to segregate much of the Torah, see Deuteronomy 11:1 and Genesis 26:5. Unfortunately, many English Bibles are not consistent in the way they translate each Hebrew word.

[142] This is a typical example of the inconsistent translation, or even mistranslation, of the words mentioned in the previous footnote. The Hebrew text reads, "to teach you the חקים (*khuqqim*) and the מפטים (*mishpatim*)."

[143] Deuteronomy 9:9,11.

in the commandments. In addition, all of them can be understood as categories for related offenses both major and minor. In all but three categories, there is a corresponding major offense that could result in a death penalty.[144]

The Judgments

This section begins with a very clear and concise title regarding its contents. "These are the" מפטים (*mishpatim*) "you are to set before them."[145] The translation of *mishpatim* varies among the English versions. Based on the Hebrew root, it would be more accurate to translate it as "judgments" or "rulings." Exodus 21:1–22:20 lists God's rulings regarding personal injury, property damage, theft, bailment, and specific capital offenses. His decision in these cases sets a legal precedent for human judges and provides general guidelines for legal retaliation (*lex talionis*), along with some examples of acceptable deviations from those guidelines.

The first topic of this section is the rights of Hebrew slaves.[146] Admittedly, it appears to be an awkward place to discuss such a topic. However, its placement in this context helps us to understand an important part of ancient Jewish law. Most of the rulings for a non-capital offense resulted in fines intended to compensate the victims for their losses. One's inability

---

[144] Exodus 20:3 (Deut. 13:1–18, 17:2–7), Exodus 20:8–11 (Exod. 31:14, 35:2), Exodus 20:12 (Exod. 21:15,17; Deut. 21:18–21), Exodus 20:13 (Exod. 21:12), Exodus 20:14 (Lev. 20:10), Exodus 20:15 (Exod. 21:16; Deut. 24:7), Exodus 20:16 (Deut. 19:15–21). Two of the three commandments not in this list are the idol prohibition in Exodus 20:4–6 and the false oath prohibition in Exodus 20:7. It is interesting that both lack a judicial ruling like the others but carry within the commandment itself a promise of God's personal involvement in punishing the violator. The last commandment in Exodus 20:17 has neither a judicial ruling nor a clause regarding God's response to its violators. However, by observing the commandment to not covet, one would most likely avoid breaking the commandments in verses 13–16. For more explanation, see James R. Ward, *The Mountain Yeshiva* (Maitland: Xulon Press, 2020), 32–35.

[145] Exodus 21:1.

[146] Exodus 21:2–11.

to pay the penalty did not relieve them of their obligation. Someone else could pay the debt for him, but then he would be obligated to the benefactor to work off the debt via indentured servitude.[147] The rulings on this topic, among other things, address the maximum duration of such servitude.

The second topic is personal injury.[148] The rulings begin with the ultimate personal injury: murder. The penalty has not changed since God first ruled on this matter back in the Noahic Covenant.[149] God provides a very simple principle for judging personal injury cases.

> But if there is serious injury, you are to take life for
> life, eye for eye, tooth for tooth, hand for hand, foot for
> foot, burn for burn, wound for wound, bruise for bruise
> (Exod. 21:26).

Regarding personal injury in general, there is a one-to-one correspondence between the crime and the penalty. When the punishment fits the crime, the victim would be compensated for his loss (except in the case of murder, of course) and the perpetrator would incur the loss himself. Misunderstanding this principle, or even outright misuse of scripture, has caused some to misinterpret this to support vigilantism. On the contrary, this was carried out methodically in a court of law, and the penalty was imposed in the form of a fine based on the value of the body part.[150] This was also the understanding of the Aramaic translator for the same verse.

> The value of an eye for an eye, the value of a tooth for
> a tooth, the value of a hand for a hand, the value of a
> foot for a foot, all equivalent of the pain of burning for

Exodus 21:2 of Targum Jonathon says, "If thou shalt have bought a son of Israel, on account of his theft ..." See *The Targums of Onkelos and Jonathan Ben Uzziel On the Pentateuch*, http://www.targum.info/pj/psjon.htm.

[148] Exodus 21:12–36

[149] Exodus 21:12 (Gen. 9:6), Exodus 21:28 (Gen. 9:5).

[150] Bava Kamma 8:1.

burning, and of wounding for wounding, and of blow for blow.[151]

In conjunction with other verses in Exodus 21:12–36, the judges of the Mishnaic period factored in the victim's pain, medical costs, recuperation, and loss of time when determining the totality of the fine for personal injury.[152]

The third topic is property, specifically addressing the areas of damage, theft, and bailment.[153] As with personal injury cases, there is a general principle when making rulings in property cases. Here, however, instead of one-to-one, there is a two-to-one correspondence between the crime and the penalty.

> In all cases of illegal possessions, whether for an ox, a donkey, a sheep, a garment, or any kind of lost item, about which someone says "This belongs to me," the matter of the two of them will come before the judges, and the one whom the judges declare guilty must repay double to his neighbor" (Exod. 22:9).

The verses before and after this one provide the exceptions to this principle by either increasing the penalty or by reducing it to simple restitution. Also, in the case of bailment, when the guardian pleads innocent and the actual thief cannot be identified, the guardian is afforded the option of making restitution or protecting himself with an oath.

The fourth and least comprehensive topic is idolatrous practices.[154] This list of offenses is limited to sorcery, bestiality, and sacrifices.

---

[151] See Targum Jonathon (not the case in Onkelos), *The Targums of Onkelos and Jonathan Ben Uzziel on the Pentateuch*, http://www.targum.info/pj/psjon.htm.
[152] Bava Kamma 8:1.
[153] Exodus 22:1–17.
[154] Exodus 22:18–20.

The Decrees

Exodus 22:21–23:19 make up the final section of the Book of the Covenant. This category of directives from God is often called "decrees," stemming from the Hebrew word חק (khoq, masc.) or חקה (khuqqah, fem.). Various English versions of the Bible will also translate it as "statue," "ordinance," or "rule." Often, these decrees provide clarity and specificity to the generality of the Ten Commandments. They also cover areas specific to life in the promised land, kosher laws, offerings, war, and more. Unfortunately, neither form of the word appears in the Hebrew text of this section. However, many of the topics found here are replicated in the decrees (חקים—khuqqim) and judgments (מפטים—mishpatim)[155] section of Deuteronomy (see chapters 12–26).[156]

After the ratification of the covenant in Exodus chapter 24, there would be additional decrees (חקים—khuqqim), judgments (מפטים—mishpatim), instructions (תורות—toroth), and responsibilities (משמרת—mishmaroth). The majority of these were given during their yearlong stay on Mount Sinai and included directives regarding the building and service of the tabernacle, diet, offerings, sexual practices, public health, and holidays.

The three-part Book of the Covenant concludes with God's promises to guard the Israelites on their way to the promised land, to help them defeat the inhabitants of the land, and to establish their borders.[157]

---

[155] Deuteronomy 12:1

[156] Comparisons include Exodus 22:21–22 (Deut. 24:17–18), Exodus 22:25-27 (Deut. 23:19–20, 24:10–13), Exodus 22:28 (Deut. 17:12), Exodus 22:29 (Deut. 26:1–17), Exodus 22:29–30 (Deut. 15:19–20), Exodus 23:1–3 (Deut. 19:16–21), Exodus 23:6–9 (Deut. 16:18–20), and Exodus 23:4–5 (Deut. 22:1–4). The shmitah the seventh year in which there is to be no sowing or harvesting in Exodus 23:10–11, is not mentioned in Deuteronomy. However, the other two events of that same year are recorded: the cancellation of debts (Deut. 15:1–6) and the release of one's servants (Deut. 15:12–18). Also, the three feast days (חג—khag) mentioned in Exodus 23:14–17 are called everlasting decrees (חקת עולם-khuqqath olam) in Leviticus 23:14, 23:21, 23:41.

[157] Exodus 23:20–33.

The Covenant with Israel: The Ratification

As we observed with God's covenants with Noah and Abraham, the final step in the process was for all parties to recognize the terms of the agreement by way of ceremony. After Moses descended from Mount Sinai, he relayed to the people what God had told him. They reaffirmed their consent by saying, "Everything the LORD has said we will do."[158] Then Moses wrote all the words of the LORD in a document that would be used later in the ceremony.

> He got up early the next morning and built an altar at the foot of the mountain and set up twelve stone pillars representing the twelve tribes of Israel. Then he sent young Israelite men, and they offered burnt offerings and sacrificed young bulls as fellowship offerings to the LORD. Moses took half of the blood and put it in bowls and the other half he sprinkled on the altar. Then he took the Book of the Covenant and read it to the people. They responded, "We will do everything the Lord has said; we will obey."
>
> Moses then took the blood, sprinkled it on the people and said, "This is the blood of the covenant that the LORD has made with you in accordance with all these words" (Exod. 24:4–8).

As with the earlier examples, the terms were announced, and the sacrifices were made—burnt offerings to signify dedication and fellowship offerings denoting communion between the parties. The sprinkling of the blood of the offerings on the participants was also symbolic. The altar represented God, and the pillars represented the people. Thus, the agreement was finalized.

---

[158] Exodus 19:8, 24:3, 24:7.

The Covenant with Israel: The Sign

The Noahic Covenant had the rainbow and the Abrahamic Covenant had circumcision. The Covenant with Israel also had a sign.

> Then the Lord said to Moses, "Say to the Israelites, 'You must observe my *Sabbaths. This will be a sign between me and you for the generations to come,* so you may know that I am the Lord, who makes you holy. Observe the *Sabbath* because it is holy to you. Anyone who desecrates it must be put to death; whoever does any work on that day must be cut off from his people. For six days, work is to be done, but the seventh day is a *Sabbath* of rest, holy to the Lord. Whoever does any work on the Sabbath must be put to death. The Israelites are to observe the *Sabbath,* celebrating it for the generations to come as a lasting covenant [ברית־עולם—*brit olam*]. *It will be a sign between me and the Israelites forever,* for in six days the Lord made the heavens and the earth, and on the seventh day he had abstained from work and rested" (Exod. 31:12–17, *italics and Hebrew text added*).

> Therefore I led them out of Egypt and brought them into the desert. I gave them my decrees [חקות—*khuqqoth*] and made known to them my laws [מפטים—*mishpatim*], for the man who obeys them will live by them. Also, I gave them *my Sabbaths as a sign between us,* so they would know that I the Lord made them holy (Ezek. 20:10–12, *italics and Hebrew text added*).

> Keep my *sabbaths* holy, that *they may be a sign between us.* Then you will know that I am the Lord your God (Ezek. 20:20, *italics added*).

Regarding the passage from Exodus 31, the placement of the command in the text is noteworthy. God gave the Sabbath directive to Moses immediately after chapters 25–31, where he gave him instructions regarding the construction of the tabernacle. The command to remember the Sabbath was already given in Exodus 20:8–11. However, it is repeated here to emphasize that it takes precedence over this sacred work. Even during the construction of the tabernacle, the Sabbath must be observed.[159]

The phrase from Exodus 31:13 above is a clear statement of its purpose: that the Jewish people "may know that I am the Lord, who makes you holy." It correlates the sign with God's original covenant promise: "Out of all the nations you will be my treasured possession."[160]

The great Jewish commentator Rav Hirsch explains:

> דעת (*to know*) is the purpose of every sign ...; for an
> אות (*sign*) is a means of making something known ...,
> and the knowledge to be made known by שמירת שבת
> (*Sabbath observance*) is כי אני ה' מקדשכם (*that I am
> the* LORD *who sanctifies you*), that God *sanctifies* us—i.e.,
> *separates* us entirely and places us *at the ready* for His
> service.
>
> Through שמירת שבת [*Sabbath observance*]—i.e., by
> refraining from all constructive work—we lay ourselves,
> our whole world, and all the powers God has granted us
> so that we should master our world in homage before
> God, and we acknowledge and avow that we and our
> world and our power to act are sacred unto God, i.e.,
> belong exclusively to Him for the fulfillment of His
> will.[161] (*Hebrew translation added*)

---

[159] Rav Samson Raphael Hirsh, *The Hirsch Chumash: Sefer Shemos* (New York: Feldheim Publishers, 2005), 738.
[160] Exodus 19:5.
[161] Rav Samson Raphael Hirsh, *The Hirsch Chumash: Sefer Shemos* (New York: Feldheim Publishers, 2005), 739–740.

God had set apart the Israelites, as a nation, for himself. As each Israelite observes the sign of the covenant, the Sabbath, they are essentially setting themselves apart for God in recognition of the covenant between them.

The Covenant with Israel: Permanence, Renewability, Revisability

The permeance of the relationship between God and Israel is observed throughout scripture. Even during Israel's many cycles of apostasy and renewal, God's commitment to his covenant is demonstrated by his decision to bless or to punish his people accordingly, but never to abandon them. As the apostle Paul expounded on the subject in the eleventh chapter of his epistle to the Romans, "I ask then: Did God reject his people? By no means! ... For God's gifts and his call are irrevocable."[162] Like the previous covenants with Noah and Abraham, God's covenant with Israel is an everlasting one.

> He remembers his covenant forever,
> the word he commanded, for a thousand generations,
> the covenant he made with Abraham,
> the oath he swore to Isaac.
> He confirmed it to Jacob as a decree,
> to Israel as an everlasting covenant [עולם ברית—*brit olam*]:
> "To you I will give the land of Canaan as the portion you will inherit" (Ps. 105:8–11; 1 Chron. 16:15–18, *Hebrew text added*).

> The earth[163] is defiled by its people;

---

[162] Romans 11:1, 11:29.

[163] The subject matter of this portion of Isaiah focuses on the coming Assyrian threat that will lead to the destruction and exile of Israel and its neighbors. Because the prophecies in previous chapters include the neighboring countries, some have concluded that Isaiah 24 is broader in scope and have chosen to translate the Hebrew word ארץ (*erets*) as "earth" in every occurrence. However, the use of the

they have disobeyed the laws [תורת—*toroth*],
violated the statutes [חק—*khoq*]
and broken the everlasting covenant [ברית עולם—*brit olam*] (Isa. 24:5, *Hebrew text added*).

As we observed earlier, the sign for the Israelite Covenant is also permanent.

The Israelites are to observe the Sabbath, celebrating it for the generations to come as a lasting covenant [עולם ברית—*brit olam*]. It will be a sign between me and the Israelites forever [עולם—*olam*] (Exod. 31:16–17, *Hebrew text added*).

Interestingly, there is a priestly responsibility that includes both the people of the covenant and the sign of the covenant. There was a table in the holy place of the tabernacle, specifically placed on the north side opposite the menorah. Once each week, the priest would place twelve fresh loaves of bread upon it. The loaves represented the tribes of Israel. Their presence within the tabernacle, separated from the ark of the covenant by only a curtain, was a continual reminder of God's watchful eye over the nation and of the close covenantal relationship between them. Even the day of the week in which the bread was replaced had significance.

This bread is to be set out before the Lord regularly, Sabbath after Sabbath, on behalf of the Israelites, as a lasting covenant [ברית עולם—*brit olam*] (Lev. 24:8, *Hebrew text added*).

---

words "laws" (תורת—*toroth*) and "statutes" (חק—*khoq*) in verse 5 seems to indicate that the judgments are directed at Israel, specifically at the northern kingdom at this time. Therefore, it would be better to translate the word ארץ (*erets*) as "land" in each occurrence (vv. 1, 3–6, 11) prior to verse 13. Thereafter, "earth" would be the better translation.

In this one verse, the participants of the covenant, the symbols in the tabernacle that represent them, and the sign of the covenant are forever united in a permanent ritual.

The renewability of the covenant is observed early, unfortunately, even while the Israelites were still encamped at Mount Sinai. While Moses was on the mountain the second time receiving instructions regarding the building of the tabernacle, the people were already violating the terms of the covenant.

> Then the Lord said to Moses, "Go down, because your people, whom you brought up out of Egypt, have become corrupt. They have been quick to turn away from what I commanded them and have made themselves an idol cast in the shape of a calf. They have bowed down to it and sacrificed to it and have said, 'These are your gods, Oh Israel, who brought you up out of Egypt.'
>
> I have seen these people," the Lord said to Moses, "and they are a stiff-necked people. Now leave me alone so that my anger may burn against them and that I may destroy them. Then I will make you into a great nation" (Exod. 32:7–10).

The people were very quick to violate their oath, "We will do everything the LORD has said. We will obey."[164] God had every right to destroy them because, by breaking the covenant via disobedience, they had divorced themselves from it. However, whereas God's covenant with Abraham was with his descendants, his covenant with Israel was with a nation. At any time, individuals could be "cut off" from it because they violated specific laws.[165] Even an entire generation could be excluded, as we will soon see. However, it would have no effect on the permanency of the

---

[164] Exodus 19:8, 24:3, 24:7.

[165] I.e., Numbers 9:13 (not observing Passover). For a complete list, see page 406 of Excursus 36 in Jacob Milgrom, *The JPS Torah Commentary: Numbers* (Philadelphia: the Jewish Publication Society, 1990).

covenant because it was national and transgenerational. Notice the last sentence of Exodus 32:10, where God says to Moses, "Then I will make you into a great nation." Had God destroyed all the Israelites that day, Abraham's line would have continued, and the national covenant would also have continued as God proceeded to rebuild the nation using just one man and his family. He had already done it previously.[166]

Given the right circumstances and the right mediator, the covenant can be renewed with the offending generation. In this case, Moses interceded on Israel's behalf, and "the LORD relented and did not bring upon his people the disaster he had threatened."[167] Consequently, the covenant was renewed with the current generation. However, there was also a slight revision. Exodus 34 is a record of this covenant renewal/revision. First, there was a new set of stone tablets, chiseled by Moses and written upon by God.[168] They contained the same ten commandments as the first set. This would by necessity include all the decrees and judgments that delineated them. Second, God reiterated the decrees he had given Moses previously that concluded the Book of the Covenant.[169] However, there is a third observation that denotes a revision.

> Then the Lord said to Moses, "Write down these words, for in accordance with these words I have made a covenant *with you* and with Israel" (Exod. 34:27, *italics added*).

It appears that God was including a contingency plan in this version of the covenant by adding a cosigner. God's plan to make Moses into a great nation and Moses's request for forgiveness are both woven into the fabric of this version of the covenant. If the Israelites were to rebel against God again, he would now have the covenantal right to enforce what might be called the Exodus 32:10 clause. Actually, if either cosigner

---

[166] Genesis 12:2.
[167] Exodus 32:11–14.
[168] Exodus 34:1, 34:28; Deuteronomy 10:1–5.
[169] cf. Exodus 34:10–16 (Exod. 23:20–33); Exodus 34:18–26 (Exod. 23:10–19).

disobeyed God from this point forward, they would forfeit entrance into the promised land.

The renewability of the covenant is observed again about a year later, not long after what was only an eleven-day journey to the southern border of the promised land.[170] The story of this rebellion is found in Numbers 13 and 14. The Israelites were encamped at Kadesh and had sent spies into the land of Canaan. The spies brought back a good report about the produce of the land, but also a bad report about the size of the inhabitants. This bad report terrified the leadership so much that they discussed how they might depose Moses and Aaron, elect new leaders, and return to Egypt. This action was enough for God to invoke the Exodus 32:10 clause.

> The Lord said to Moses, "How long will these people treat me with contempt? How long will they refuse to believe in me, in spite of all the miraculous signs I have performed among them? I will strike them down with a plague and destroy them, but I will make you into a nation greater and stronger than they" (Num. 14:11–12).

Once again, Moses successfully interceded for the people, and the Israelites were spared. However, even though they received forgiveness, the relationship with this generation did not return to its previous state.

> The Lord said to Moses and Aaron: "How long will this wicked community grumble against me? I have heard the complaints of these grumbling Israelites. So tell them, 'As surely as I live, declares the Lord, I will do to you the very things I heard you say: In this desert your bodies will fall—every one of you twenty years old or more who was counted in the census and who has grumbled against me. Not one of you will enter the land I swore with uplifted hand to make your home, except Caleb son of Jephunneh and Joshua son of Nun.

---

170 Deuteronomy 1:2.

As for your children that you said would be taken as plunder, I will bring them in to enjoy the land you have rejected. But you—your bodies will fall in this desert. Your children will be shepherds here for forty years, suffering for your unfaithfulness, until the last of your bodies lies in the desert. For forty years—one year for each of the forty days you explored the land—you will suffer for your sins and know what it is like to have me against you.' I, the Lord, have spoken, and I will surely do these things to this whole wicked community, which has banded together against me. They will meet their end in this desert; here they will die" (Num. 14:26–35).

As stated earlier, individuals, or even an entire generation, can be "cut off" without affecting the permanency of the covenant. Such actions serve to demonstrate the national and transgenerational nature of the agreement. Over the next forty years, God was going to use the current generation to raise the next one and then have them die naturally in the desert. God was willing to wait until the next generation was ready to accept the terms of the covenant. Later, when they reached the Plains of Moab, after they had defeated the two Amorite kings east of the Jordan River, and after the plague in Numbers 25, God gave Moses the order to take another census.[171] You might say that there was an outstanding accounting issue and the books needed to be settled. Also, the reliability of God's word would be documented for future generations.

These are the ones counted by Moses and Eleazar the priest when they counted the Israelites on the plains of Moab by the Jordan across from Jericho. Not one of them was among those counted by Moses and Aaron the priest when they counted the Israelites in the desert of Sinai. For the Lord had told those Israelites they would surely die in the desert and not one of them was left except Caleb son of Jephunneh and Joshua son of Nun (Num. 26:63–65).

---

[171] Numbers 26:1–4.

And so the covenant would continue with the next generation. The children of those who died in the desert would grow to be a believing generation. They would ratify a new and revised version of the covenant that included all the terms of the covenant at Sinai, along with additional decrees and judgments applicable to life in the promised land. The details of this version and the details of the final version, often called the New Covenant, will be discussed in subsequent chapters.

It should also be noted that there would be covenant renewals initiated by the Israelites. One very good example happened during the reign of Josiah. After Hilkiah, the high priest (father of Jeremiah the prophet) discovered the Book of the Law in the temple, Josiah publicly renewed the covenant and subsequently followed up on his commitment to abide by it.[172] Another example happened after the Babylonian exile. Nehemiah returned to Jerusalem to rebuild the city with the full approval of King Artaxerxes. After Ezra read the law during the Feast of Tabernacles, the Israelites renewed their commitment to the covenant.[173]

---

[172] 2 Kings 22 and 23.
[173] Nehemiah 8–10.

THE COVENANT WITH ISRAEL: AT MOAB AND SHECHEM

The events that occurred at Kadesh after the spies returned essentially sealed the fate of an entire generation. Those whose names were included in the first census would not live to see the fulfillment of God's promise to bring them into their inheritance. Thirty-eight years after the divine pronouncement that they would die in the desert, their children crossed the Zered valley on their way to the Plains of Moab.[174] The biblical record of this period is minimal. What has been preserved is found in Numbers 15:1–21:12. The complete itinerary from Egypt to Moab is found in Numbers 33. Shortly after crossing the Arnon valley, the Israelites began their conquest by defeating the two Amorite kings whose kingdoms were located on the eastern side of the Jordan River. Afterward, they encamped on the Plains of Moab until the day Joshua led them across the river.[175] It was here that Moses expounded his great discourses found in the book of Deuteronomy. His final message, combined with what had already been delivered to him at Sinai, completed the terms of the covenant[176] and prepared the new generation of Israelites for life in the promised land.

---

[174] Deuteronomy 2:14–15.
[175] Numbers 22:1; Joshua 3:1.
[176] Deuteronomy 29:1.

Order of Events

The book of Deuteronomy is organized according to Moses's discourses. His first discourse is found in Deuteronomy 1:1–4:43 and serves as a prologue to the book. In it, he recounts the events of the last forty years. The second discourse is found in Deuteronomy 4:44–29:1. It has two major sections. First, in Deuteronomy 4:44–11:32, Moses begins by reiterating the Ten Commandments, the foundation of the covenant. Second, in Deuteronomy 12:1–29:1, he lists the additional terms of the covenant. The very first verse of chapter 12 states, "These are the decrees (חקים—*khuqqim*) and judgments (מפטים—*mishpatim*) you must be careful to follow." Finally, the third discourse found in Deuteronomy 29:2–30:20 includes Moses's admonishments for this generation to ratify the covenant and to internalize the Torah.[177]

Although Deuteronomy is organized in this manner, the chronology of events probably happened differently. In regard to the covenant revisions found in Deuteronomy 12:1–29:1, the following can be suggested:

Moses documented them[178]	Deuteronomy 31:24
He gave a copy to the priests	Deuteronomy 31:25–26
He ordered the assembly of the elders and officials	Deuteronomy 31:28

The purpose of assembling the leaders was to "speak these words in their hearing." This would imply that Moses read the document publicly to them as representatives of the people who would subsequently disseminate the information to their respective groups. In time, the

---

[177] The actual terms used to denote the internalization of Torah are "take them to heart" (Deut. 30:1), "with all your heart and soul" (Deut. 30:2, 30:6, 30:10), and "the word is very near you; it is in your mouth and in your heart" (Deut. 30:14). All these harken back to the Shemah of Deuteronomy 6:4–5. Also, Moses uses the phrase "circumcise your hearts" (Deut. 30:6), a phrase first used in Deuteronomy 10:16.

[178] This document would have included at least Deuteronomy 12–28. It might have also included the other discourses or the document from Sinai (Exod. 24:4, 24:7). However, this document is called the Book of the Law, whereas the earlier document was called the Book of the Covenant.

individual documents written by Moses during this period were compiled into one book, possibly by Ezra the scribe after the exile.[179] This particular document has been passed down to us in the pages of Deuteronomy 12:1–29:1.

The Revisions

Deuteronomy chapters 12 through 26 contain what might be called "revisions"[180] to the existing covenant with Israel. The details of these revisions are outside the scope of this book. However, a broad overview of the material will provide the reader a road map for further study if desired. (Note: Verses in brackets are the corresponding verses from the Hebrew text.)

Sanctuary and Religious Matters (Deut. 12:2-16:17)

One place of worship	12:1–32
Worshiping other gods	13:18–14:2
Kosher laws	14:3–21 (Lev. 11)
Tithes	14:22–29 (also Deut. 26:12–15)
The seventh year	15:1–18
Cancelling debts	15:1–11
Freeing servants	15:12–18 (Exod. 21:2–4)
Firstborn animal	15:19–23 (Exod. 13:11–16, Num. 18:14–19)
Feasts	16:1–17
Passover (Feast of Unleavened Bread)	16:1–8 (Exod. 12, Lev. 23:4–8, Num. 9:1–14, 28:16–25)
Feast of Weeks	16:9–12 (Lev. 23:15–22, Num. 28:26–31)
Feast of Tabernacles	16:13–17 (Lev. 23:33–43, Num. 29:12–38)

---

[179] Tigay, *JPS Torah Commentary: Deuteronomy*, xix.

[180] It should be noted that the topic at hand, "Revisions," does not include the elimination of any previous decree or judgment. It does include things not previously stated such as new decrees and additional details to existing ones.

Civil and Religious Authorities (Deut. 16:18–18:22)

Local courts	16:18–17:13
The King	17:14–20 (1 Sam. 8:5, 8:19, 8:20)
Priests and Levites	18:1–8 (Num. 18)
Prophets	18:9–22

Judicial and Military Matters (Deut. 19:1–21:9)

Cities of refuge (relates to murder)	19:1–13 (Exod. 21:12–14, Num. 35, Deut. 4:41–43)
Respect for boundaries (relates to property theft)	19:14
Witnesses (relates to perjury)	19:15–21
Going to war	20:1–20
Atonement for an unsolved murder	21:1–9

Protections (of various individuals and aspects of society) (Deut. 21:10–25:19)

Of a captive woman	21:10–14
Of the right of the firstborn	21:15–17
Of society from a rebellious son	21:18–21
Of the land regarding an execution	21:22–23
Of your neighbor from your indifference	22:1–4
Of society from gender confusion	22:5
Of natural proliferation	22:6–7
Of your neighbor from your construction hazards	22:8
Of your crops from defilement	22:9
Of _____ [181]	22:10–11 (Lev. 19:19)

---

[181] "The reason for these laws is uncertain. To Rashi they are sovereign decrees of God, for which no reason need to be given. Many commentators believe that their aim is to preserve the species distinctions that God established at creation, as described in Genesis 1:11–12, 1:21, 1:24–25. Though all these laws deal with forbidden combinations, it is probable that each of them originally had its own specific purpose... Precisely which practices and species are covered by these laws, where they apply, and what may or may not be done with the products of such

Of _____[182]	22:12 (Num. 15:37–41)
Of a woman's dignity	22:13–29
Of your father's honor	22:30
Of the citizenry	23:1–23:8
Of the camp regarding sanitation	23:9–14
Of foreign slaves	23:15–16
Of the temple treasury	23:17–18
Of Israelite debtors	23:19–20
Of those making vows	23:21–23
Of individuals regarding crop consumption	23:24–25
Of a divorced woman	24:1–4
Of newlyweds	24:5
Of a debtor (collateral, security)	24:6 (Exod. 22:26)
Of society regarding kidnapping	24:7
Of society regarding public health	24:8–9
Of the dignity of the debtor	24:10–13
Of the day worker	24:14–15
Of family members of lawbreakers	24:16
Of the alien, orphan, and widow	24:17–22 (Exod. 22:21–24)
Of one receiving physical punishment	25:1–3
Of work animals (possibly proverbial)	25:4 (1 Cor. 9:9, 1 Tim. 5:18)
Of childless widows	25:5–10
Of a man's dignity	25:11–12
Of commerce regarding equal weight and measures	25:13–16
Of future generations	25:17–19

---

mixtures is discussed in detail in tractate Kil'ayim." Tigay, *JPS Torah Commentary: Deuteronomy*, 202.

[182] There is a fair amount of explanations offered in Jewish commentaries regarding this statute, which, in my opinion, provide valuable insight as to its purpose. However, I have chosen to leave it blank since the reason is not discernable from the plain reading of the text.

Liturgical Declarations (Deut. 26:1–15)

First Fruits   26:1–11

Tithes   26:12–15

The Renewal

What happens next will be, for this generation of Israelites, a first-time ratification of the covenant. However, regarding all the post-Exodus Israelites (which would include their parents), it will be a renewal. This ratification/renewal was documented and has become the postscript to Moses's aforementioned list of decrees (חקים—*khuqqim*) and judgments (מפטים—*mishpatim*).

> The Lord your God commands you this day to follow these decrees and laws[183]; carefully observe them with all your heart and with all your soul. You have declared this day that the Lord is your God and that you will walk in obedience to him, that you will keep his decrees, commands and laws[184] and that you will obey to him. And the Lord has declared this day that you are his people, his treasured possession as he promised, and that you are to keep all his commands. He has declared that he will set you in praise, fame and honor high above all the nations he has made and that you will be a people holy to the Lord your God, as he promised (Deut. 26:16–19).

As you might have noticed, this reads like the final paragraph of a contract. The party of the first part states its commitment to the applicable terms ("You have declared this day that ..."). The party of the second part declares its commitment to the applicable terms ("He has

---

[183] More accurately translated as "decrees (חקים—*khuqqim*) and judgments (מפטים—*mishpatim*)."

[184] More accurately translated as "decrees (חקים—*khuqqim*), commands (מצות—*mitsvoth*), and judgments (מפטים—*mishpatim*)."

declared that ...”). Although there have been revisions to the details of the covenant, the agreement between the two parties has not changed since the original offer forty years earlier.

> Then Moses went up to God, and the Lord called to him from the mountain and said, “This is what you are to say to the descendants of Jacob and what you are to tell the people of Israel: ‘You yourselves have seen what I did to Egypt, and how I carried you on eagles’ wings and brought you to myself. Now if you obey me fully and keep my covenant, then out of all nations you will be my treasured possession. Although the whole earth is mine, you will be for me a kingdom of priests and a holy nation.’ These are the words you are to speak to the Israelites” (Exod. 19:3–6).

What is considered by many to be the covenant renewal ceremony, that led to what is documented in Deuteronomy 26:16–19, is recorded later in the twenty-ninth and thirtieth chapters. There, Moses explained to the Israelites that they were summoned to make their decision regarding the covenant.

> Carefully follow the terms of this covenant, so that you may prosper in everything you do. All of you are standing today in the presence of the Lord your God—your leaders and chief men, your elders and officials, and all the other men of Israel, together with your children and your wives, and the foreigners living in your camps who chop your wood and carry your water. You are standing here in order to enter into a covenant with the Lord your God, a covenant the Lord is making with you this day and sealing with an oath, to confirm you this day as his people, that he may be your God as he promised you and as he swore to your fathers, Abraham, Isaac and Jacob. I am making this covenant, with its oath, not only with you who are

standing here with us today in the presence of the Lord our God but also with those who are not here today (Deut. 29:9–15).

The phrase "not only with you who are standing here … but also with those who are not here today" indicates that the covenant is transgenerational. The inability of this generation's parents to uphold the terms of the covenant did not remove God's offer to this or future generations. The blessings or punishments incurred by each generation of Israelites would be determined by the decision of each generation to uphold the terms. The covenant itself was as everlasting as the one who offered it to them.

We can assume that if this was indeed a covenant ceremony, there would have been fellowship and burnt offerings.[185] Unfortunately, these were not logged in the biblical record. However, there would be another renewal ceremony after the Israelites entered the promised land. Moses gave explicit instructions about it, including the burnt offerings and fellowship offerings and the altar upon which they were to present them.[186]

These two renewals are very important in this stage of Israel's history. The covenant renewal on the plains of Moab demonstrated that this was indeed a believing generation. Their commitment to the terms of the agreement, and consequently to the God of the covenant, permitted them entrance into Canaan. The covenant renewal within Canaan's borders demonstrated their commitment to complete the task of the conquest.[187] But there is another reason for this second renewal. It is a

---

[185] Genesis 8:20, 9:8–17; Exodus 24:4–8. Also, when Abraham was instructed to bring certain animals prior to the covenant ceremony (Gen. 15:9–10, 17–19), Jubilees states, "And the day passed, and Abram offered the pieces, and the birds, and their fruit offerings, and their drink offerings, and the fire devoured them" (Jub. 14:19).

[186] Deuteronomy 27:1–8.

[187] On more than one occasion, they were instructed to destroy the inhabitants of the land. (Exod. 23:23–33, Deut. 7:1–6).

reason that carries with it great historical and personal significance for both parties.

The covenant renewal ceremony would happen just after the victories at Jericho and Ai, but before the southern and northern military campaigns.[188] Its location was specified by Moses when he gave these instructions:

> When you have crossed the Jordan, these tribes shall stand on Mount Gerizim to bless the people: Simeon, Levi, Judah, Issachar, Joseph and Benjamin. And these tribes shall stand on Mount Ebal to pronounce curses: Ruben, Gad, Asher, Zebulun, Dan and Naphtali (Deut. 27:12–13).

The ceremony included a component where half of the tribes were to stand on neighboring mountains and recite the blessings and curses of the covenant. The interesting, but unspoken, detail of this arrangement is what lay in the valley between the mountains, the ancient city of Shechem. About four and a half centuries earlier, their ancestor left his homeland in Ur of the Chaldeans, without much more than a promise.[189] He was seventy-five years old when he entered Canaan and made his way as far as the great tree of Moreh at Shechem. It was there that the Lord appeared to him again to add another promise, "To your offspring I will give this land."[190] Afterward, Abraham built an altar, and there, at Shechem between Mount Gerizim and Mount Ebal, sacrificed to the God who brought him safely to this land. And now, many years later, his offspring were standing in the same place renewing the covenant that the Lord made with them, making similar offerings. Afterward, they would begin the campaign to take the promised land for their very own. The significance of the moment is undeniable. The magnitude of the moment is almost incomprehensible.

---

[188] Joshua 8:30–35.
[189] Genesis 12:2–3.
[190] Genesis 12:7.

Ultimately, the covenant renewals on the Plains of Moab and at Mount Gerizim and Ebal constitute the response of that Israelite generation to the everlasting covenant that God offered to the nation at Mount Sinai.[191]

---

[191] There was one other covenant renewal at Shechem. However, it was not like the one that is described in Joshua 8:30–35. It was a renewal that appeared to address a particular issue. The people failed to obey the Lord regarding his instructions to not make treaties with the previous inhabitants and to break down their altars. As expected, they had begun to embrace the local deities, not necessarily to the exclusion of the Lord, but simultaneously with their worship of him. This covenant renewal is documented in Joshua 24. In order to understand the issue at hand, one needs to be aware of the chronological overlap that exists between Joshua 13:1–24:33 and Judges 1:1–3:6. Although the tribal allotments were decided prior to Joshua's death, the acquisition of the land transpired over many years. Over time their successes became stifled and most of the tribes west of the Jordan river were unable to drive out completely the previous inhabitants (Judg. 1:19, 1:21, 1:27–35). The angel of the Lord spoke to them at Bokim and explained that their failures were due to their disobedience regarding his command to "not make a covenant with the people of this land, but you shall break down their altars" (Judg. 2:1–3). The key to understanding that this renewal was about this particular point of disobedience is found in Joshua 24:25, where it states, "He drew up for them decrees and laws." This is similar to what was presented earlier (i.e., Deut. 12:1) where the terms "decrees" (חקים—khuqqim) and "judgments" (מפטים—mishpatim) are used. However, here the Hebrew words are singular, not plural, and should read "decree (חק—khoq) and judgment (מפט—mishpat). The decree refers to the repeated phrase in Joshua 24: "serve the LORD." Making treaties with the inhabitants and not breaking down their altars will lead to a logical conclusion; the Israelites would be enticed to follow the local deities. The judgment or ruling from God for such behavior is that "he will turn and bring disaster on you and make an end of you, after he has been good to you" (Josh. 24:20). Consequently, the covenant drawn up by Joshua, with this one decree and judgment, was in response to their failure to drive out the inhabitants and the subsequent explanation given by the angel of the Lord at Bokim.

THE COVENANT WITH ISRAEL'S ROYAL LINE

God's covenant with the royal line begins much like previous ones. The process began with Noah and Abraham when God chose them, called them, and subsequently entered a covenant relationship with them. Later, based on his promises to Abraham, God chose the Israelites, called them out of bondage, and led them to Mount Sinai to enter a covenant relationship with them as a nation. We shall see this same pattern of events occur regarding God's covenants with Israel's royal and priestly lines. However, the full story of these covenants cannot be fully appreciated without consulting both biblical and extrabiblical sources. Judaism has a rich literary history. Although the apocryphal and pseudepigraphal works are subordinate to the sacred scriptures, they have been consulted and maintained throughout history and often illuminate what in the Bible might be a very succinct story. Some of these documents were preserved by the Qumran community that brought us the Dead Sea Scrolls.

The Origin of the Royal Line

It could be said that God's choice of the royal line in Israel began when, about a year before Isaac was born, he gave Abraham the sign of the covenant, or circumcision. To Abraham, he said:

> I will make you very fruitful; I will make nations of you,
> and kings will come from you (Gen. 17:6).

And about Sarah, he said,

> I will bless her and will surely give you a son by her. I will
> bless her so that she will be the mother of nations; Kings
> of peoples will come from her (Gen. 17:16).

God's announcement to Abraham was fulfilled in a very broad sense,
for he sired children with Hagar,[192] Sarah,[193] and Keturah.[194] Hagar's
son Ishmael became the father of the Arab people, who survive to this
day and have produced many kings and kingdoms throughout history.
Abraham's grandson Esau, brother of Jacob, became a nation and
produced a line of kings.[195] Abraham's son Midian became the father
of the Midianites. Shortly before the conquest of Canaan, the Israelites
battled a Midianite nation and defeated their five kings.[196]

However, God's announcement about Sarah being the mother of nations
and kings brought specificity to the promise, because it would have to
be fulfilled through her only son, Isaac. Later, after Isaac's son Jacob
acquired the birthright from his brother Esau[197] and the blessing of the
firstborn from his father,[198] both the covenant and the promise of a royal
line were firmly in the hands of Jacob and his descendants. After serving
his father-in-law, Laban, for twenty years, Jacob returned to Bethel to
fulfill his vow to God[199] and ratify the covenant God made with his
fathers Abraham and Isaac. It was there that God said to him:

> I am God almighty; Be fruitful and increase in number.
> A nation in the community of nations will come from
> you, and kings will come from your body (Gen. 35:11).

---

[192] Genesis 16:4.

[193] Genesis 21:2.

[194] Genesis 25:1–2.

[195] Genesis 36:31–43 (1 Chron. 1:43–50).

[196] Numbers 31:8.

[197] Genesis 25:29–34.

[198] Genesis 27:1–29.

[199] Genesis 28:20–22.

From Abraham, through Sarah, and on to Jacob flowed the promise of a royal lineage. However, it appears that during the lifetime of Jacob, another degree of specificity was added. For during his final days on earth, Jacob summoned his sons and said, "Gather around so I can tell you what will happen to you in the days to come."[200] What he said about Judah is of particular interest:

> Judah, your brothers will praise you;
> your hand will be on the neck of your enemies;
> your father's sons will bow down to you …
> The scepter will not depart from Judah,
> nor the ruler's staff from between his feet,
> until he comes to whom it belongs
> and the obedience of the nations is his (Gen. 49:8, 10).

It is evident from the metaphors, scepter, and ruler's staff that Jacob understands that the royal line would be passed to Judah. In addition, there appears to be an intended recipient of this kingship. The phrase "to whom it belongs" is equivalent to the Hebrew word שׁילה (shiloh). The meaning of the word is debated in both Christianity and Judaism. However, many interpreters in both groups understand it to be messianic in nature. In other words, there may be many kings throughout Israel's history who are of the tribe of Judah. But ultimately, the position is intended for the last one.[201] And unlike his predecessors, he will not only be the ruler of Israel but also "of the nations."

One might ask regarding Jacob's statement, "How did he know this?" There is not a record in the biblical text relating a story about Jacob having a dream, vision, or direct revelation from God about it. It is necessary for us, then, to turn to the extrabiblical records for insight.

---

[200] Genesis 49:1.

[201] This seemed to be the understanding of the prophet Isaiah when he said, "The government will be upon his shoulders… of the increase of his government and peace there will be no end. He will sit upon David's throne and over his kingdom, establishing and upholding it with justice and righteousness from that time on and forever" (Isa. 9:6–7).

One such document is the Testaments of the Twelve Patriarchs. In it, each son of Jacob provides a short narrative of his life, sometimes emphasizing certain events. He might focus on his own successes or failures in an effort to exhort his children to imitate a positive characteristic or to avoid a bad one. At times, he might retell a biblical event from his own perspective, and even provide information known only to him. One such example is found in the Testament of Judah:

> And the Lord shall bring upon them divisions one against another. And there shall be continual wars in Israel; And among men of another race shall my kingdom be brought to an end, Until the salvation of Israel shall come, Until the appearing of the God of righteousness, That Jacob [and all the Gentiles] may rest in peace. And He shall guard the might of my kingdom forever; For the Lord swore to me with an oath that He would not destroy the kingdom from my seed forever.[202]

One might be quick to notice the similarities between Judah's statement and the previous reference to Genesis 49:8, 10. What was said there regarding "to whom it belongs," or שׁילה (shiloh), is comparable to the phrases here that begin with "until." It appears that Judah recognized that there would be a temporary halt in the royal line, "men of another race shall my kingdom be brought to an end" until something/someone arrives, "the salvation of Israel/the God of righteousness." The last line is also interesting. He states that "the Lord swore to me with an oath" regarding his kingdom. As with Jacob's statement about Judah in Genesis chapter 49, we must also inquire here: "How did he know this?" When did the Lord make such an oath to Judah? Unfortunately, a record of such an event has yet to be discovered.[203] However, earlier in his testament,

---

[202] Sefaria Library, https://www.sefaria.org/The_Testaments_of_the_Twelve_Patriarchs, Judah 22:1–3.

[203] In the Testaments of the Twelve Patriarchs, Levi states that he had a prophetic dream regarding his priesthood. Could Judah have had such dream as well but simply did not record it in his last testament?

Judah mentioned an event that, unfortunately, never became part of the biblical record:

> And Isaac, the father of my father, blessed me to be king in Israel, and Jacob further blessed me in like manner. And I know that from me shall the kingdom be established.[204]

Fortunately, this story was recorded in the Book of Jubilees. It was about a time when Jacob went to visit his father, Isaac, and he brought with him two of his sons, Judah and Levi. If, perchance, Judah had an encounter with God prior to that journey, his vision/dream was confirmed by his grandfather's blessing.

Jacob was in Shechem when God told him to go to Bethel and build an altar.[205] Jacob was to return to the place where the Lord first appeared to him and fulfill his vow. God had been with him and prospered him during his time with Laban, and now he was going to personally ratify the Abrahamic Covenant and make the Lord his God. The thirty-first chapter of the Book of Jubilees picks up the story:

> And he went up on the new moon of the seventh month to Bethel. And he built an altar at the place where he had slept, and he set up a pillar there, and he sent word to his father Isaac to come to him to his sacrifice, and to his mother Rebekah. And Isaac said: Let my son Jacob come, and let me see him before I die."[206] Jacob went to his father Isaac and to his mother Rebekah, to the house

---

[204] Sefaria Library, https://www.sefaria.org/The_Testaments_of_the_Twelve_Patriarchs, Judah 17:5–6.

[205] Genesis 33:18, 35:1.

[206] We learn later that Jacob had invited his father to the covenant ratification ceremony at Bethel to be part of the momentous event. However, Isaac was 165 years old and could no longer make such a journey. He instructed his wife, Rebekah, to go with him (Jub. 31:26–30). She brought her handmaiden, Deborah, with her. This would explain why the Bible records the death of Deborah at Bethel (Gen. 35:8).

of his father Abraham and he took two of his sons with him, Levi and Judah, and he came to his father Isaac and to his mother Rebekah.[207]

After their visit and as the time for their departure approached, possibly during the time Isaac was bestowing a blessing upon his grandsons, "the spirit of prophecy came down into his mouth,"[208] and he said to Judah,

> May the Lord give the strength and power to tread down all that hate thee; A prince shalt thou be, thou and one of thy sons, over the sons of Jacob; May thy name and the name of thy sons go forth and traverse every land in region. Then shall the gentiles fear before thy face, and all the nations shall quake. In thee shall be the help of Jacob, and indeed be found the salvation of Israel. And when thou sittest on the throne of honor of thy righteousness there shall be great peace for all the seed of the sons of the beloved; Blessed be he that blesseth thee, and all that hate thee and afflict thee and curse thee shall be rooted out and destroyed from the earth and be accursed.[209]

The reference in the prophecy about being "a prince" and sitting "on the throne of honor" clearly demonstrates that the royal line had been bestowed upon Judah. Whether or not Judah was aware of this via some previous encounter with God is uncertain. However, this could very well be the reason Jacob knew about it and declared it years later to his children just before his death.[210] He had heard it straight from the mouth of his father, Isaac.

---

[207] Charles, *Apocrypha and Pseudepigrapha of the Old Testament*, Jubilees 31:3–5.
[208] Jubilees 31:12.
[209] Charles, *Apocrypha and Pseudepigrapha of the Old Testament*, Jubilees 31:18–20.
[210] Genesis 49:8, 49:10.

The Early Development of the Royal Line

The royal line of Judah was developed and protected throughout history by what could be nothing short of divine providence. It is interesting how, in the years before the Davidic dynasty, some faithful women played a prominent role in the process. Conversely, the royal line would also be threatened. Understanding God's choice of the line of Judah and his eventual covenant with David helps us to appreciate the importance of some otherwise trivial, even confusing, stories in scripture.

Tamar

In the Testament of the Twelve Patriarchs, Judah recounts a story from Genesis 38 and provides some additional information:

> And after these things my son Er took to wife Tamar, from Mesopotamia, a daughter of Aram. Now Er was wicked, and he was in need concerning Tamar, because she was not of the land of Canaan. And on the third night an angel of the Lord smote him. And he had not known her according to the evil craftiness of his mother, for he did not wish to have children by her. In the days of the wedding-feast I gave Onan to her in marriage; and he also in wickedness knew her not, though he spent with her a year. And when I threatened him, he went in unto her, but he spilled the seed on the ground, according to the command of his mother, and he also died through wickedness. And I wished to give Shelah also to her, but his mother did not permit it; for she wrought evil against Tamar, because she was not of the daughters of Canaan, as she also herself was.[211]

---

[211] Sefaria Library, https://www.sefaria.org/The_Testaments_of_the_Twelve_Patriarchs, Judah 10:1–7.

And I knew that the race of the Canaanites was wicked, but the impulse of youth blinded my mind. And when I saw her pouring out wine, owing to the intoxication of wine I was deceived, and took her although my father had not counselled (it). And while I was away, she went and took for Shelah a wife from Canaan. And when I knew what she had done, I cursed her in the anguish of my soul. And she also died through her wickedness together with her sons.[212]

Unlike his father and grandfather, Judah did not marry a woman from his own people in Paddan Aram. He married a Canaanite woman, who bore him three sons. It was a choice he obviously regretted. It seemed that she was very influential regarding her sons' choices of wives, and even matters of procreation. Her agenda was clear. She wanted her sons to marry Canaanites, and assuming that her control continued with her grandsons, they would also marry women from her people. Within three or four generations, Judah's Semitic ethnicity would have been all but eradicated from his descendants, as would the royal line. The genetic line to David, and ultimately the Messiah, would have ended before it had begun. The seriousness of such consequences might cause one to wonder if there were forces involved in this story beyond the physical.

Tamar was a Mesopotamian[213] woman who was acquired by Judah for his son Er. According to Judah's testament above, Er did not desire her because she was not a Canaanite. Because of the "evil craftiness of his mother," "he did not wish to have children by her." Both Judah's testament and the Genesis record[214] agree that Er's death on the third night of the wedding feast was a judgment from God. By the law of the

---

[212] Sefaria Library, Judah 11:1–5.

[213] Sefaria Library, Judah 10:1 states that she was "from Mesopotamia, a daughter of Aram," or מאָרַם נַהֲרִים בַּת־אָרָם (me-aram naharim bat-aram), or literally "from Aram of the rivers, the daughter of Aram." This would imply that she was a descendant of Aram and not that her father's name was Aram. Aram was a son of Seth (Gen. 10:22) and settled in the land between the rivers (Tigris and Euphrates). Thus, she was Semitic.

[214] Genesis 38:7.

levirate marriage,[215] one of Er's brothers was obligated to marry her, since Er died without producing a male heir. Consequently, Onan married her but, "according to the command of his mother," spilled his seed on the ground.[216] He was subsequently judged by God and died as well.

Judah wanted to give Tamar to his remaining son, Shelah, but "his mother did not permit it; for she wrought evil against Tamar, because she was not of the daughters of Canaan." Once, when Judah "was away she went and took for Shelah a wife from Canaan." This angered him greatly. It apparently angered God as well for Judah's testament declares "And she also died through her wickedness together with her sons."

At some point, probably before Shelah's marriage, Judah becomes hesitant to give Tamar to his remaining son. If Shelah were to follow his brother's example and avoid impregnating her, he would lose his only son to the judgment of God. And so he sent Tamar back to her father under the pretext that Shelah was too young to marry and that she should wait for him to grow up.[217] After Shelah's marriage to the woman who was his mother's choice and after the death of Judah's wife,[218] Tamar understood that she had been cast aside. She had waited long enough, and no doubt knew her rights. The time had come for her to act.

Most Bible students are familiar with the rest of the story as it is unveiled in Genesis 38. It often makes modern readers uncomfortable. It tells how she disguised herself as a prostitute, traveled to city where Judah was conducting business, and seduced him. She acquired his seal, cord, and staff as collateral for payment of her services. Later, when she was three months pregnant and about to be judged for her perceived immorality,

---

[215] Normally, this relationship between a man and his sister-in-law was forbidden (Lev. 18:16). However, if his brother died without fathering a male child, a brother was obligated to marry his widow and father a son in his name (Deut. 25:5–10). This law was not codified until the renewal of the covenant on the Plains of Moab. Nonetheless, the Judah/Tamar story in Genesis 38 demonstrates that the practice was already understood.

[216] T12P Judah 10:6, Genesis 38:9.

[217] Genesis 38:11.

[218] Genesis 38:12.

she produced the same three items to publicly identify the unborn child's father. Judah could do nothing but exonerate her and admit that his poor judgment caused her to take such drastic action saying, "She is more righteous than me, since I wouldn't give her to my son Shelah."[219]

However, the importance of this story becomes clear six months later when she gives birth to twins, Perez and Zerah. If our suggestion that dark spiritual forces could have been behind the efforts of Judah's wife to eradicate his ethnicity from their descendants (and the chosen royal line as well), then it would be reasonable to assume that, ultimately, Tamar's actions were used by God to maintain that line. Having survived an early attack, the royal line of Judah would proceed as planned:

> Perez was the father of Hezron,
> Hezron was the father of Ram,
> Ram was the father of Amminadab,
> Amminadab was the father of Nahshon,
> Nahshon was the father of Salmon,
> Salmon was the father of Boaz,
> Boaz was the father of Obed,
> Obed was the father of Jesse,
> And Jesse was the father of David (Ruth 4:18–22).

Rahab

We find the story of Rahab in chapters 2 and 6 of the book of Joshua. The story begins:

> Then Joshua the son of Nun secretly sent two spies from Shittim. "Go, look over the land," he said, "especially Jericho." So they went and entered the house of a prostitute named Rahab and stayed there (Josh. 2:1).

---

[219] Genesis 38:26.

As often is the case in the biblical narrative, we are given only a very succinct description of events. Details are left to the imagination so that the story can progress. This is the reason that Bible students consult extrabiblical literature, hoping to glean those details to possibly broaden one's view of the story and to more fully understand the reason for certain events. When there is no such literature to cross-reference, we are forced to ask questions regarding the missing details and make comparisons with other biblical events to help collect possible answers. Such is the case with the opening verse of Joshua 2.

First, why were the spies sent to explore the land, especially Jericho? Was this merely standard pre-battle military protocol? Joshua would not receive specific instructions about the battle until Joshua 6:2–5. Did he dispatch the spies on his own initiative or had the Lord instructed him to do so? Forty years earlier, spies were sent to explore the land. Was that reconnaissance mission initiated by God or by the Israelites? The answers to these questions are important because they could affect the way we interpret the Rahab story.

We are able to answer at least one of these questions. When Moses was speaking to the Israelites on the Plains of Moab, recounting the story of the spies forty years earlier, he said,

> Then all of you came to me and said, "Let us send men ahead to spy out the land for us and bring back a report about the route we are to take and the towns we will come to."
>
> The idea seemed good to me; so I selected twelve of you, one man from each tribe (Deut. 1:22–23).

But when we check the parallel passage from the book of Numbers, we find this:

> The LORD said to Moses, "Send some men to explore the land of Canaan, which I am giving to the Israelites.

From each ancestral tribe send one of its leaders" (Num. 13:1–2).

It appears that the idea to send spies originated with the people. God directed Moses on how many should be sent and from which tribes. Moses was the one who chose which leaders would be sent.[220] So with regard to our aforementioned questions, it is fair for us to entertain both the possibility that Joshua sent the spies of his own initiative and that he sent them because of a divine directive. If the latter is true, why?

Another question we might ask pertains to their final destination. How is it that they stayed in the home of the only person in the city who revered the God of Israel? Was this destination included in the instructions given to them by Joshua? Or did Rahab identify them as Israelites, as did Jericho's king,[221] and invite them to stay with her in order to protect them?[222] In light of the fact that her entire city would be destroyed in a matter of days, were her actions directed by God?

All these questions are worth pondering but will have to remain unanswered. Consider, however, the long inquiry of Abraham with God regarding the fate of Sodom and Gomorrah.[223] God was willing to spare the cities if ten righteous people could be found there. In the end, the cities were destroyed, for there was only one such righteous person— Abraham's nephew Lot. However, not one ounce of fiery judgment was allowed to fall from heaven until he and his family found refuge in a neighboring town.[224] Could the encounter between the two Israelite spies and Rahab parallel the similar encounter between the two angels and Lot? Was this also a rescue operation? If so, *why* and for *what* ultimate purpose?

---

[220] Each tribe had many leaders. We should not assume that these men were the supreme heads of the tribe. Notice that the list of the tribal leaders who were sent to spy on the land (Num 13:4–16) did not include the same tribal leaders who were chosen to assist Moses and Aaron with the census (Num. 1:2–16).

[221] Joshua 2:2–3.

[222] Joshua 2:4–7.

[223] Genesis 18:16–33.

[224] Genesis 19:21–22.

We might be able to answer this last question: The immediate reason for her deliverance from Jericho's destruction was the fact that she was a believer.

Consider her statement to the spies that evening:

> "I know that the LORD has given this land to you and that a great fear of you has fallen on us, so that all who live in this country are melting in fear because of you. We have heard how the LORD dried up the water of the Red Sea for you when you came out of Egypt, and what you did to Sihon and Og, the two kings of the Amorites east of the Jordan, whom you completely destroyed. When we heard of it our hearts melted and everyone's courage failed because of you, for the *Lord your God is God in heaven above and on the earth below*" (Josh. 2:8–11, *italics added*).

Her words to the spies were nothing short of a statement of faith. Even an event that was forty years old factored in her decision to recognize the God of Heaven and his nation of choice. She knew that the only hope for survival for her and her family was to plead for mercy in return for the kindness she had shown them by hiding them from the Jericho authorities.[225] The spies agreed, and the two parties sealed it with an oath.[226] On the day of Jericho's destruction, Rahab and her family were spared.[227] It is interesting that the last words written about Rahab in the book of Joshua are as follows:

> And she lives among the Israelites to this day (Josh. 6:25).

In what capacity did she live among the Israelites? Was her story in the book of Joshua just about a rescue operation? As was asked earlier, "For what ultimate purpose?"

---

[225] Joshua 2:12–14.
[226] Joshua 2:17–21.
[227] Joshua 6:22–25.

Judah the father of Perez and Zerah, whose mother was
Tamar,
Perez the father of Hezron,
Hezron the father of Ram,
Ram the father of Amminadab,
Amminadab the father of Nahshon,
Nahshon the father of Salmon,
Salmon the father of Boaz, whose mother was Rahab,
Boaz the father of Obed, whose mother was Ruth,
Obed the father of Jesse,
and Jesse the father of King David (Matt. 1:3–6).

Her faith in the God of Israel did not go unnoticed. In the light of God's foreknowledge and sovereignty, Rahab's story was about more than God rescuing a woman of faith from imminent death. She and her husband, Salmon, produced a family that included the great-grandfather of King David. God had a role for her to play as he continued to develop the royal line of Judah.

Ruth

Ruth lived in the country of Moab. The Moabites were ancient relatives of the Israelites, descendants of Abraham's nephew Lot.[228] Mahlon, the man who would become her husband, lived in Israel during the time of the judges. In the course of time, due to a famine, he and his family decided to move to the neighboring country of Moab. The group included his parents, Elimelech and Naomi, and his brother Kilion. Ruth married Mahlon. Kilion also married a Moabite woman named Orpah. Unfortunately, Elimelech died, and within ten years, both Mahlon and Kilion died, leaving three widows to survive on their own.

News from back home reached Naomi that the famine was over. As she planned her trip back to Bethlehem, her daughters-in-law pleaded to go with her. She explained to them that it would be better for them to stay

---

[228] Genesis 19:36–38.

in Moab and to find new husbands. She was prepared to face the rest of her days being alone and wanted them to start over and to be happy. Kilion's widow, Orpah, followed Naomi's advice. However, Ruth refused to break ties with the mother-in-law she had come to love, as well as her people and her faith, stating,

> Do not urge me to leave you or to turn back from you. Where you go I will go, and where you stay I will stay. Your people will be my people and your God my God. Where you die I will die, and there I will be buried. May the LORD deal with me, be it ever so severely, if anything but death separates you and me" (Ruth 1:16–17).

Obviously, Naomi's Israelite influence on her Moabite daughter-in-law had been both strong and positive. It was enough to persuade Ruth to leave family and country in order to take care of Naomi and to become part of the covenant people of God. Her plea to Naomi was a simple statement of faith. It would not go unnoticed by God.

The two of them traveled together back to Israel, back to the property in Bethlehem that Elimelech and his family left during the famine. They arrived during the time of the barley harvest. Since they were not there during the planting season, there was nothing for them to harvest. Thus, their destitution continued as they became part of the nation's poor. This status permitted them to enter the fields of others and to reap from the edges of the field or from whatever might have been dropped by the harvesters. This practice was established by God in the Torah, specifically to aid those who were in economic distress, like the poor and the alien.[229]

---

[229] Leviticus 19:9–10, 23:22; Deuteronomy 24:19–22. There is an entire tractate in Talmud that addresses the details of this practice. It is called Peah, which means "corner" or "side," referring to the portion of the field that should not be harvested by the property owner but left for the poor.

While gathering the sheaves in this manner, Ruth met the property owner, Boaz, who showed her great kindness because of what she had done for Naomi. He told her,

> I've been told all about what you have done for your mother-in-law since the death of her husband—how you left your father and mother and your homeland and came to live with the people you did not know before. May the LORD repay you for what you have done. May you be richly rewarded by the LORD, the God of Israel, under whose wings you have come to take refuge (Ruth 2:11–12).

Bible students are familiar with the rest of the story. The two of them fell in love and together worked through a legal process whereby Boaz purchased Naomi's property using his rights as a relative of Elimelech ("kinsman redeemer").[230] In the end, Naomi's property stayed in the family, and both women were no longer destitute.

Once again, a woman who was not Jewish was accepted into the Israelite community because of her faith and character. When Boaz blessed Ruth that day, he probably did not realize just how she would "be richly rewarded by the LORD" and that he would also play a role in that blessing. Actually, God not only blessed Ruth, but he also blessed the royal line of Judah, for

> Boaz the father of Obed,
> Obed the father of Jesse,
> and Jesse the father of David (Ruth 4:21–22).

---

[230] This practice is explained in detail in Levi 25:25–55. The land was to remain within the respective tribal allotments. The sale of property gave the buyer the right to plant and harvest crops during the years that remained until the year of the Jubilee. At that time, the ownership of the land would revert to the original owner or his heir. The text tells us that the owner is selling the property because of hardship. If at any time he comes out of debt, he has the right to redeem the property he sold. Even if he is unable to redeem it himself, someone—a relative, for instance, can redeem it for him.

The Chosen Pedigree of the Royal Line

We must remind ourselves that the prophecies we have examined so far regarding the royal line seem to have the final recipient of the kingship in mind.

> And among men of another race shall my kingdom be brought to an end, Until the salvation of Israel shall come, Until the appearing of the God of righteousness, That Jacob [and all the Gentiles] may rest in peace. And He shall guard the might of my kingdom forever.[231]

> A prince shalt thou be, thou and one of thy sons, over the sons of Jacob; May thy name and the name of thy sons go forth and traverse every land in region. Then shall the Gentiles fear before thy face, and all the nations shall quake. In thee shall be the help of Jacob, and indeed be found the salvation of Israel. And when thou sittest on the throne of honor of thy righteousness there shall be great peace for all the seed of the sons of the beloved.[232]

> The scepter will not depart from Judah,
> nor the ruler's staff from between his feet,
> until he comes to whom it belongs
> and the obedience of the nations is his (Gen. 49:10).

In the first reference, "the salvation of Israel" and "the God of righteousness" act as titles of the individual who will "guard the might of my kingdom forever." In the second reference, from the Book of Jubilees, the individual is "one of thy sons" who bears the title "the help of Jacob" and "the salvation of Israel."[233] In the final reference, from Genesis, the

---

[231] Sefaria Library, https://www.sefaria.org/The_Testaments_of_the_Twelve_Patriarchs, Judah 22:2–3.

[232] Charles, *Apocrypha and Pseudepigrapha of the Old Testament*, Jubilees 31:18–20.

[233] The construction of both phrases is identical (יוושע יעקב ובך יפדה ישׂראל בך) from the Sefaria Library, https://www.sefaria.org/Book_of_Jubilees, Jubilees 31:31.

individual is simply called שִׁילֹה (*shiloh*), which is usually translated "to whom it belongs." In each reference, there is mention of the Gentiles or the nations indicating that he will have world dominion.

Although these prophecies look forward to the final king and the final kingdom, God anticipated the Israelites' desire to "be like the other nations" and request a king of their own in the interim.

> When you enter the land the LORD, your God is giving you and have taken possession of it and settle in it, and if you say, "Let us set a king over us like all the nations around us," be sure to appoint over you the king the LORD your God chooses. He must be from among your own brothers. Do not place a foreigner over you, one who is not a brother Israelite. The king, moreover, must not acquire great numbers of horses for himself or make the people return to Egypt to get more of them, for the Lord has told you, "You are not to go back that way again." He must not take many wives, or his heart will be led astray. He must not accumulate large amounts of silver and gold. When he takes the throne of his kingdom, he is to write for himself on a scroll a copy of this law, taken from that of the priests, who are Levites. It is to be with him, and he is to read it all the days of his life so that he may learn to revere the LORD his God and follow carefully all the words of this law and these decrees and not consider himself better than his brothers and turn from the law to the right or to the left. Then he and his descendants will reign a long time over his kingdom in Israel (Deut. 17:14–20).

The presence of a king in Israel was not mandated by the Torah; it only specified the responsibilities of the office holder. Until such a time when Israel would make the request for a king, the LORD was their king.[234] He

---

[234] Consequently, anyone sitting on the throne in either Israel or Judah would rule with delegated authority from Israel's true king, the Lord himself. This fact,

had given them their laws. He disciplined them and protected them. He spoke to them through the prophets and the Urim and Thummim.[235] However, Israel eventually did ask for a king, and it was seen by God as a personal rejection.[236] It happened during the latter years of the prophet Samuel. He was displeased with them, but he brought their request to God anyway.

> And the LORD said to him: "Listen to all that the people are saying to you; It is not you they have rejected, but they have rejected me as their king. As they have done from the day I brought them up out of Egypt until this day, forsaking me and serving other gods, so they are doing to you. Now listen to them; but warn them solemnly and let them know what the king who will reign over them will do" (1 Sam. 8:7–9).

Samuel obeyed God and proceeded to warn the people about how a king would draft their young men and women into his service and heavily tax them through the confiscation of their herds, flocks, fields, and vineyards.[237] They replied by reiterating their request, and so God instructed Samuel to grant it.

Regarding the overall topic of kingship, it is noteworthy that the first king of Israel was from the tribe of Benjamin.[238] The next three kings were from the tribe of Judah, David, Solomon, and Rehoboam. During the reign of Rehoboam, the Israelite nation was divided into two kingdoms. The southern kingdom would continue to be ruled by the descendants of David. However, the first king of the northern kingdom

---

in addition to his sovereignty over the world in general, is the basis for his right to determine who ascends to the throne and to judge the kings based on their obedience to him. The chronicler said it plainly, "So Solomon sat on the *throne of the* LORD as king in place of his father David." (1 Chron. 29:23, *italics added*)

[235] Exodus 28:30.
[236] "So in my anger I gave you a king" (Hos. 13:11).
[237] 1 Samuel 8:10–18.
[238] 1 Samuel 9:15–17, 10:20–24, 11:14–15.

was Jeroboam from the tribe of Ephraim.[239] He was chosen by God and was informed of God's decision through the prophet Ahijah.[240] There would be other northern kings who were not from the tribe of Judah but were nonetheless appointed by God.[241] However, the northern kingdom eventually broke the covenant and rebelled against God's law and "set up kings without my consent" and chose "princes without my approval."[242]

The prophet Samuel made an interesting comment to King Saul, the Benjamite, after his first act of disobedience during a battle with the Philistines at Gilgal. He said, "You have not kept the command the LORD your God gave you; if you had, he would have established your kingdom over Israel for all time (עַד עוֹלָם —ad olam)."[243] Had Saul been obedient, God was prepared to give him a permanent dynasty. How is this to be reconciled with the royal prophecies to date regarding the tribe of Judah? In the same way, how are we to understand God's involvement in the royal history of the northern kingdom? It is important to understand the context of the kingdoms at this time, united or divided. Had Israel not requested a king, it would have had no effect on the timing nor the tribal identification of that final king previously identified as "the help of Jacob," "the salvation of Israel," and שִׁילֹה (shiloh).

All the kings, from Saul until the exile of the northern and southern kingdoms, existed for only one reason; The Israelites had asked for a king. Any dynasties during that time, permanent or short-term, should be understood in the context of that period, the time when Israel requested a king. But the tribal identity of the final king during the end of days was revealed by God when Jacob and his family were still living as strangers in the land of Canaan. It should come as no surprise to anyone that God would use this period of the kings in Israel's history to further delineate the progeny of the royal line of Judah. For it was during this time that God found "a man after his own heart and appointed him

---

[239] 1 Kings 11:26.
[240] 1 Kings 11:29–39.
[241] 1 Kings 16:2; 2 Kings 9:1–13.
[242] Hosea 8:4.
[243] 1 Samuel 13:13

leader of his people."[244] Not only would God establish a dynasty for this man, but he would also make an everlasting covenant (עולם ברית—*brit olam*) with him.

The exact identity of the next king had not yet been revealed to the prophet Samuel. He was simply told to travel to Bethlehem, to the home of a man named Jesse, who had seven sons. He was told to bring oil with him for he would be anointing one of Jesse's sons as the next king. When he arrived, he offered a sacrifice, and Jesse proceeded to present his sons in birth order.[245] Samuel was directed by God to reject the first six sons. The youngest son, David, was still tending the flocks and had to be summoned. When he arrived, the Lord said to Samuel, "Rise and anoint him; he is the one."[246]

The process of becoming a king was not always immediate. After David was anointed by Samuel, he continued with life as usual. Eventually, he entered the service of King Saul, first as a musician[247] and then as a military official.[248] However, over time, the relationship between them deteriorated because of David's successes and Saul's jealousy. Saul's reign came to an end when he took his own life on the battlefield.[249] Afterward, David was anointed king over Judah at Hebron,[250] but Saul's son Ish-Bosheth maintained control over his father's reign until he was murdered by two of his own military leaders.[251] It was at that time that the elders of all the tribes of Israel came to Hebron and anointed David king over Israel.[252]

David obeyed the Lord in all that he did. Even when Saul was seeking his life, David refused to kill him when he had the opportunity because

---

[244] 1 Samuel 13:14
[245] 1 Samuel 16:6–12; 1 Chronicles 2:13–14.
[246] 1 Samuel 16:12.
[247] 1 Samuel 16:14–23.
[248] 1 Samuel 18:5.
[249] 1 Samuel 31:1–6; 1 Chronicles 10:1–7.
[250] 2 Samuel 2:1–7.
[251] 2 Samuel 4:1–12.
[252] 2 Samuel 5:1–5; 1 Chronicles 11:1–3.

of the great respect he had for him as the anointed leader of Israel.[253] It was after he brought the ark of the covenant to Jerusalem and God had given him rest from all his enemies that the Lord revealed to David his long-term plans for his faithful servant.

> The LORD declares to you that the LORD himself will establish a house for you: when your days are over and you rest with your fathers, I will raise up your offspring to succeed you, who will come from your own body, and I will establish his kingdom. He is the one who will build a house for my name, and I will establish the throne of his kingdom forever [עד עולם—*ad olam*]. I will be his father and he will be my son ... my love will never be taken away from him, as I took it away from Saul, whom I removed from before you. Your house and your kingdom will endure forever [עד עולם—*ad olam*] before me; Your throne will be established forever [עד עולם— *ad olam*] (2 Sam. 7:11–13, 15–16, *Hebrew text added*).

God addressed the matter of David's successor first. David had wanted to build the temple in Jerusalem but was forbidden by God. The task would be accomplished by his son Solomon.[254] Also, regarding his son's dynasty, God promised to establish the throne of "his kingdom" forever [עולם עד—*ad olam*]. As will be observed later, this promise was understood as having a condition. However, when God addressed David's future, he spoke of "your house," "your kingdom," and "your throne," indicating a distinction between his plans for the two men. That distinction is found in the qualifying phrase "before me."[255] At the very least, it can be said that Solomon's dynasty applied to the time of the kings. His progeny continued to rule the southern kingdom until the Babylonian

---

[253] 1 Samuel 24:1–22, 26:1–25.

[254] 1 Chronicles 28:2–3, 5–6.

[255] It must be noted that there are scribal inconsistencies with this phrase. Also, the passage from 2 Samuel 7:16 is not included in the parallel passages of 1 Chronicles 17:10–14. However, David attests to the phrase in his responsive prayer in both 2 Samuel 7:26 and 1 Chronicles 17:24.

exile. His dynasty has become part of the earthly historical record. However, David's house/kingdom/throne would endure forever before God. It could be said that his dynasty is part of the heavenly record. This minute detail could very well be the reason that God's statements about David were understood to be a promissory covenant. Later, in what are understood to be David's last words, he says,

> Is not my house right with God? Has he not made with me an everlasting covenant [עולם ברית—*brit olam*], arranged and secured in every part? (2 Sam. 23:5, *Hebrew text added*).

God's promise to David was an everlasting covenant (ברית—עולם *brit olam*). However, God's promise to establish the throne of David's offspring forever (עד עולם—*ad olam*) is similar to the statement made by the prophet Samuel to Saul, "You have not kept the command the LORD your God gave you; if you had, he would have established your kingdom over Israel for all time (עד עולם—*ad olam*)."[256] The potential of a dynasty for Saul existed, but he failed to obey God in all he did. The promise of a dynasty for Solomon, or any descendant for that matter, was understood to be conditional. On the day that David summoned his officials to declare that his son Solomon would be building the temple and turned the temple plans over to him, he said,

> And you, my son Solomon, acknowledge the God of your father, and serve him with wholehearted devotion and with a willing mind, for the LORD searches every heart and understands every motive behind the thoughts. *If* you seek him, he will be found by you; but *if* you forsake him, he will reject you forever (1 Chron. 28:9, *italics added*).

Later, after David's death, Solomon completed the temple and included these words during his public prayer of dedication:

---

[256] 1 Samuel 13:13.

> You have kept your promise to your servant David my
> father; With your mouth you have promised and with
> your hand you have fulfilled it- as it is today. Now LORD,
> God of Israel, keep for your servant David my father the
> promises you made to him when you said, "You shall
> never fail to have a man to sit before me on the throne
> of Israel, *if only* your sons are careful in all they do to
> walk before me according to my law as you have done
> (2 Chron. 6:15–16, *italics added*).

Sometime after the temple dedication, the Lord appeared to Solomon at
night (presumedly in a dream) and said,

> I have heard your prayer and have chosen this place for
> myself as a temple for sacrifices ...

> As for you, *if* you walk before me as David your father
> did, and do all I command, and observe my decrees and
> laws, I will establish your royal throne, as I covenanted
> with David your father when I said, "You shall never fail
> to have a man rule over Israel (2 Chron. 7:12, 7:17–18,
> *italics added*).

Even within one of the songs of ascents,[257] the permanency of the throne
to David and the conditionality of the throne to others is recognized.

> The Lord swore an oath to David,
> a sure oath that he will not revoke:
> "One of your own descendants I will place on your
> throne—
> *if* your sons keep my covenant
> and the statutes I teach them,

---

[257] See also Psalm 89, where in verses 19–37, Ethan, the Ezrahite, cites a vision
from God to the people. Note especially the conditional statements in verses 30–32
regarding the royal offspring but with the many reiterations of his commitment to
David.

then their sons will sit on the throne forever and ever"
(Ps. 132:11–12, *italics added*).

The condition for maintaining the dynasty from Solomon onward was
clear: each heir to the throne must walk in the ways of their ancestor
David, keeping the covenant between God and Israel. Unfortunately,
many of them failed to meet the standard. During those administrations
when the king did not observe God's decrees and laws, or even worshiped
other gods, God could have justifiably terminated the dynasty. Eventually,
the kingdom was divided because of Solomon's unfaithfulness, but the
Davidic line would continue to rule in the south. There were many kings
who did not wholeheartedly serve the Lord. Despite this, God permitted
the Davidic line to continue ruling Judah until the exile. The reason for
this appears to be founded in the relationship between God and "a man
after his own heart."

When Solomon's heart had turned away from the Lord, God said to him,

> Since this is your attitude and you have not kept my
> covenant and my decrees, which I commanded you,
> I will most certainly tear the kingdom away from you
> and give it to one of your subordinates. Nevertheless,
> *for the sake of David* your father, I will not do it during
> your lifetime. I will tear it out of the hand of your son.
> Yet I will not tear the whole kingdom from him, but will
> give him one tribe *for the sake of David* my servant and
> for the sake of Jerusalem, which I have chosen (1 Kings
> 11:11–13, *italics added*).

When the Ahijah prophesied to Jeroboam about becoming the first king
of the northern tribes, he said,

> See, I am going to tear the kingdom out of Solomon's
> hand and give you ten tribes. But *for the sake of my
> servant David* and the city of Jerusalem, which I have
> chosen out of all the tribes of Israel, he will have one
> tribe (1 Kings 11:31–32, *italics added*).

Regarding the reign of Rehoboam's son Abijah (Solomon's grandson), the Bible states,

> He committed all the sins his father had done before him; his heart was not fully devoted to the Lord as God, as the heart of David his forefather had been. Nevertheless, *for David's sake* the LORD his God gave him a lamp in Jerusalem by raising up a son to succeed him and by making Jerusalem strong (1 Kings 15:3–4, *italics added*).

Regarding King Jehoram:

> He did evil in the eyes of the Lord. Nevertheless, *for the sake of his servant David*, the Lord was not willing to destroy Judah. He had promised to maintain a lamp for David and his descendants forever (2 Kings 8:18–19; 2 Chron. 21:6–7, *italics added*).

In time, both the northern and southern Israelite kingdoms were conquered by their enemies. Both were warned by the prophets well in advance of their demise. They spoke of the opportunity to repent and to return to the God of their forefathers, but ultimately, the people and their leaders passed the point of no return. In 722 BCE, the Assyrians conquered the northern kingdom and drove many of the people into exile. The exile of the southern kingdom happened in stages. However, the end came in 586 BCE when the Babylonians destroyed Jerusalem and the temple and exiled many of the leaders and prominent citizens (i.e., the royal family and the prophets Daniel and Ezekiel).

The prophet Jeremiah brought forth two prophecies around this time that were relevant to the future of the Davidic line. The first prophecy was nothing short of an announcement regarding the end of the royal line of David during this period of the kings, specifically that of Judah. The second prophecy concerned a future time of restoration of both the nation of Israel and its king. That king would be the final one anticipated by the ancient prophecies, and he would be a descendant of David.

The last king of Judah who inherited the throne from his father was Jehoiachin. His administration was as evil as his father's and grandfather's.[258] Most of the twenty-third chapter of Jeremiah is devoted to God's denunciation of these kings. The extent of Jehoiachin's wickedness can be observed from the fact that he was only eighteen years old and reigned for just three months. At that time, Nebuchadnezzar laid siege to the city of Jerusalem. Jehoiachin, his mother, his attendants, his nobles, and officials surrendered to him and were carried off to Babylon.[259] During his short reign as king of Judah, Jeremiah records this word from the Lord:

> "As surely as I live," declares the LORD, "even if you, Jehoiachin son of Jehoiakim king of Judah, were a signet ring on my right hand, I would still pull you off. I will hand you over to those who seek your life, those you fear—Nebuchadnezzar king of Babylon and to the Babylonians. I will hurl you and the mother who gave you birth into another country, where neither of you was born, and there you both will die. You will never come back to the land you long to return to."
>
> Is this man Jehoiachin, a despised, broken pot, an object no one wants?
>
> Why will he and his children be hurled out, cast into a land they do not know?
>
> Oh land, land, land, hear the word of the LORD!
>
> This is what the LORD says: "Record this man as if childless, a man who will not prosper in his lifetime, for none of his offspring will prosper, none will sit on the throne of David or rule anymore in Judah" (Jer. 22:24–30).

---

258 2 Kings 23:32, 23:37, 24:9.
259 2 Kings 24:10–11, 24:15.

The Lord's displeasure with Jehoiachin is most evident,[260] but his final statement is notable. Although there are various opinions about it, the idea that of his offspring "none will sit on the throne of David or rule anymore in Judah" presents a chilling reality regarding this particular branch of David's descendants.[261] It must imply more than what is obvious, that Jehoiachin was about to be deported and the nation of Judah, along with the dynasty, would cease to exist within eleven years. Its meaning must be understood to be far-reaching, that the final ruler of the Messianic kingdom ("the help of Jacob," "the salvation of Israel," and שׁילה (*shiloh*) would not be a descendant of Jehoiachin, possibly implying the end of Solomon's royal line.[262]

The last man to rule Judah was not the heir to the throne. He was Jehoiachin's uncle Mattaniah, a puppet ruler who was appointed by Nebuchadnezzar and subsequently renamed Zedekiah. He was only twenty-one years old and reigned for eleven years.[263] Against the backdrop of a dying nation and a failed dynasty, Jeremiah made an astounding prophecy:

---

[260] In Babylon, Jehoiachin was imprisoned for thirty-seven years until the reign of Evil-Merodach, who released him and treated him kindly (2 Kings 25:27–30). Some have understood this as an indication of God's mercy toward one who had repented. His release would have given him the opportunity to influence his grandson, Zerubbabel (1 Chron. 3:17–19; Ezra 3:2; Matt. 1:12), who would lead the exiled Israelites back to Jerusalem years later to rebuild the temple. It is worth noting that regarding Jehoiachin, the Lord said, "If you … were a signet ring on my right hand, I would still pull you off" (Jer. 22:24), but regarding Zerubbabel, he said, "I will make you like my signet ring, for I have chosen you" (Hag. 2:23).

[261] If Jesus/Jeshua had not been born of a virgin, this prophecy could have disqualified him from being the Messiah. According to Matthew 1:11–12, he was a descendant of Jeconiah/Jehoiachin the king by way of Joseph's lineage. However, according to Mary's lineage in Luke 3:23–38, his nearest male ancestor was Heli, Mary' father. Heli was a descendant of David's son Nathan (v. 31). God's covenant was with David, not with the royal line during the time of the kings in Israel/Judah.

[262] For a more thorough explanation, see Rabbi Dr. Barney Kasdan, *Matthew Presents Yeshua, King Messiah: A Messianic Commentary* (Clarksville: Lederer Books, 2011), 10–12.

[263] 2 Kings 24:17-18.

"The days are coming," declares the Lord, "when I will fulfill the gracious promise I made to the house of Israel and the house of Judah.

In those days and at that time I will make a righteous Branch sprout from David's line;

He will do what is just and right in the land.

In those days Judah will be saved and Jerusalem will live in safety.

This is the name by which it will be called:

The LORD Our Righteousness."

For this is what the LORD says: "David will never fail to have a man sit on the throne of the house of Israel ...

If you can break my covenant with the day and my covenant with the night, so that day and night no longer come at their appointed time, then my covenant with David my servant ... can be broken and David will no longer have a descendant to reign on the throne" (Jer. 33:14–21).

The prophecy was made in the tenth year of Zedekiah,[264] about a year before the destruction of Jerusalem. The "gracious promise" to which the Lord refers is contained in the phrases above that begin with the words "in those days." Actually, he was repeating an earlier prophecy given to Jeremiah.[265] This repetition helps to reinforce the fact that he was not finished with Israel in spite of the current situation, nor would it have any effect on the messianic lineage of the "righteous Branch."[266]

---

[264] Jeremiah 32:1.

[265] Jeremiah 23:5-6.

[266] This term for the messianic king of the end-times is also found in Jeremiah 33:15, Isaiah 4:2, and Zechariah 3:8 and 6:12.

God's covenant with Israel and with David was everlasting (ברית עולם—
brit olam). God's development of the royal line began when he chose the
tribe of Judah and was sealed when he made the covenant with David.
David understood his place in the overall process, for he stated, "Yet the
LORD, the God of Israel, chose me from my whole family to be king over
Israel forever. He chose Judah as the leader, and from the house of Judah
he chose my family, and from my father's sons he was pleased to make
me king over all Israel."[267] However, after the destruction of Jerusalem
and the Solomonic dynasty ending with a curse, it remained to be seen
just which son of David would be the ancestor of "the help of Jacob," "the
salvation of Israel," and שילה (*shiloh*).

The Lord used the life of the prophet Hosea to illustrate the estranged
relationship between God and Israel. Just as Hosea's marriage to an
unfaithful wife was eventually restored, so would the relationship
between God and the nation be restored. After the ordeal, the Lord
left Hosea with a message of hope for the future that is relevant to our
subject.

> For the Israelites will live many days without king or
> prince, without sacrifice or sacred stones, without ephod
> or idol. Afterward, the Israelites will return and seek the
> Lord their God and David their king. They will come
> trembling to the Lord and to his blessings in the last
> days (Hos. 3:4–5).

---

[267] 1 Chronicles 28:4.

THE COVENANT WITH ISRAEL'S PRIESTLY LINE

The tribe of Levi has played a special role in Israel's history. They are part of a long line of individuals who transmitted, protected, and taught sacred history. Sometimes they were required to fill the role of enforcers and to be the arm of judgment upon God's enemies. Eventually, they would become the protectors and servants of the tabernacle and temple, entering a covenant relationship with the Lord that would be as permanent as all the others we have studied.

The Caretakers of Sacred History

The record of divine history, laws, and practices that would eventually be entrusted to the care of the Levites was first passed from father to son. Enoch is the first person on record to transmit his writings to his descendants. When he was three hundred, the Lord "took him away" so that he did not experience death.[268] During the time preceding the biblical flood, he documented the things he saw and heard in the heavenly realms regarding events of his day and of the future. The part of his writings that remains to this day is known to us as the book of 1 Enoch. In it, he mentions how he passed his books to his son Methuselah,[269] his great-grandson Noah,[270] and, ultimately, to future generations. Consequently,

---

[268] Genesis 5:21-24.
[269] 1 Enoch 82:1, 108:1.
[270] 1 Enoch 68:1.

one would expect such important documents to have been part of Noah's cargo during the Great Flood. Later, in the book of Jubilees, we read,

> And in the twenty-eighth jubilee Noah began to enjoin upon his sons' sons the ordinances and commandments, and all the judgments that he knew, and he exhorted his sons to observe righteousness, and to cover the shame of their flesh, and to bless their creator, and honor father and mother, and love their neighbor, and guard their souls from fornication and uncleanness and all iniquity ...

> For thus did Enoch, the father of your father command Methuselah, his son, and Methuselah his son Lamech, and Lamech commanded me all the things which his fathers commanded him.[271]

Hundreds of years later, God called Abraham to leave his country and go to the land of Canaan. Jubilees records the Abrahamic promise just as it appears in Genesis chapter 12. However, it includes this additional instruction from the Lord to the angelic messenger:

> "Open his mouth and his ears, that he may hear and speak with his mouth, with the language which has been revealed"; for it had ceased from the mouths of all the children of men from the day of the overthrow (of Babel).[272]

The angel states,

> And I opened his mouth, and his ears and his lips, and I began to speak with him in Hebrew in the tongue of the creation.

---

[271] Charles, *Apocrypha and Pseudepigrapha of the Old Testament*, Jubilees 7:20–39.
[272] Charles, Jubilees 12:25.

And he took the books of his fathers, and these were written in Hebrew, and he transcribed them, and he began from henceforth to study them, and I made known to him that which he could not (understand), and he studied them during the six rainy months.[273]

What were these "books of his fathers"? From whom did his ancestors acquire them? Could they have been the writings of Enoch that survived the deluge?

As Abraham approached the end of his life, he called Isaac to his side to pass on his knowledge of the commandments, ordinances, and judgments of God. The twenty-first chapter of the book of Jubilees documents this event. Abraham's list included detailed instructions regarding offerings. He even identified his source documents:

"For thus I have found it written in the books of my forefathers, and in the words of Enoch, and in the words of Noah."[274]

This information helps us to understand why God, when confirming his covenant with Isaac, told him it was because,

"Abraham obeyed me and kept my requirements, my commands, my decrees and my laws," (Gen. 26:5).

Undoubtedly, the books that Abraham had acquired were transferred to Isaac, and from Isaac to Jacob. When the book of Jubilees records the death of Jacob, it states,

And he slept with his fathers, and he was buried in the double cave in the land of Canaan … And he gave all his books and the books of his fathers to Levi his son that

---

[273] Charles, Jubilees 12:26–27.
[274] Charles, Jubilees 21:10.

he might preserve them and renew them for his children until this day.[275]

The Jewish literature known as the Testament of the Twelve Patriarchs, understood to be the final words of Jacob's sons, does not reference the laws given to Moses, as would be expected since they predate that event. However, there are numerous references to the book of Enoch,[276] confirming the patriarchs' familiarity with it.

Since the Levites had become the caretakers of sacred history, it would seem reasonable that when Moses finished documenting the terms of the covenant, both at Sinai and on the Plains of Moab,[277] he gave the scroll to the priests, who were Levites. He instructed them to place it beside the ark of the covenant.[278] He also instructed them to read it to the people every seven years when they gathered together to celebrate the Feast of Tabernacles.[279] It would now be their responsibility "to teach the Israelites all the statues that the LORD has spoken to them through Moses."[280]

The Origin of the Priestly Line

The story of the priestly line begins shortly after Jacob and his family returned to the land of Canaan. Jacob had fled to Paddan Aram, both to escape his brother and to acquire a wife from his mother's family.[281] He stayed there twenty years, marrying twice and having eleven sons and one daughter. By the Lord's instruction,[282] he gathered his family and

---

[275] Charles, Jubilees 45:15–16.
[276] T12P Simeon 5:4; Levi 10:5, 14:1; Zebulon 3:4; Dan 5:6; Naphtali 4:1; Benjamin 9:1.
[277] Deuteronomy 29:1.
[278] Deuteronomy 31:24–25.
[279] Deuteronomy 31:9–13.
[280] Leviticus 10:11.
[281] Genesis 27:41–28:2.
[282] Genesis 31:3, 13.

returned to home, settling near a city called Shechem.[283] Bible students are familiar with the story that follows. The thirty-fourth chapter of Genesis recounts the disturbing story of the rape of Jacob's daughter[284] and the subsequent violence against the men of Shechem. Regarding the defilement of his daughter, we are told,

> When Jacob heard that his daughter Dinah had been defiled, his sons were in the fields with his livestock; so he kept quiet about it until they came home (Gen. 34:5).

Indeed, he knew where his sons were, but he was not aware that one of them was having a life-changing moment. Levi was eighteen years old at that time.[285] He recounts his experience in the Testament of the Twelve Patriarchs:

> And when I was feeding the flocks in Abel-Maul, the spirit of understanding of the Lord came upon me, and I saw all men corrupting their way, and that unrighteousness had built for itself walls, and lawlessness sat upon towers. And I was grieving for the race of the sons of men, and I prayed to the Lord that I might be saved. Then there fell upon me a sleep, and I beheld ...[286]

What Levi beheld was phenomenal, to say the least. A heavenly messenger escorted him through the various "heavens," seven in all, providing commentary along the way. Eventually, he was given an answer to his inquiry.

> Therefore the Most High hath heard thy prayer, to separate thee from iniquity, and that thou shouldst become to Him a son, and a servant, and a minister of His presence. The light of knowledge shalt thou light up

---

[283] Genesis 33:18–19.
[284] According to Jubilees 30:2, she was twelve at the time.
[285] T12P Levi 12:5.
[286] Sefaria Library, Levi 1:3–5.

in Jacob, and as the sun shalt thou be to all the seed of
Israel. And there shall be given to thee a blessing, and
to all thy seed, until the Lord shall visit all the Gentiles
in His tender mercies forever. And therefore there have
been given to thee counsel and understanding, that thou
mightst instruct thy sons concerning this; Because they
that bless Him shall be blessed, and they that curse Him
shall perish. And thereupon the angel opened to me the
gates of heaven, and I saw the holy temple, and upon a
throne of glory the Most High. And He said to me: Levi,
I have given thee the blessings of the priesthood until I
come and sojourn in the midst of Israel.[287]

Levi's expression of grief regarding the sinfulness of humankind and
plea for help to avoid it was answered most definitively. He and his
descendants would have a major role in the sanctity of the nation. It
seemed to be a fitting responsibility for the tribe that was to be the
caretaker of its sacred history. The Most High had officially selected the
priestly tribe for his chosen people.[288]

---

[287] Sefaria Library, Levi 4:2–5:2. This divine decree appears to be referenced in
Jubilees 31:18–19.

[288] The timing of this event is confirmed by the fact that Levi was tending his flocks
just prior to the massacre at Shechem. For after the vision, Levi states that the
angel, who had been his guide, gave him a sword and a shield and said, "Execute
vengeance on Shechem because of Dinah, thy sister, and I will be with thee because
the Lord hath sent me" (T12P, Lev. 5:3). This is confirmed by a statement in Jubilees
in the aftermath: "For judgment is ordained in heaven against them that they
should be destroyed with the sword all the men of the Shechemites because they
had wrought shamed in Israel" (Jub. 30:5–6). Regarding the practices of the men
of Shechem, Levi adds, "And thus they did to all strangers, taking away their wives
by force, and they banished them" (the men) (T12P Lev. 6:10). Thus, the story of
Dinah is indicative of the practices of the Shechemites. The plan of Shechem's leader
to intermarry with Jacob's family (Gen. 34:6–23) was not an acceptable option for
God. Based on the extrabiblical literature, the massacre at Shechem was God's
judgment, and the order to do so was given directly to Levi. This would not be
the last time that Levi would be the sword-bearer of God's judgment. During the
incident of the golden calf at the foot of Mount Sinai, it was the Levites who sided
with the Lord and, on Moses's order, executed three thousand idolaters (Exod.

After the incident at Shechem, Jacob and his family moved to Bethel. This had been his intended destination ever since leaving Paddan Aram. For he had made a vow to God at Bethel twenty years earlier after having a vison:

> "If God will be with me and will watch over me on this journey I am taking and will give me food to eat and clothes to wear and so that I return safely to my father's house, then the LORD will be my God ... and of all that you give me I will give you a tenth" (Gen. 28:20–22).

According to Levi's testament, seventy days after arriving in Bethel, he had another vision.[289]

> And I saw seven men in white raiment saying unto me: Arise, put on the robe of the priesthood, and the crown of righteousness, and the breastplate of understanding, and the garment of truth, and the plate of faith, and the turban of the head, and the ephod of prophecy.

> And they severally carried (these things) and put (them) on me, and said unto me: From henceforth become a priest of the Lord, thou and thy seed for ever.

> And the first anointed me with holy oil, and gave to me the staff of judgment.

> The second washed me with pure water, and fed me with bread and wine (even) the most holy things, and clad me with a holy and glorious robe.

32:26–29). Also, Numbers 18:1–7 is understood by many to be the implementation of tabernacle/temple security, an assignment given to the Levites to protect it from encroachment in response to the recent attempt by Korah and his followers to take over the priesthood (Num. 16).

[289] This second dream is mentioned briefly in Jubilees 32:1, but after their return from Hebron. It should probably be understood as a past event and mentioned only to explain the reason why Jacob paid his tithes to Levi.

The third clothed me with a linen vestment like an ephod.

The fourth put round me a girdle like unto purple.

The fifth gave me a branch of rich olive.

The sixth placed a crown on my head.

The seventh placed on my head a diadem of priesthood, and filled my hands with incense, that I might serve as priest to the Lord God ...

Therefore, every desirable thing in Israel shall be for thee and for thy seed, And ye shall eat everything fair to look upon, And the table of the Lord shall thy seed apportion.

And some of them shall be high priests, and judges, and scribes; For by their mouth shall the holy place be guarded.

And when I awoke, I understood that this (dream) was like the first dream.

And I hid this also in my heart, and told it not to any man upon the earth.[290]

It would appear that this event was the heavenly counterpart and precursor to what would happen to Aaron and his sons only three generations later.[291] He went on to say,

And after two days I and Judah went up with our father Jacob to Isaac our father's father. And my father's father blessed me according to all the words of the visions which I had seen.[292]

---

[290] Sefaria Library, https://www.sefaria.org/The_Testaments_of_the_Twelve_Patriarchs, Levi 8:2–18.
[291] Exodus 29:4–9; Leviticus 8:5–13.
[292] Sefaria Library, Levi 9:1–2.

This journey to Hebron to visit Isaac was mentioned in our previous chapter when discussing Judah and the origins of the royal line. The ceremony that Jacob had planned at Bethel regarding his vow to God was momentous, and he wanted his parents to be present. However, Isaac was too old to travel, but he did send Rachel.[293] Before they returned to Bethel, Isaac blessed both Judah and Levi. His words to Judah were discussed previously. To Levi, he said,

> May the God of all, the very Lord of all the ages, bless thee and thy children throughout all the ages. And may the Lord give to thee and to thy seed greatness and great glory, and cause thee and thy seed, from among all flesh, to approach him to serve in His sanctuary as the angels of the presence and as the holy ones. Even as they, show the seed of thy sons be for glory and greatness and holiness, and may He make them great unto all the ages. And they shall be judges and princes, and chiefs of all the seed of the sons of Jacob; They shall speak the word of the Lord in righteousness, and they shall judge all His judgments in righteousness. And they shall declare My ways to Jacob and My paths to Israel. The blessing of the Lord shall be given in their mouths to bless all the seed of the beloved.[294]

The prophetic words of Isaac, "to approach him to serve in His sanctuary," confirmed the accuracy of Levi's visions. In addition, Levi states in his testament that after returning to Bethel,

> my father saw a vision concerning me, that I should be their priest unto God. And he rose up early in the morning, and paid tithes of all to the Lord through me.[295]

---

[293] Jubilees 31:27.

[294] Charles, *Apocrypha and Pseudepigrapha of the Old Testament*, Jubilees 31:13–15.

[295] Sefaria Library, Levi 9:3–4.

The details of Jacob's tithe (oxen, rams, sheep, lambs, goats) and an additional thank offering are recounted in Jubilees 32:2–10. This act fulfilled the vow he made when he stated, "The LORD will be my God … and of all that you give me I will give you a tenth."[296]

After the ceremony at Bethel, Jacob and his family journeyed back to Hebron to live near Isaac.[297] Now Isaac and Levi could begin the transference of the sacred history and traditions. Levi states:

> And Isaac called me continually to put me in remembrance of the law of the Lord, even as the angel of the Lord showed unto me. And he taught me the law of the priesthood, of sacrifices, whole burnt-offerings, First Fruits, freewill-offerings, peace-offerings. And each day he was instructing me, and was busied on my behalf before the Lord …[298]

What was first transcribed by Enoch, carried by Noah, transferred to Abraham via the books of his forefathers, and given to Isaac had now arrived at its destination—the chosen priestly line of Levi.[299]

The Chosen Pedigree of the Priestly Line

After God announced his commandments to the Israelites from the dense cloud covering Mount Sinai and his subsequent delivery to Moses

---

[296] Genesis 28:21–22.

[297] T12P Levi 9:5, Genesis 35:27.

[298] Sefaria Library, Levi 9:6–8.

[299] All this background information from the extrabiblical literature helps to resolve two confusing references to priests in Exodus 19:22–24. Aaron and his sons are not mentioned as God's chosen priests until Exodus 28:1. So the priests mentioned here must be the Levites, who were currently performing the priestly duties during the interim between Levi's ordination and Aaron's ordination. On a separate note, could this group have included Korah, the son of Kohath, the son of Levi? And could it explain his jealousy for the priesthood after the selection of Aaron and his sons (Num. 16:1–11)?

of what would later become the Book of the Covenant,[300] Moses returned and ascended the mountain to receive from God the stone tablets of the commandments[301] and the details regarding the construction of the tabernacle.[302] It would seem reasonable that at that time, the Lord would reveal his choice of personnel to serve in the tabernacle.

> Have Aaron your brother brought to you from among the Israelites, with his sons Nadab and Abihu, Eleazar and Ithamar, so that they may serve me as priests (Exod. 28:1).

Just as David was chosen as the specific line of Judah that would produce the Messiah, the final king, so Aaron and his sons were chosen as the specific line of Levi that would serve the Lord in the tabernacle and the temple. The rest of Exodus 28 recounts God's instructions to Moses regarding the special priestly garments. Chapter 29 lists detailed instructions regarding their ordination ceremony, most of which are duplicated in Leviticus 8, when the ordination was performed. The section of the text regarding the donning of the garments is noteworthy.

> Then bring Aaron and his sons to the entrance to the Tent of Meeting and wash them with water. Take the garments and dress Aaron with the tunic, the robe of the ephod, the ephod itself and the breastpiece. Fasten the ephod on him by its skillfully woven waistband. Put the turban on his head and attach the sacred diadem to the turban. Take the anointing oil and anoint him by pouring it on his head. Bring his sons and dress them in tunics and put headbands on them. Then tie sashes on Aaron and his sons (Exod. 29:4–9 [Lev. 8:6-9, 8:13]).

This part of the ceremony very closely resembles the ceremony experienced by Levi in his second vision. Though the former might be

---

[300] Exodus 24:4, 24:7.
[301] Exodus 24:12.
[302] Exodus 25:1–31:18.

prophetic of the latter, it is more likely that they are to be understood as two independent ceremonies. The first served to confirm God's choice of Levi, and the second confirmed the earthly reality of that decision upon the specific lineage of Aaron.[303] Even though both the general and the specific divine choices had been made, another forty years would pass before God would mention the topic of covenant (ברית—*brit*) regarding the priestly line of Levi.

After the Israelites left Mount Sinai, they traveled to Kadesh, where they camped and sent a small reconnaissance team into Canaan. In response to the negative report by most of that team, the leadership talked of choosing a new leader to replace Moses and to lead them back to Egypt. The subsequent wandering in the wilderness was God's judgment upon their rebellion against his appointed leader and their refusal to proceed with the conquest of the promised land. Consequently, that generation would die in the wilderness and God would start anew with the next generation. Toward the end of the forty years, the Israelites made their way around Edom to the south and proceeded north along its eastern border up to Moab. They defeated two Amorite kings on the battlefield and finally settled on the Plains of Moab, their final stop before renewing the covenant and crossing the Jordan River into Canaan.

It is at this time that we encounter the story of Balaam in Numbers 22–24. He ultimately failed to accommodate the request of the Moabite/Midianite leaders to curse the Israelites. However, before returning to his country, he advised the leaders on how to weaken the Israelites by sending their own women to the Israelite camp to entice the men and lead them to idolatry.[304] They followed his advice. As the Israelite men followed these women and sacrificed to their gods, "the LORD's

---

[303] These comparable ordination experiences between Levi and Aaron, being four generations apart (1 Chron. 6:1–3), provide an interesting link back to the Abrahamic Covenant. God told Abraham during his covenant ceremony in Canaan, "In the fourth generation, your descendants will come back here" (Gen. 15:16). It is interesting that the one who received the heavenly ordination belonged to the generation that immigrated to Egypt and the one who received the earthly ordination belonged to the generation of the Exodus.

[304] Numbers 31:16, 25:1–3.

anger burned against them." The Lord instructed Moses to execute the idolaters, a task he immediately delegated to the judicial system.[305] Oddly, this is where the covenant story continues.

> Then an Israelite man brought to his family a Midianite woman right before the eyes of Moses and the whole assembly of Israel while they were weeping at the entrance to the tent of meeting. When Phinehas son of Eleazer, the son of Aaron the priest, saw this, he left the assembly, took a spear in his hand and followed the Israelite into the tent. He drove the spear through both of them—through the Israelite and into the woman's body. And then the plague against the Israelites stopped; But those who died in the plague numbered 24,000 (Num. 25:6–9).

Had the idolatry gone unchecked, it could have jeopardized the entire operation as the rebelliousness of their fathers had forty years earlier at Kadesh. It was here that this generation of Israelites would re-ratify their covenant with God and enter the promised land. The cancer of idolatry had the potential to deprive them of that opportunity. Ultimately, 24,000 were executed for their national/spiritual act of treason.[306] In this crucial moment, Phinehas, the grandson of Aaron, acted with the righteous indignation exhibited by Levi at Shechem and the Levites at Mount Sinai after the golden calf incident. His actions were noticed by God.

> The Lord said to Moses, "Phinehas son of Eleazar, the son of Aaron, the priest, has turned my anger away from the Israelites; For he was as zealous as I am for my honor among them, so that in my zeal I did not put an end to them. Therefore tell him I am making my covenant of peace [ברית שלום—*brit shalom*] with him. He and his

---

[305] Numbers 25:4–5, in keeping with what would be later codified in Deuteronomy 13.
[306] Unfortunately, the NIV translated the word מגפה as "plague," which is correct in certain contexts. The root of the word is נגף and means "to strike, smite." Thus, in this context, it refers to the executions.

descendants will have a covenant of a lasting priesthood [ברית כהנת עולם—*brit kohanoth olam*], because he was zealous for the honor of his God and made atonement for the Israelites" (Num. 25:10–13, *Hebrew text added*).

It seemed that something special was bestowed upon the line of Phinehas. It was very similar to what God had said earlier about Aaron's lineage in general just after the tabernacle was erected.

"Bring Aaron and his sons to the entrance to the Tent of Meeting and wash them with water. Then dress Aaron in the sacred garments, anoint him and consecrate him so that he may serve me as priest. Bring his sons and dress them in tunics. Anoint them just as you anointed their father, so that they may serve me as priests. Their anointing will be to a priesthood that will continue [עולם כהנת—*kohanoth olam*] for all generations to come" (Exod. 40:12–15, *Hebrew text added*).

Aaron had four sons and, quite sadly, lost two of them soon after his ordination.[307] The remaining sons, Eleazer and Ithamar, carried on the duties of the priesthood after the passing of Aaron. However, all the high priests in the future would be descendants of Phinehas.[308] What began with the request of one man to be delivered from the sinfulness that besets all men had now been sealed by way of a covenant with one of his progenies. Levi sought the Lord in his youth and procreated a lineage of service to God.[309] With the zeal of his ancestor, Phinehas acquired for himself and his descendants the prominent role in that service to God,

---

[307] Leviticus 10:1–5.

[308] Rav Samson Raphael Hirsch, *The Hirsch Chumash: Sefer Bemidbar* (New York: Feldheim Publishers, 2005), 529.

[309] The chronicler documented the role of the Levites in the service of the temple. Some of their more general duties are listed in 1 Chronicles 23:28–32. The priests were divided into twenty-four groups (1 Chron. 24:1–19). Others were dedicated to the task of musician (1 Chron. 25:1–31), gatekeeper (1 Chron. 26:1–19), treasurer, or other duties (1 Chron. 26:20–32).

a lasting priesthood confirmed by a divine everlasting covenant (עולם ברית—*brit olam*).[310]

Additional Observations

The permanency of the priestly covenant was confirmed "point in time" by God's statement to Phinehas. However, God's intention for Aaron and his sons to have a permanent role in his service was conspicuous from their assigned duties well before the covenant was mentioned. Many of these duties were designated as being עולם(*olam*), which was variously translated as being "permanent," "everlasting," "perpetual," or "forever."

Most of what we often consider to be commands in the Bible were delivered to Moses as "decrees," "statutes," and "ordinances." In fact, chapters 12–26 of Deuteronomy are so designated as the decrees of the Lord and the judgments, or rulings, for disregarding them.[311] The words "decree," "statute," and "ordinance," henceforth used interchangeably, are all translated from the same two Hebrew words: חק (*khoq*) or חקה (*khuqqah*), which are merely the masculine and feminine forms of the same word. When we see these words together with *olam*, חק עולם (*khoq olam*) and חקת עולם (*khuqqath olam*), or their plural forms עולם חקים (*khuqqim olam*) and חקות עולם (*khuqqoth olam*), we understand that the decree God issued was neither frivolous nor temporary. It is both permanent and an integral part of the covenant relationship he has with the intended recipient.[312] In the case of the priesthood, the

---

[310] After the Babylonian exile, God begins using the more generalized phrase of the/my "covenant with Levi" (Mal. 2:4–5, 8).

[311] Deuteronomy 12:1.

[312] The word "covenant" (ברית) and "decree" (חק) are even paired in some cases, for example: "So the Lord said the Solomon, 'Since this is your attitude and you have not kept my covenant (ברית) and my decrees (חק), which I commanded you, I will most certainly tear the kingdom away from you and give it to one of your subordinates'" (1 Kings 11:11); "They rejected his decrees (חק) and the covenant (ברית) he had made with their fathers and the warnings he had given them" (2 Kings 17:15); "But to the wicked, I say: 'What right have you to recite my laws (חק) or take my covenant (ברית) on your lips?'" (Ps. 50:16); and "This is what the LORD

everlasting or permanent nature of the decrees for Aaron and his sons probably indicated·that God's intention all along was to culminate their relationship with him with an everlasting covenant.

What follows is a list of most of those decrees that are specific to Aaron and his sons. They are permanent in nature and address various aspects of the priesthood. You will notice that the NIV translation generally uses the word "ordinance" for חק (*khoq*) and חקה (*khuqqah*). It also tends to favor the phrase "regular share" in those passages about the priest's portion of the offerings.

Regarding the lamps of the tabernacle:

> In the Tent of Meeting, outside the curtain that is in front of the Testimony, Aaron and his sons are to keep the lamps burning before the LORD from evening till morning. This is to be a lasting ordinance [חקת עולם] among the Israelites for the generations to come (Exod. 27:21, *Hebrew text added*).

> Outside the curtain of the Testimony in the Tent of Meeting, Aaron is to tend the lamps before the LORD from evening till morning, continually. This is to be a lasting ordinance [חקת עולם] for the generations to come (Lev. 24:3, *Hebrew text added*).

Regarding the priestly garments:

> Aaron and his sons must wear them whenever they enter the Tent of Meeting or approach the altar to minister in the Holy Place so that they will not incur guilt and die. "This is to be a lasting ordinance [חקת עולם] for Aaron and his descendants (Exod. 28:43, *Hebrew text added*).

---

says: 'If I have not established my covenant (ברית) with day and night and the fixed laws (חקה) of heaven and earth'" (Jer. 33:25).

Regarding the priestly portion of the offerings:

This is always to be the regular share [חק עולם] from the Israelites for Aaron and his sons. It is the contribution the Israelites are to make to the LORD from their fellowship offerings (Exod. 29:28, *Hebrew text added*).

Any male descendant of Aaron may eat it. It is his regular share [חק עולם] of the offerings made to the LORD by fire for the generations to come. Whatever touches it will become holy (Lev. 6:18, *Hebrew text added*).

From the fellowship offerings of the Israelites, I have taken the breast that is waved and the thigh that is presented and have given them to Aaron the priest and his sons as their regular share [חק עולם] from the Israelites (Lev. 7:34, *Hebrew text added*).

On the day they were anointed, the LORD commanded that the Israelites give this to them as their regular share [חקת עולם] for the generations to come" (Lev. 7:36, *Hebrew text added*).

"The thigh that was presented and the breast that was waved must be brought with the fat portions of the offerings made by fire, to be waved before the LORD as a wave offering. This will be the regular share [חק עולם] for you and your children, as the LORD has commanded" (Lev. 10:15, *Hebrew text added*).

Whatever is set aside from the holy offerings the Israelites present to the LORD I give to you and your sons and daughters as your regular share [חק עולם]. It is an everlasting covenant of salt before the LORD for both you and your offspring (Num. 18:19, *Hebrew text added*).

Regarding the ordination ceremony:

The priesthood is theirs by a lasting ordinance [עולם חקת]. In this way, you shall ordain Aaron and his sons (Exod. 29:9, *Hebrew text added*).

Regarding the ceremonial washing:

Whenever they enter the Tent of Meeting, they shall wash with water so that they will not die. Also, when they approach the altar to minister by presenting an offering made to the LORD by fire, they shall wash their hands and feet so that they will not die. This is to be a lasting ordinance [חק עולם] for Aaron and his descendants for the generations to come (Exod. 30:20–21, *Hebrew text added*).

Regarding their sobriety when serving:

You and your sons are not to drink wine or other fermented drink whenever you go into the Tent of Meeting, or you will die. This is a lasting ordinance [עולם חקת] for the generations to come (Lev. 10:9, *Hebrew text added*).

Regarding the Bread of the Presence:

This bread is to be set out before the LORD regularly, Sabbath after Sabbath, on behalf of the Israelites, as a lasting covenant. It belongs to Aaron and his sons, who are to eat it in a holy place, because it is a most holy part of their regular share [חק עולם] of the offerings made to the LORD by fire (Lev. 24:8–9, *Hebrew text added*).

Regarding the blowing of the trumpets:

"The sons of Aaron, the priests, are to blow the trumpets. This is to be a lasting ordinance [חקת עולם] for you and the generations to come," (Num. 10:8, *Hebrew text added*).

Regarding the role of tabernacle security:

"From now on the Israelites must not go near the Tent of Meeting, or they will bear the consequences of their sin and will die. It is the Levites who are to do the work at the Tent of Meeting and bear the responsibility for offences against it. This is a lasting ordinance [חֻקַּת עוֹלָם] for the generations to come. They will receive no inheritance among the Israelites," (Num. 18:22–23, compare with Num. 18:1–7, *Hebrew text added*).

There is another very important piece of evidence that supports the permanency of the priestly covenant that must not go unmentioned. This passage from Jeremiah was cited in the previous chapter. However, only the part that applied to the royal covenant was quoted. Let us read the entire section so that we might gain clarity regarding the priestly covenant.

"The days are coming," declares the LORD, "when I will fulfill the gracious promise I made to the house of Israel and the house of Judah.

In those days and at that time I will make a righteous Branch sprout from David's line;

He will do what is just and right in the land.

In those days Judah will be saved and Jerusalem will live in safety.

This is the name by which it will be called:

The LORD Our Righteousness."

> For this is what the LORD says: "David will never fail to
> have a man sit on the throne of the house of Israel *nor*
> *will the priests, who are Levites, ever fail to have a man*
> *to stand before me continually to offer burnt offerings, to*
> *burn grain offerings and to present sacrifices."*

> The word of the LORD came to Jeremiah: "This is what
> the LORD says: 'If you can break my covenant with the
> day and my covenant with the night, so that day and
> night no longer come at their appointed time, then my
> covenant with David my servant—*and my covenant with*
> *the Levites who are priests ministering before me*—can
> be broken and David will no longer have a descendant
> to reign on his throne. I will make the descendants of
> David my servant *and the Levites who minister before me*
> as countless as the stars of the sky and as measureless as
> the sand on the seashore'" (Jer. 33:14–22, *italics added*).

If the Bible student does not understand the permanent nature of both
the royal and priestly covenants, the importance of this portion of
Jeremiah can easily be overlooked. Each one is an everlasting covenant
(ברית עולם—*brit olam*). Both are as permanent as God's covenant with
the day and the night. It is no accident that these two covenants are
addressed together in these verses. They are to be understood and
interpreted exactly the same way.[313] To do otherwise would reveal an
inconsistent method of interpretation and expose the reader's bias. It
is interesting that many Christian theologians, both Covenantalists
and Dispensationalists and all the flavors in between, make little or no
mention of the priestly covenant or of its parity with the royal covenant.
We are not at liberty to interpret what Jeremiah says about one in a
literal way and then to interpret the other by some other means. The
pairing of these two everlasting covenants forces Bible students to face

---

[313] It is interesting that the phrase "covenant of salt" (ברית מלח) is mentioned only
twice in the Hebrew scriptures. The first occurrence in Numbers 18:19 is in relation
to the Levitic Covenant. The second occurrence in 2 Chronicles 13:5 is in relation
to the Davidic Covenant.

the consistent or inconsistent nature of both their hermeneutic and eschatological choices. Obviously, the current state of both throughout history is determined by the existence of a nation with a monarchy and a functioning temple. However, as we have seen from our various sources, the God of both covenants has the endgame in view. What will be the status of both during the last millennium of history when his kingdom on earth is finally realized? According to Jeremiah, a descendant of David will be on the throne, and the priestly line of Levi will be serving in the third temple.

THE COVENANT
WITH ISRAEL: IN
THE FUTURE

The New Covenant is a very useful topic because it helps us to segregate theologians into neat little groups. It enables us to discern one's hermeneutical principles, eschatological preferences, and even one's ability to maintain a consistent definition of the phrase "everlasting covenant" (ברית עולם—*brit olam*). It is only fair that this author's ideas, though they are not new, likewise be drawn, quartered, and labeled accordingly. And so let us begin.

The New Covenant, or God's covenant with Israel in the future, should not be understood as a complete replacement of the current everlasting covenant with his chosen people. Rather, it will be a covenantal renewal for a future generation in which the nation of Israel will finally internalize the Torah and, once and for all, "circumcise their hearts." It will not be the first time a renewal has taken place. Previously, we discussed the renewal that happened after the golden calf incident.[314] At that time, the terms of the covenant did not change. However, God incorporated a contingency plan to make Moses into a great nation[315] should the Israelites fail a second time to live up to the terms. Essentially, he accomplished this by making Moses a cosigner.

> Then the LORD said to Moses, "Write down these words, for in accordance with these words I have made a covenant with *you and Israel*" (Exod. 34:27, *italics added*).

---

[314] Exodus 32:1–34:35.
[315] Exodus 32:9–10.

Later, on the Plains of Moab, the covenant was renewed by the generation of Israelites that had grown up during the forty years in the wilderness. Unlike their parents, they were ready to trust the Lord and conquer the promised land. This covenant renewal included additional decrees and judgments that prepared them to live as a holy nation in the new land.[316] It was documented that these additions should not be understood as something separate from what had been previously delivered.

> These are the terms of the covenant the LORD commanded Moses to make with the Israelites in Moab, in addition to the covenant he had made with them at Horeb (Deut. 29:1).

The everlasting covenant (עולם ברית—*brit olam*) made at Mount Sinai had not been replaced; it had simply been updated for a new situation and a believing generation. Unfortunately, the generation of Israelites that ratified the covenant on the Plains of Moab had enough faith to enter Canaan, but not enough to pass it on to the next generation.

> After that whole generation had been gathered to their fathers, another generation grew up, who knew neither the LORD nor what he had done for Israel (Judg. 2:10).

Moses

Moses anticipated this cycle of believing and unbelieving generations throughout Israel's history and addressed it during his third discourse in the book of Deuteronomy.[317] The "blessings and curses"[318] were part of the

---

[316] Deuteronomy 12:1–26:19.

[317] The third discourse, found in Deuteronomy 29:2–30:20, is understood by many to be the precursor to the documented covenant ratification found in Deuteronomy 26:16–19. Notably, in Deuteronomy 29:9–15 he explains to them that they are about enter into a covenant with the Lord and that it is transgenerational. In Deuteronomy 29:16–28, Moses warns them about future apostasy, both personal and national, and how it will stand as a testimonial to future generations.

[318] Deuteronomy 30:1.

covenant and were based upon the nation's obedience or disobedience to God's laws. However, a total rejection of his people was never an option for God. In a parallel passage,[319] God states unequivocally,

> "I will not reject them or abhor them so as to destroy them completely, breaking my covenant with them. I am the LORD their God. But for their sake, I will remember the covenant with their ancestors whom I brought out of Egypt in the sight of the nations to be their God. I am the LORD" (Lev. 26:44–45).

And later, through the prophet Isaiah, he states,

> "To me this is like the days of Noah, when I swore that the waters of Noah would never again cover the earth. So now I have sworn not to be angry with you, never to rebuke you again. Though the mountains be shaken and the hills be removed, yet my unfailing love for you will not be shaken nor my covenant of peace [שלום ברית—brit shalom] be removed," says the LORD, who has compassion on you (Isa. 54:9–10, Hebrew text added).

Moses also foresaw an end to the cycles of disobedience and anticipated that glorious day in the future when Israel would return to their Lord once and for all. In that day, the Torah would not only be the law of the land, but it would be internalized by its citizens.

> When all these blessings and curses I have set before you come upon you and you take them to heart wherever the LORD your God disperses you among the nations, and when you and your children return to the LORD your God and obey him with all your heart and with all your soul according to everything I command you today, then the LORD your God will restore your fortunes and have

---

[319] The whole twenty-sixth chapter of Leviticus is a good chapter to read in parallel with Deuteronomy 29 and 30.

compassion on you and gather you again from all the nations where he scattered you. Even if you have been banished to the most distant land under the heavens, from there the LORD your God will gather you and bring you back. He will bring you to the land that belonged to your father's, and you will take possession of it. He will make you more prosperous and numerous than your fathers. The LORD your God *will circumcise your hearts* and the hearts of your descendants, so that you may love him *with all your heart* and *with all your soul,* and live. The Lord your God will put all these curses on your enemies who hate and persecute you. You will again obey the LORD and follow all his commands I am giving you today. Then the LORD your God will make you most prosperous in all the work of your hands and in the fruit of your womb, the young of your livestock and the crops of your land. The LORD will again delight in you and make you prosperous, just as he delighted in your fathers, if you obey the LORD your God and keep his commands and decrees that are written in this Book of the Law and turn to the LORD your God *with all your heart* and *with all your soul* (Deut. 30:1–10, *italics added*).

It is very clear from the "heart" and "soul" metaphors that the Torah, the Book of the Law, was intended to be both the law of the land and the law of the heart. The Israelite presence in the promised land and its national prosperity would depend on it. The teachings of Moses were all they had at the time with which to know and understand their God.[320] To understand the Torah was to understand the mind of God, and it was accessible to the average Israelite. They were instructed to discuss it with each other and with their children during normal daily

---

[320] Whatever extrabiblical literature that might have existed at that time would not have addressed their specific national obligations to God and life in the promised land.

activities.[321] It was read publicly during the three feasts every seven years.[322] The internalization of the Torah was really a joint effort. God was always ready to "circumcise their hearts."[323] However, the Israelites were also instructed, "Circumcise your hearts, therefore, and do not be stiff-necked any longer."[324] Moses foresaw the day when God and Israel would work together to that end. When that happens, the time of restoration and prosperity can begin, and, unlike Israel's intermittent cycles of obedience throughout ancient times, it will be permanent.

The apostle Paul seems to echo Moses's statements when he instructed the Messianic Jews of the church in Rome. He uses the term "circumcision" in a general sense, not referring specifically to the practice but, rather, to the way it designates someone as being under the Sinai Covenant and obligated to keep its laws.

> Circumcision has value if you observe the law, but if you break the law, you have become as though you had not been circumcised. So then, if those who are not circumcised keep the law's requirements, will they not be regarded as though they were circumcised? The one who is not circumcised physically and yet obeys the law will condemn you who, even though you have the written code and circumcision, are a lawbreaker. A man is not a Jew who is one only outwardly, nor is circumcision merely outward and physical. No, a man is a Jew if he is one inwardly; and circumcision is *circumcision of the heart*, by the Spirit, not by the written code. Such a man's praise is not from men, but from God. (Rom. 2:25–29, *italics added*).

This time of Israel's permanent return to God as prophesied by Moses is probably the earliest reference to what would later be called the New

---

[321] Deuteronomy 6:6–9.
[322] Deuteronomy 31:9–13.
[323] Deuteronomy 30:6.
[324] Deuteronomy 10:16.

Covenant. It will be the final renewal of an agreement by two parties long ago on Mount Sinai.

Isaiah, Hosea, and Ezekiel

The prophets continued this theme of Israel's permanent return to God and the final restoration of the nation. In addition, they associated these events with a renewed covenant.

In the book of Isaiah, the prophet wrote a great deal about the impending Assyrian threat in chapters 6–37. Then from chapter 38 to 47, he turned his attention to Babylon, speaking comfort to the exiled Jews. It is important to note that it would be over one hundred and thirty years before such exiles existed. In his foreknowledge, God was sending them words of consolation over one century in advance. Then, in chapters 49–55, Isaiah speaks to the exiles about Israel's future and final restoration. He uses the term "covenant" twice in these chapters.

In the first occurrence, he says,

> This is what the LORD says: "In the time of my favor I will answer you, and in the day of salvation I will help you; I will keep you and we'll make you to be a covenant for the people, to restore the land and to reassign its desolate inheritances, to say to the captives, 'Come out,' and to those in darkness, 'Be free'" (Isa. 49:8–9).

The four occurrences of the pronoun "you" are singular and mostly likely refer to the servant mentioned the previous seven verses. There are various opinions regarding the identity of this individual. However, it is this author's opinion that it was none other than God's special messenger who has been the mediator of the covenants[325] up until now and will embody the covenant itself ("*to be* the covenant for the people")[326] in the

---

[325] The topic, Mediator of the Covenants, will be addressed in the next chapter.
[326] This same phrase is also used in Isaiah 42:6.

latter days as the Messiah. The mediator of the covenant will be assigned the tasks "to restore the land and to reassign its desolate inheritances."

Then, in the second occurrence he says,

> I will make an everlasting covenant [ברית עולם—*brit olam*] with you, my faithful love promised to David (Isa. 55:3, *Hebrew text added*).

In this passage, the future renewal of the covenant with Israel is associated with the Davidic Covenant. Thus, the permanence of both covenants is associated with the final restoration of Israel.

The prophet Hosea, a contemporary of Isaiah, spoke in similar terms.

> In that day, I will make a covenant for them with the beasts of the field and the birds of the air and the creatures that move along the ground. Bow and sword and battle I will abolish from the land, so that all may lie down in safety. I will betroth you to me forever; I will betroth you in righteousness and justice, in love and compassion. I will betroth you in faithfulness, and you will acknowledge the LORD. In that day I will respond," declares the Lord, "I will respond to the skies, and they will respond to the earth; and the earth will respond to the grain, the new wine and oil, and they will respond to Jezreel. I will plant her for myself in the land; I will show my love to the one I called 'Not my loved one.' I will say to those called 'Not my people,' 'You are my people'; and they will say, "You are my God" (Hos. 2:18–23).

Through the prophet, the Lord associates with the future covenant renewal various characteristics in addition to the restored relationship with his chosen nation. First, he mentions the restored harmony with nature. This is akin to Isaiah's statements, "The wolf will lie down with the lamb, the leopard will lie down with the goat ....”[327] Hosea also mentions the abolition of war from the land and the sufficiency of rain and the abundance of crops. This harkens back to the terms of the original covenant.[328]

Through the prophet Ezekiel, the Lord spoke to the exiles in Babylon about the hope that the nation has in the future. He had not forgotten them, nor would he abandon his covenant with them. He addressed the many facets of the restoration we have seen earlier, including the promise of the final Davidic ruler:

> I will save my flock, and they will no longer be plundered. I will judge between one sheep and another. I will place over them one shepherd, my servant David, and he will tend them; he will tend them and be their shepherd. I the Lord will be their God, and my servant David will be prince among them. I the Lord have spoken. I will make a covenant of peace [שלום ברית—*brit shalom*] with them and rid the land of wild beasts so that they may live in the desert and sleep in the forests in safety. I will bless them and the places surrounding my hill. I will send down showers in season; there will be showers of blessing. The trees of the field will yield their fruit and the ground will yield its crops; the people will be secure in their land. They will know that I am the Lord, when I break the bars of their yoke and rescue them from the hands of those who enslaved them. They will no longer be plundered by the nations, or will wild animals devour them. They will live in safety, and no one will make them afraid. I will provide for them a land renowned for its crops, and they will no longer be victims of famine in the land or bear the scorn of the nations. Then they will know that I, the Lord their God, am with them and that they, the house of Israel, are my people, declares

---

[327] Isaiah 11:6–9.
[328] Leviticus 26:3–8.

the sovereign Lord. You are my sheep, the sheep of my pasture, and I am your God, declares the Sovereign Lord" (Ezek. 34:22–31, *Hebrew text added*).

In Ezekiel 37, the prophet received the well-known vision about the valley of dry bones. In it, the Lord spoke of the future restoration of the formerly divided Israelite kingdoms. After the Babylonian captivity, the exiles who were mostly from the tribe of Judah returned to the land of Israel. The Bible does not record any such return of the exiles of the Assyrian captivity. However, Ezekiel's vision speaks of a complete nation in the future.

> This is what the Sovereign LORD says: "I will take the Israelites out of the nations where they have gone. I will gather them from all around and bring them back into their own land. I will make them one nation in the land, on the mountains of Israel. There will be one king over all of them and they will never again be two nations or be divided into two kingdoms. They will no longer defile themselves with their idols and vile images or with any of their offenses, for I will save them from all their sinful backsliding, and I will cleanse them. They will be my people, and I will be their God. My servant David will be king over them, and they will all have one shepherd. They will follow my laws and be careful to keep my decrees. They will live in the land I gave to my servant Jacob, the land where your fathers lived. They and their children and their children's children will live there forever, and David my servant will be their Prince forever. I will make a covenant of peace [שָׁלוֹם בְּרִית—*brit shalom*] with them; It will be an everlasting covenant [עוֹלָם בְּרִית—*brit olam*]. I will establish them and increase their numbers, and I will put my sanctuary among them forever. My dwelling place will be with them; I will be their God, and they will be my people. Then the nations will know that I the Lord make Israel

holy, when my sanctuary is among them forever" (Ezek. 37:21–28, *Hebrew text added*).

Before the fall of Jerusalem, God spoke extensively about the city with the sentiment of a loving but estranged husband in Ezekiel 16. He used the same metaphors of a prostitute and an unfaithful wife as are found in the book of Hosea. At one point, he even compared Jerusalem with ancient Sodom.[329] After the Lord finished the reminiscence of her earlier years and chastisement of her later years, he concluded positively with the anticipation of her future restoration and renewed covenant.

> This is what the Sovereign LORD says: "I will deal with you as you deserve, because you have despised my oath by breaking the covenant. Yet I will remember the covenant I made with you in the days of your youth, and I will establish an everlasting covenant [ברית עולם—*brit olam*] with you ... So I will establish my covenant with you, and you will know that I am the LORD. Then when I make atonement for you for all you have done, you will remember and be ashamed and never again open your mouth because of your humiliation," declares the Sovereign LORD" (Ezek. 16:59–63, *Hebrew text added*).

The nation will be united again. The final king will be a descendant of David. The people will follow God's laws and keep his decrees because their hearts will be circumcised. The covenant that God made with them "in the days of your youth" was an everlasting covenant. The covenant he will make with them in the latter days will also be everlasting. There will not be two coexisting covenants. The future covenant will be a renewal of the existing one, with at least one modification, as we will now see.

---

[329] Ezekiel 16:44–58.

Jeremiah

Jeremiah and Ezekiel were contemporaries who served the Lord and the people of Judah in different locations. Ezekiel was probably among the people deported to Babylon by Nebuchadnezzar eleven years before the fall of Jerusalem.[330] He received his vision by the Kebar river in Babylon in the fifth year of the exile of King Jehoiachin.[331] However, Jeremiah remained in Judah, warning the leadership and the people that Judah would not be rescued from the hand of Nebuchadnezzar. He warned the inhabitants of Judah of the coming destruction. He wrote a letter to those who had already been exiled, advising them to settle in Babylon, build houses, marry, and have children because the Lord's order for their return would not happen for seventy years.[332] The devastation of both Israel and Judah and the fall of Jerusalem were not unexpected, for both the blessings and the curses were terms of the covenant.

> "If in spite of this you still do not listen to me but continue to be hostile toward me, then … I will scatter you among the nations and will draw out my sword and pursue you. Your land will be laid waste, and your cities will lie in ruins" (Lev. 26:27, 26:33).

Jeremiah also spoke of the final restoration of the nation and the renewal of the covenants.[333] He dedicated three entire chapters to the subjects.[334] It is from his writings that we acquire the term "new covenant."

> "The time is coming," declares the LORD, "when I will make a new covenant (ברית חדשה—*brit khadashah*) with the house of Israel and with the house of Judah. It will not be like the covenant I made with their forefathers when I took them by the hand to lead them out of

---

[330] 2 Kings 24:8–17, 25:2
[331] Ezekiel 1:2.
[332] Jeremiah 29:1–23.
[333] The covenants with Israel, David, and Levi.
[334] Jeremiah 30, 31, 33.

Egypt, because they broke my covenant, though I was a husband to them," declares the LORD (Jer. 31:31–32, *Hebrew text added*).

It is very important that we understand God's intention when he says, "It will not be like the covenant I made with their forefathers ...." This should not be understood as a replacement of the previous covenant. All the covenants we have examined thus far were designated as "everlasting." We understand that "God is not a man, that he should lie, nor the son of man, that he should change his mind."[335] And so this statement must be interpreted in the context of the permanent covenant that preceded it.

The translators of the Greek Septuagint understood this, as evidenced by the way they translated the phrase "new covenant" in Jeremiah 31:31 above. When translating the word "new," they could have used either νεος (*neos*) or καινος (*kainos*). The word *neos* means something that has never existed previously. The word *kainos* carries overtones of freshness and renewal of something which has existed.[336] The writers of the Septuagint used the Greek word *kainos* to translate the Hebrew word חדשה (*khadashah*). No doubt, the translators understood that the covenant God made with Israel on Mount Sinai was everlasting, and thus the choice between *neos* and *kainos* was obvious.

Consequently, if the New Covenant "will not be like the covenant I made with their forefathers" and is a renewal of the former covenant and not a replacement of it, then in what manner is it "not like" it. What exactly is the difference?

> "This is the covenant I will make with the house of Israel after that time," declares the LORD. "*I will put my law in their minds and write it on their hearts. I will be their God and they will be my people. No longer will a man teach his neighbor, or a man his brother, saying, 'Know

---

[335] Numbers 23:19.

[336] David H. Stern, *Jewish New Testament Commentary* (Clarksville: Jewish New Testament Publications, Inc.), 690.

the LORD,' because they will all know me, from the least of them to the greatest," declares the LORD. "For I will forgive their wickedness and will remember their sins no more" (Jer. 31:33–34, *italics added*).

In addition to whatever other modifications there may be when the New Covenant is ratified by Israel in the future, we know that the medium upon which it will be written will be different. It will not be external, written on stone tablets, and subsequently disobeyed as in previous generations. The Torah will be internalized by a believing generation of Israel, circumcised in heart and knowing the Lord. As we have seen, this is the covenantal relationship that God wanted with his chosen people from the beginning. The two parties have experienced much turmoil through the centuries, and God has been forthright in expressing his feelings about the relationship. In the end, through divine sovereignty and unconditional love, the Lord will have his bride.

But one might ask, how will this affect God's plan for the rest of humanity? Those who are under the Noahic Covenant? Or, as he promised Abraham, how will "all the peoples of the earth"[337] to be blessed through him and his descendants?

---

[337] Genesis 12:3.

THE MEDIATOR
OF THE
COVENANTS

God has spoken throughout recorded history in various ways. Sometimes he has communicated directly via a face-to-face encounter.[338] At other times, he spoke through dreams, visions,[339] or the Urim and the Thummim.[340] With each of these methods, except the last one, the recipient has at times seen the Lord on his throne,[341] standing at the top of a heavenly staircase,[342] or even sharing his meal with him.[343] However, both Moses and the apostle John have clearly stated that God has not been seen by anyone.[344] It is important that we recognize the existence of God's special messenger and understand the special relationship that exists between the two of them. This understanding will not only help us interpret scripture more accurately but will also lead us to a greater appreciation of the Bible's main character.

---

[338] Genesis 18:1–2; Numbers 12:8.

[339] Numbers 12:6.

[340] Exodus 28:30.

[341] Isaiah 6:1; 2 Chronicles 18:18.

[342] Genesis 28:12–13

[343] Genesis 18:3–8.

[344] Deuteronomy 4:12, 4:15; John 1:18.

Definition of Terms

Angel

The Hebrew word that is often translated as "angel" is מלאך (*malakh*). The writers of the Septuagint used the Greek word αγγελος (*aggelos*) to translate it. The English word "angel" is simply a transliteration of the Greek word. It would be better and more consistent to use the word "messenger"[345] to refer to a person who has been sent by someone else. The same Hebrew word is used to denote both heavenly and earthly messengers. With this understanding, we can see that a messenger/ angel, whether earthly or heavenly, is not a type of being but, rather, a job description. When sent by the Lord, they will either carry a message to someone or seek information that they will carry back and report.[346] This latter reconnaissance work is in view when they are called "watchers" in the book of 1 Enoch and are called the "eyes of the Lord" in the biblical text.[347]

We should also not assume, at least for heavenly messengers, that such individuals necessarily have feathers and wings, for not all heavenly beings in scripture are depicted as such.

God

The Hebrew words that are often translated as "God/god" are אלוה (*eloah*) and אל (*el*), along with their plural forms אלהים (*elohim*) and אלים (*elim*). These two words are not synonyms. However, there is not yet a consensus regarding the exact difference between them. The word *elohim* is the form most frequently used in biblical Hebrew.

---

[345] The word מלאך (*malakh*) is used in Genesis 32:1, 3. In both verses, the same Hebrew word is used, and in both cases, the LXX translates it using the word αγγελος (*aggelos*). However, the English translators decided to translate it as "angels" in the first verse and "messengers" in the second verse.

[346] Job 1:6, 2:1. Here, they are called "sons of God," as in Genesis 6:2, 6:4.

[347] Proverbs 15:3; 2 Chronicles 16:9.

Interestingly, it is the plural form, but as the subject in a sentence, it often takes a singular verb.[348] It is notable that *elohim* is used in the Bible to refer not only to the creator but also to other heavenly beings,[349] to human leadership,[350] to deceased human beings (including the prophet Samuel),[351] and even to Moses.[352] With such varied usage, it is easy to see that we must embrace a much broader understanding of these words, possibly as a title or function. The ancient form of the Hebrew alphabet was pictographic, and the meaning of the letters might help us gain that understanding. The words אלוה (*eloah*) and אל (*el*) have two letters in common (reading from right to left) א and ל. The character from that ancient alphabet that would later become the letter א was the caricature of an ox head. The ancient predecessor to the letter ל was a shepherd's staff. The ox was the strongest of all the domesticated animals, and its ancient alphabetic character symbolized strength. The shepherd's staff character symbolized direction and leadership. This understanding should help us broaden our definition of these two Hebrew words. Whether the terms are used in a heavenly or earthly context, they should convey some aspect of strong leadership.[353]

---

[348] I.e., Genesis 1:1.

[349] Psalm 82:1.

[350] Exodus 22:28.

[351] 1 Samuel 28:13–15.

[352] Exodus 4:16. Many translations use the phrase "as God" to accommodate the more limited understanding of the word *elohim*. However, the Hebrew text does not read כאלהים, using the prepositional prefix כ, meaning "as." Rather, it reads לאלהים, using a ל, as is done repeatedly when the author is specifically referring to God (i.e., Exod. 29:45, Lev. 26:12, Jer. 30:22).

[353] Jeff A. Benner, *The Ancient Hebrew Language and Alphabet* (College Station: Virtualbookworm.com Publishing Inc.), 40, 50, and 58. It is interesting how some other words follow this line of thinking. Used as a metaphor for the "high and mighty" by the prophet Isaiah (Isa. 2:13), the word for oak tree is spelled אלון. The leader of the ovine flock is the ram, the word for which is spelled איל.

God Speaks from Heaven

There have been occasions when God has spoken directly to a group of people. Upon examination, those occasions help to demonstrate the need for a mediator, someone who can speak and interact with people, personally and privately. The most well-known public announcement from God was at Mount Sinai. After he revealed his Ten Commandments to the Israelites in a loud voice, accompanied by a thick cloud, thunder, and lightning, the people were terrified and said to Moses, "Speak to us yourself and we will listen. But do not have God speak to us or we will die" (Exod. 20:19).

On this occasion, the voice of God caused the Israelites to fear for their lives. Whether it was because of the intensity of his voice or simply the effects of the accompanying weather conditions on the mountain, they understood the seriousness of direct communication with God.

On what has been called the Mountain of Transfiguration, Peter, James, and John witnessed the face of Jesus shine like the sun and his clothes become white as light. Moses and Elijah appeared and spoke with Jesus. The experience was evidently not terrifying enough to stop Peter from asking a silly question. However, when God spoke,

> a bright cloud enveloped them, and a voice from the cloud said, "This is my Son, whom I love; with him I am well pleased. Listen to him!" When the disciples heard this, they fell face down to the ground, terrified (Matt. 17:5–6).[354]

Like the Sinai event, the experience was terrifying.

Just before Jesus was to enter Jerusalem for the last time, he spoke to his disciples:

---

[354] They had experienced some degree of fear prior to the voice from heaven, for Mark 9:6 states parenthetically, "For they were afraid, and he did not know what to say." Luke 9:32 indicates that they were sleeping just before all this transpired.

"Now my heart is troubled, and what shall I say? 'Father, save me from this hour'? No, it was for this very reason I came to this hour. Father, glorify your name!" Then a voice came from heaven, "I have glorified it, and will glorify it again." The crowd that was there and heard it said it had thundered; others said an angel had spoken to him (John 12:27–29).

On this occasion, the voice of God did not cause life-threatening fear. However, to some, the voice was undiscernible, and they interpreted it as a weather phenomenon. Others, apparently, were able to understand what was said but misidentified the speaker.

Finally, God spoke audibly for all to hear when Jesus was at the Jordan River being baptized by John. We are told only that as Jesus came up from the water, "a voice from heaven said …"[355] There is no mention of fear and trembling.

These examples demonstrate that the voice from heaven was not seen, could not be touched, could at times be unbearable, and could be misidentified. Conceivably, it would be very difficult to relate with someone under these conditions. For humans to interact with the Divine, there needed to be a mediator, a person who could relate with both parties and stand in the gap.

God Speaks Through a Mediator

We shall examine seven passages of scripture that tell of instances when a messenger communicated God's words to various biblical characters. You will notice very quickly that there will appear to be some inconsistencies in the texts that can be confusing. If we allow the confusion to cause us to dig more deeply, we might just unveil a character in the story that is often overlooked. Be aware that when you read the word "LORD" in all

---

[355] Matthew 3:16–17, Mark 1:10–11, Luke 3:21–22.

capital letters, it represents the actual name of God in the Hebrew text, sometimes translated as *Yahweh* or *Jehovah*.

Let us begin with the story of Moses and the burning bush.

> Now Moses was tending the flock of Jethro his father-in-law, the priest of Midian, and he led the flock to the far side of the desert and came to Horeb, the mountain of God. There the *angel of the* LORD appeared to him in flames of fire from within a bush. Moses saw that though the bush was on fire it did not burn up. So Moses thought, "I will go over and see this strange site–why the bush does not burn up."

> When the LORD saw that he had gone over to look, *God* called to him from within the bush, "Moses! Moses!"

> And Moses said, "Here I am."

> "Do not come any closer," *God* said. "Take off your sandals, for the place where you are standing is holy ground." Then he said, "I am the *God* of your father, the *God* of Abraham, the *God* of Isaac and the *God* of Jacob." At this, Moses hid his face, because he was afraid to look at *God* (Exod. 3:1–6, *italics added*).

You might have already begun to see what appears to be inconstancies in the text just by reading the italicized words. Who appeared to Moses in flames of fire from within the bush? Who saw that Moses had gone over to look? Who called to him from within the bush and said, "Take off your sandals"? Why would the angel of the LORD say, "I am the God of your father"? Who was Moses afraid to look at? But then again, who was in the burning bush?

The next example is from an earlier time, when there was discord between Abraham's wife, Sarai (Sarah), and her maidservant, Hagar.

Hagar fled from Sarai and journeyed to her homeland in Egypt. On the way, she stopped by a spring.

> The *angel of the* LORD found Hagar near a spring in the desert; it was the spring that is beside the road to Shur. And he said, "Hagar, servant of Sarai, where have you come from, and where are you going?"
>
> "I'm running away from my mistress Sarai," she answered.
>
> Then *the angel of the* LORD told her, "Go back to your mistress and submit to her." The angel added, "*I will* so increase your descendants that they will be too numerous to count."
>
> *The angel of the* LORD also said to her: "You are now with child and you will have a son. You shall name him Ishmael, for the LORD has heard of your misery. He will be a wild donkey of a man; His hand will be against everyone and everyone's hand against him, and he will live in hostility toward all his brothers."
>
> She gave this name to the LORD, who spoke to her: "You are the *God* who sees me," for she said, "I have now seen the one who sees me." That is why the well was called Beer Lahai Roi; it is still there, between Kadesh and Bered (Gen. 16:7–14, *italics added*).

By now, I am sure that you are anticipating the questions. Who found Hagar near the spring in the desert and told her, "Go back to your mistress"? Who said, "I will so increase your descendants that they will be too numerous to count," mimicking the words spoken to Abraham by the LORD?[356] Who "heard of her misery"? Why did Hagar give "this name to the LORD who spoke to her" when it was the angel of the LORD

---

[356] Genesis 13:16, 15:5, 22:17.

who actually spoke? And why did she refer to the person who spoke to her as "the God"?

Hopefully, all these questions help you to sense that there is something just beneath the surface that we need to uncover. The problem is a combination of how we understand the main character and how the Hebrew text was translated. Someone once said, "Reading a story through a translation is like kissing the bride through the veil." Oddly, if we continue to ask the questions, we will discover that we have a set of consistent inconsistencies. That discovery, along with the terms we defined earlier, will help us to remove the veil.

Next, we will examine the story about the time God tested Abraham. God told Abraham to take his son to the region of Moriah and sacrifice him on one of the mountains. With great anguish and difficulty, Abraham obeyed God and accomplished the task, just up to the point of raising the knife, when he was stopped.

> The *angel of the* LORD called out to him from heaven, "Abraham! Abraham!"
>
> "Here I am," he replied.
>
> "Do not lay a hand on the boy," he said. "Do not do anything to him. Now I know that you fear *God*, because you have not withheld from *me* your son, your only son."
>
> Abraham looked up and there in a thicket he saw a ram caught by its thorns. He went over and took the ram and sacrificed it as a burnt offering instead of his son. So Abraham called that place the LORD will provide. And to this day it is said, "on the mountain of the LORD it will be provided."
>
> The *angel of the* LORD called to Abraham from heaven a second time and said, "I swear by myself, declares the LORD that because you have done this and have not

withheld your son, your only son, I will surely bless you and make your descendants as numerous as the stars in the sky and as the sand on the seashore. Your descendants will take possession of the cities of their enemies, and through your offspring all the nations on the earth will be blessed, because you have obeyed me" (Gen. 22:11–18, *italics added*).

The inconsistencies in this passage are fewer. In the final section, the angel of the LORD is clearly passing a message from the LORD to Abraham for he includes the phrase, "declares the LORD." However, when he stopped Abraham from sacrificing Isaac, he said, "I know that you fear God." But then he says, "You have not withheld *from me* your son." Who then gave Abraham the order to perform this act?

We now move to the time after the Exodus, the conquest of Canaan, and after the death of Joshua, when the Israelites were fighting the remaining people of the land. The Israelites had not done everything the Lord had commanded and were about to be reprimanded.

The *angel of the* LORD went up from Gilgal to Bokim and said, "*I brought* you up out of Egypt and lead you into the land that *I swore* to give to your forefathers. *I said*, '*I will never break* my covenant with you, and you shall not make a covenant with the people of this land, but you will break down their altars.' Yet you have disobeyed *me.* Why have you done this? Now therefore I tell you that I will not drive them out before you; they will be thorns in your sides and their gods will be a snare to you.

When the *angel of the* LORD had spoken these things to all the Israelites, the people wept aloud, and they called the place Bokim. There they offered sacrifices to the LORD (Judg. 2:1–5, *italics added*).

Why is the angel of the LORD using the first-person singular pronoun "I" when referring to these events? Who brought them out of Egypt?[357] Who made the oath with their forefathers? Who made a covenant with them? What distinctions should we make between the LORD and the angel of the LORD?

The next example is from the story of Gideon.

> The *angel of the LORD* came and sat down under the oak in Ophrah that belonged to Joash the Abiezrite, where his son Gideon was threshing wheat in a wine press to keep it from the Midianites. When the *angel of the LORD* appeared to Gideon, he said, "The LORD is with you, mighty warrior."
>
> "But sir," Gideon replied, "if the LORD is with us, why has all this happened to us? Where are all his wonders that our fathers told us about when they said, "Did not the LORD bring us up out of Egypt?" But now the LORD has abandoned us and put us into the hand of Midian."
>
> The LORD turned to him and said, "Go in the strength you have and save Israel out of Midian's hand. Am I not sending you?"
>
> "But Lord," Gideon asked, "how can I save Israel? My clan is the weakest in Manasseh, and I am the least in my family." The LORD answered, "I will be with you, and you will strike down all the Midianites together."
>
> Gideon replied, "If now I have found favor in your eyes give me a sign that it is really you talking to me. Please

---

[357] These verses indicate the angel of the Lord brought them out of Egypt (Exod. 14:19, Num. 20:16). The Exodus passage is interesting when compared to another verse in the same chapter. Verse 19 speaks of the "angel of God" in relation to the pillar of cloud that preceded the Israelite camp. However, in verse 24, it says, "The LORD looked down from the pillar of fire and cloud."

do not go away until I come back and bring my offering and set it before you."

And he said, "I will wait until you return."

Gideon went in, prepared a young goat and from the flour he made bread without yeast. Putting the meat in a basket and its broth in a pot, he brought them out and offered them to him under the oak.

The *angel of God* said to him, "Take the meat and the unleavened bread, place them on this rock, and pour out the broth." and Gideon did so. With the tip of the staff that was in his hand, the *angel of the* LORD touched the meat and the unleavened bread. Fire flared from the rock, consuming the meat and the bread. And the *angel of the* LORD disappeared. When Gideon realized that it was the *angel of the* LORD, he exclaimed, "Ah, *Sovereign* LORD! I have seen the *angel of the* LORD face to face!"

But the LORD said to him, "Peace! Do not be afraid. You are not going to die."

So Gideon built an altar to the LORD there and called it The LORD is Peace. To this day it stands in Oprah of the Abiezrites (Judg. 6:11–24, *italics added*).

Who came and sat under the oak tree? Who appeared to Gideon and spoke to him? Who turned to Gideon and said, "Go in the strength you have" and answered his subsequent question? Who instructed Gideon to "take the meat and the unleavened bread" and touched it, setting it on fire? Who told him, "Peace! Do not be afraid"?

Be patient. We are almost done. Sometimes Bible study can be tedious, but it is worth it.

The next example involves the parents of Samson. The angel of the LORD appeared to the woman who would be his mother, the wife of Manoah, to tell her that she would conceive and have a child, and that the child would be a Nazirite[358] from birth. She relayed this information to Manoah, who subsequently prayed and ask the Lord to send the "man of God" back to them so he could instruct them on how the child should be brought up. So the messenger returned and gave them the instructions he requested. Then ...

> Manoah said to the *angel of the* LORD, "We would like you to stay until we prepare a young goat for you."

> The *angel of the* LORD replied, "Even though you detain me, I will not eat any of your food. But if you prepare a burnt offering, offer it to the LORD." (Manoah did not realize that it was the angel of the LORD.)

> Then Manoah inquired of the *angel of the* LORD, "What is your name, so that we may honor you when your word comes true?"

> He replied, "Why do you ask my name? It is beyond understanding." Then Manoah took the young goat, together with the grain offering, and sacrificed it on a rock to the LORD. And the LORD did an amazing thing while Manoah and his wife watched: As the flame blazed up from the altar toward heaven, the *angel of the* LORD ascended in the flame. Seeing this, Noah and his wife fell with their faces to the ground. When the *angel of the* LORD did not show himself again to Manoah and his wife, Minoah realized that it was the *angel of the* LORD.

> "We are doomed to die!" he said to his wife. "We have seen *God!*"

---

[358] Numbers 6:1–21.

But his wife answered, "If the LORD had meant to kill us he would not have accepted a burnt offering and grain offering from our hands, nor shown us all these things or now told us this" (Judg. 13:15–23, *italics added*).

Who appeared to Manoah and his wife? Why did they say "We have seen God!"? What amazing thing did the LORD do? Or was it the angel of the LORD doing something amazing by ascending in the flame?[359] When Manoah asked for the messenger's name, they received a response similar to Jacob when he asked the same question of the "man" with whom he wrestled.[360] In like manner, after the encounter Jacob claimed he had seen God.[361] It almost seems as though the lines between the terms, "angel of the LORD," "LORD," and "God" are being blurred.

Our final example comes from the latter years of the life of Jacob. Joseph brought his two sons to him so he could bless them. Jacob placed his hands on them and said,

> "May the *God* before whom my fathers
>   Abraham and Isaac walked,
> the *God* who has been my shepherd
>   all my life to this day,
> the *Angel* who has delivered me from all harm
>   —may he bless these boys.
> May they be called by my name
>   and the names of my fathers Abraham and Isaac,
> and may they increase greatly upon the earth" (Gen.
> 48:15–16, *italics added*).

This passage has been presented last because it begins to bring to a climax the perceived inconsistencies we have seen so far. First, we should be

---

[359] The angel of the Lord was "in flames of fire from within a bush" (Exod. 3:2). The angel of God, or the Lord, was in the pillar of fire and cloud (Exod. 14:19, 14:24). There seems to be a pattern.

[360] Genesis 32:29.

[361] Genesis 32:30.

aware that the phrase "May he bless these boys" is significant. The word "he" is not actually in the Hebrew text. It has been added for readability in English because the Hebrew verb for "bless" is in the masculine form. However, the word "bless" in Hebrew is, in fact, singular. This is important because it clarifies the subjects in the previous phrases to be one and the same person. The God before whom his fathers walked and who had been his shepherd, and the angel who delivered him are *not* two different entities. Again, they are one and the same person. This is why we needed to define these terms early in this chapter. This person of whom Jacob spoke is both מלאך (*malakh*) and אלהים (*elohim*). These are the words that Jacob used in this blessing. We must acknowledge the broader definition of the word אלהים (*elohim*), or else this, and all the previous passages we have examined, may become a source of anxiety for the serious Bible student. The messenger, no doubt, was sent by someone greater than himself. So then the messenger is not the creator who sent him, and yet he is אלהים (*elohim*). Therefore, the "God," whose blessing Jacob is invoking, is not the creator but the מלאך (*malakh*)/אלהים (*elohim*).

The Divine Messenger

This may become easier to accept if we put aside the English, with our ingrained definitions, and we view things through the Hebrew terms. There are many classifications of heavenly beings of which אלהים (*elohim*) is just one.[362] The entire council, or assembly, of God consists of אלהים (*elohim*). Psalm 82:1 may be helpful at this point. One's understanding of the words אלהים (*elohim*) and אל (*el*) has caused this verse to be translated in many ways.

---

[362] Rambam (c.1176–c.1178), in his Mishneh Torah, lists ten classifications of heavenly beings: חיות הקדש (*hayoth hakodesh*), אופנים (*ophanim*), אראלים (*erelim*), חשמלים (*hashmalim*), שרפים (*seraphim*), מלאכים (*malachim*), אלהים (*elohim*), בני אלהים (*bene elohim*), כרובים (*cherubim*), and אישים (*ishim*). See Foundations of the Torah 2:7 in the Sefaria Library, https://www.sefaria.org/Mishneh_Torah,_Foundations_of_the_Torah. The apostle Paul suggests a divine hierarchy, using terms such as "rule," "authority," "power," and "dominion," referring to the "heavenly realm" (Eph. 1:21, 6:12; 1 Cor. 15:24; Col. 2:10).

אלהים (*elohim*) stand in the council/assembly of אל (*el*);
In the midst of the אלהים (*elohim*), he judges.

If we understand the word אלהים (*elohim*) collectively, then the singular form of the verb "to stand" poses no problem. Also, since אל (*el*) is the one standing in judgment over the others, we can assume this term in this context refers to the creator himself. In Psalms 82, אל (*el*) most certainly had much to say in judgment of some of the council's members.

Now, let us ask ourselves, what would happen if a messenger were sent from this council? Would that individual not be considered a מלאך (*malakh*)/אלהים (*elohim*), being an אלהים (*elohim*) and taking on the responsibility of a מלאך (*malakh*)? Consider the LLX translation of Isaiah 9:6. No doubt the translators of the Septuagint had older Hebrew manuscripts than even those used by the writers of the Dead Sea Scrolls. The LXX reading might very well be reflecting what Isaiah actually wrote. Consider:

οτι	παιδιον	εγεννηθη	ημιν,	υιος	και	εδοθη	ημιν,
for	child	born	to us	son	and	given	to us,

ου	η	αρχη	Εγενηθη	επι	του	ωμου	αυτου,
which	the	government	has become	upon	the	shoulders	of him

και	καλειται	του	ονομα	αυτου	Μεγαλης	βουλης	αγγελος
and	be called	the	name	of him	great	council	messenger

Or, in other words,

Unto us a child is born, and a son is given, the government is upon his shoulders, and his name is called the Messenger of the Great Council.

This helps to illuminate our understanding of Jacob's words when he blessed his grandsons. This מלאך (*malakh*)/אלהים (*elohim*) is the one who had been his shepherd all his life and who delivered him from all harm. And, probably most notably, this מלאך (*malakh*)/אלהים (*elohim*) was the one before whom Isaac and Abraham walked, and, consequentially, the one who spoke to Hagar, Gideon, Manoah, and Moses.

This Messenger of the Great Council undoubtedly has played a prominent role in God's plan for humanity. His primary role in the Abrahamic Covenant and the Sinai Covenant can be established solely by his interactions with the primary characters of those covenant stories. However, this mediating messenger's preeminence could not be more evident to us once we discover the name he bears.

Toward the end of Exodus 23, God told Moses that he would send a מלאך (*malakh*) to bring the Israelites into the promised land. The text does not mention anything about this message coming from a voice in the sky. Thus, it was probably the messenger himself who was passing the information on to Moses.

> "See, I am sending an angel ahead of you to guard you along the way and to bring you to the place I have prepared. Pay attention to him and listen to what he says. Do not rebel against him; he will not forgive your rebellion, since my Name is in him" (Exod. 23:20–21).

"My Name is in him" is certainly a breathtaking statement. The seven archangels have personal names (Uriel, Raphael, Raguel, Michael, Saraqael, Gabriel, and Remiel).[363] The mission of this מלאך (*malakh*)/אלהים (*elohim*) must have been of such importance that it required the messenger to bear the very name of the one who sent him. The message he bore must have been so close to the heart of God that the authority of the name traveled with the messenger himself. To obey the messenger was to obey the one who sent him. To disobey one was to disobey the other.

We can go one step farther by reevaluating the phrase "angel of the LORD." Biblical Hebrew makes use of a literary mechanism known as construct form. Its usage accommodates the language's lack of a

---

[363] 1 Enoch 20:1–8.

preposition meaning "of." Such a preposition did not come into use until the development of Rabbinic Hebrew. Construct form is the practice of juxtaposing two nouns for the purpose of causing the second noun to have a genitive relationship to the first noun. Or simply stated, when you are translating two Hebrew nouns that appear side by side, most of the time, you can insert the word "of" in between them. For example, נביא קֹל literally means "voice prophet" but would be translated "voice of a prophet." Another example would be דבר אלהים, or "word God," which would be translated "word of God."

However, this mechanism does not always apply. In Daniel 9:21, Daniel referred to someone he had previously seen in a vision as האיש גבריאל, or "the man Gabriel." It would not be translated as "the man of Gabriel." The second word is simply the name of "the man."

Therefore, it is quite reasonable to translate מלאך יהוה not as "the messenger of the LORD (יהוה or YHVH)" or "the messenger of Yahweh," but, rather as "the messenger Yahweh." In fact, now that we understand that he bears God's name, this would seem to be the preferred translation. If we apply this knowledge to the passages we examined earlier (Gen. 16:7–14, 22:11–18, 48:15–16; Exod. 3:1–6; Judg. 2:1–4, 6:11–24, 13:15–23), those consistent inconsistencies no longer exist. When the מלאך (malakh)/אלהים (elohim), whose name is Yahweh (יהוה rendered LORD in most translations) speaks, phrases such as "the angel of the LORD said," "the LORD said," or "God said" all mean the same thing and refer to the same person.

Consequently, there are two individuals in the scriptures that bear the name Yahweh (יהוה or YHVH), the creator and his great messenger. One cannot be seen, and the other freely interacts with humanity on a personal level, representing the one that cannot be seen. For the purposes that follow, we might even refer to them as the heavenly Yahweh and the earthly Yahweh. One day, the latter appeared to Abraham by the Oak of Mamre. Abraham ran to him and invited him to lunch. After the Messenger Yahweh announced to Abraham that he would have a son, the two of them went for a walk and had a long conversation about the coming destruction of Sodom and Gomorrah. As the conversation continues, the Messenger Yahweh sent two of his companion messengers to Lot's home to rescue his family from the coming disaster. Apparently, once his family was safe in the nearby city of Zoar, the Messenger Yahweh gave the order to begin the judgment upon the evil cities.

> Then the LORD (יהוה or YHVH) rained down burning sulfur on Sodom and Gomorrah—from the LORD (יהוה or YHVH) out of the heavens (Gen. 19:24, *parenthetical gloss added*).

Clearly, there are two Yahwehs in this passage. The earthly Yahweh had been interacting with Abraham and dispatching the other two messengers to secure Lot and his family, and the heavenly Yahweh sent burning sulfur from heaven. If we simply recognize the fact that the great messenger and the one who sent him have the same name, the inconsistencies we examined previously are resolved.

Additional Sources That Recognize a Second Subordinate Authority

Talmud

Someone approached Rabbi Idith with a question about Exodus 24:1. The passage is awkward. Someone said to Moses, "Come up to the LORD." It was time for Moses to ascend Mount Sinai again to receive instructions regarding the building of the tabernacle. However, we are not told who spoke these words to Moses. It simply says, "Then he said to Moses." The person with whom Moses would eventually meet face-to-face was no doubt the messenger of LORD, as we have concluded. So, regarding the identity of the persons in question, Rabbi Idith's opinion is probably the opposite of ours. However, his answer reveals his recognition of a second subordinate authority.

Once a Min said to R. Idith: It is written, And unto Moses He said, Come up to the Lord. But surely it should have stated, Come up unto me!—It was Metatron [who said that], he replied, whose name is similar to that of his Master, for it is written, For my name is in him (Sanhedrin 38b).[364]

Metatron was the name the rabbis had given to the divine messenger. It comes from two Greek words, "meta" (μετα—"with") and "thronos" (θρονος—"throne"). It was a name that recognized the intimacy that this messenger had with God and his proximity to God's authority. Rabbi Idith also quoted Exodus 23:21, which we examined earlier, noting that Metatron bore the name of the one who sent him.

Targum

The translators of the ancient Aramaic scriptures often treated the statements or actions by the LORD (יהוה or YHVH) differently when he was interacting with people in a mundane manner. Either they found it difficult to comprehend how the creator could interact in such a way knowing that he was not a physical being, or they understood that the person in question was indeed the messenger of the LORD. Thus, in these situations, when they encountered the tetragrammaton (יהוה or YHVH) in the Hebrew text, they would translate it מימרא דיי, or the "Word (*memra*) of the Lord." No doubt, this is the Jewish origin of the New Testament's use of the term λογος (*logos*) for the same individual. Compare the following translations of the Hebrew and Aramaic texts.

Then the man and his wife heard the sound of the LORD God as he was walking in the garden in the cool of the day, and they hid from the LORD God among the trees of the garden (Gen. 3:8).

364 Tzvee Zahavy, *Halakhah.com* (based on the classic Soncino translation), https://www.halakhah.com.

And they heard the voice of the Word [*memra*] of the Lord God walking in the garden in the repose of the day; and Adam and his wife hid themselves from before the Lord God among the trees of the garden (Targum Jonathon, *parenthetical gloss added*).[365]

And

Then the LORD said, "Shall I hide from Abraham what I am about to do?" (Gen. 18:17)

And the Lord said, with His Word [*memra*], I cannot hide from Abraham that which I am about to do; and it is right that before I do it, I should make it known to him (Targum Jonathon, *parenthetical gloss added*).[366]

In addition to numerous other examples, the online Jewish Encyclopedia provides this definition in its Memra article:

"The Word," in the sense of the creative or directive word or speech of God manifesting His power in the world of matter or mind; a term used especially in the Targum as a substitute for "the Lord" when an anthropomorphic expression is to be avoided.

In the Targum the Memra figures constantly as the manifestation of the divine power, or as God's messenger in place of God Himself, wherever the predicate is not in conformity with the dignity or the spirituality of the Deity.[367]

---

[365] Sefaria Library, Genesis 3:8.
[366] Sefaria Library, Genesis 18:17.
[367] *The Jewish Encyclopedia*, https://www.jewishencyclopedia.com/articles/10618-memra.

Philo Judeus (20 BCE–50 CE)

Alexandria, Egypt, was once home of the largest Jewish population outside of Israel. It also possessed the largest library in the ancient world. It was the home of Philo Judeus, a philosopher, apologist, and even an emissary to Rome. Writing in Greek, he used the term λογος (*logos*) to refer to the מלאך (*malakh*)/אלהים (*elohim*), the great messenger.

> For God, like a shepherd and a king, governs (as if they were a flock of sheep) the earth, and the water, and the air, and the fire, and all the plants, and living creatures that are in them, whether mortal or divine … appointing as their immediate superintendent, *His own right Reason* [*logos*], *his firstborn son*, who is to receive the charge of this sacred company, as the *lieutenant of the great king*; for it is said somewhere, "Behold, I am He! I will send my messenger before thy face, who shall keep thee in the road."[368] (*italics and parenthetical gloss added*)

Notice how Philo associated this logos/son/lieutenant figure with the person who brought the Israelites out of Egypt. The verse he quoted regarding the messenger is from Exodus 23:20. The verse immediately following it is the one where God says of the messenger, "My name is in him."

In another place, Philo even mentions the λογος (*logos*) in relation to God's work of creation.

> Now the image of God is the Word [*logos*], by which all the world was made.[369] (*parenthetical gloss added*)

Compare this with the apostle Paul's statement.

---

[368] Philo Judeus, *The Works of Philo*, trans. C. D. Yonge (Peabody: Hendrickson Publishers), 178.
[369] Judeus, 541.

He is the image of the invisible God, the first born over all creation. For by him all things were created; things in heaven and on earth, visible and invisible, whether thrones or powers or rulers or authorities: all things were created by [through] him and for him (Col. 1:15–16, *parenthetical gloss added to clarify the meaning of* δια).

It is not difficult to notice how the understanding of the Word concept, λογος (*logos*)/מימרא (*memra*), was well established in Judaism by the time the apostle John used it in the opening chapter of his Gospel.

Josephus (37–100 CE)

Titus Flavius Josephus, born Yosef ben Matityahu, was a military leader and historian. After initially fighting against the Romans on the battlefield, he defected and was eventually granted Roman citizenship. His most prominent historical works were *The Jewish War* and the *Antiquities of the Jews*. However, in his *Discourse to the Greeks Concerning Hades*, he writes:

For all men, the just as well as the unjust, shall be brought before God the Word [*logos*]; for to him hath the Father committed all judgment; and he in order to fulfill the will of his Father, shall come as judge, whom we call Christ (Messiah).[370] (*parenthetical gloss added*)

In addition to what his predecessor, Philo, stated regarding the position and role of the λογος (*logos*) figure, Josephus understood the Logos to have the delegated authority from the Father to act as the judge of all. Just as we have been discussing the מלאך (*malakh*)/אלהים (*elohim*), Josephus uses the phrase "God the Word," joining the words *God* (θεος—*theos*) and *Word* (λογος—*logos*) to refer to the same person.

---

[370] Flavius Josephus, *The Works of Josephus*, trans. William Whiston (Peabody: Hendrickson Publishers), 814.

Biblical

It might be beneficial to close this section of the chapter with one additional "inconsistency" from scripture that can be resolved by our understanding of the מלאך (*malakh*)/אלהים (*elohim*) and his later identification as the λογος (*logos*). In Deuteronomy, Moses warned the Israelites about fashioning idols, even in the likeness of the God of Israel. After all, no one had ever seen him.

> Then the LORD spoke to you out of the fire. You heard the sound of words but *saw no form*; there was only a voice (Deut. 4:12, *italics added*).

> You *saw no form* of any kind the day the LORD spoke to you at Horeb out of the fire. Therefore watch yourselves very carefully, so that you do not become corrupt and make for yourselves an idol (Deut. 4:15–16, *italics added*).

However, after receiving the Book of the Covenant, Moses was instructed to return to the mountain and to bring the leaders with him.

> Moses and Aaron, Nadab and Abihu, and the seventy elders of Israel went up and *saw the God of Israel*. Under his feet was something like a pavement made of sapphire, clear as the sky itself. But God did not raise his hand against these elders of the Israelites; *They saw God*, and they ate and drank (Exod. 24:9–11, *italics added*).

When we examine these two passages in parallel, we have no choice but to conclude that the person who spoke the Ten Commandments to the Israelites and the person who was seen by Moses and the leaders were *not* one and the same. The apostle John helps us to resolve this dilemma. In the beginning of his Gospel, he speaks about the Word, or λογος (*logos*), having the same understanding of the term as Philo and Josephus. Then he makes this statement.

No one has ever seen God, but God the One and Only, who is at the Father's side, has made him known (John 1:18).

The phrase used in this text for "God the One and Only" comes from the Greek, μονογενης θεος (*monogenes theos*). A better translation would be "the uniquely begotten God." Using the English word "God" in this context might still be awkward for the reader but not so for those who have grasped the broad understanding of its Hebrew counterpart, אלהים (*elohim*). Essentially, among that class of heavenly beings known as אלהים (*elohim*), there appears to be one who is unique regarding his origins. There is no one like him in the heavenly realm. John is stating that he is the one who has been seen by human observers throughout history, not the Father.[371]

Delegated Authority

We would expect this Messenger of the Great Council, the מלאך (*malakh*)/אלהים (*elohim*), the λογος (*logos*)/מימרא (*memra*), who bears the very name of the Creator who sent him, to have sufficient authority to perform his divine responsibilities. He speaks for the Creator, but many times he speaks using the first-person pronoun "I," blurring the distinction between sender and messenger. It appears that he and the Creator have such a bond that he has even been entrusted to speak and act on his own, using the authority that has been delegated to him.

---

[371] At times, John distinguished between the Creator and the more generic use of the word for God by utilizing the definite article. In John 1:1, he used ο θεος (*ho theos*) for the first occurrence of the word "God" and the anarthrous θεος (*theos*) for the second occurrence. Also, in John 10:33, he used the anarthrous θεος, where Jesus's accusers were not suggesting he was claiming to be the creator himself, but by claiming to be his son, he was suggesting his heavenly nature and origin. However, in John 1:18, he clearly used the anarthrous θεος (*theos*) to refer to the Creator who cannot be seen and used μονογενης θεος (*monogenes theos*) to refer to the λογος (*logos*) who has been seen.

The Authority to Commission

We have seen how the messenger spoke to Moses from the burning bush. He said, "I am the God of your father, the God of Abraham the God of Isaac and the God of Jacob."[372] Also, he said, "I have indeed seen the misery of my people in Egypt."[373] But after he commissioned him to lead the Israelites out of Egypt and Moses asked him what he should say to them when they ask who sent him, he gave Moses a two- part answer.

> God said to Moses, "I AM WHO I AM. This is what you are to say to the Israelites: 'I AM has sent me to you.'"

> God also said to Moses, "Say to the Israelites, "The LORD, the God of your fathers—the God of Abraham, the God of Isaac and the God of Jacob—has sent me to you.' This is my name forever, the name by which I am to be remembered from generation to generation" (Exod. 3:14–15).

When Jacob asked the messenger who wrestled with him what his name was, he was not given a straight answer.[374] Likewise, when Samson's parents asked the messenger for his name, they were given a similar answer.[375] However, when Moses posed the question, he was given two names.

We have already determined that the messenger, the מלאך (malakh)/אלהים (elohim), can speak for the Creator, and even bears his name,[376] even in these passages that begin with "God said," for he is אלהים (elohim). Thus, the second name given by the messenger, LORD (יהוה or YHVH), is the name he bears, the name of the one who sent him. But the first name, "I AM" (אהיה or ehyeh), is something/someone different. He is clearly telling Moses the two names by which he is being sent. Moses

---

[372] Exodus 3:6.
[373] Exodus 3:7.
[374] Genesis 32:29.
[375] Judges 13:17–18.
[376] Exodus 23:21.

was instructed to tell the Israelites, "I AM has sent me to your" *and* "The LORD ... has sent me to you." If LORD (יהוה or YHVH) is the name this messenger bears, the name of the one who sent him, then it would seem logical that the name "I AM" is the phrase by which the messenger had chosen to identify himself.[377] The messenger commissioned Moses in his own name first, then proceeded to commission him in the name of the one who had sent him. By invoking the name LORD (יהוה or YHVH), the messenger demonstrated that he was working in conjunction with the will of, and in subjection to, the one who sent him. But by sending Moses to the Israelites in the name of "I AM," his own name, he demonstrated that he possessed the authority to commission.

The Authority to Forgive Sins

We examined the following verse previously for the purpose of understanding the name of God and how it is related to his messenger. Let us now focus on another point contained therein.

> "See, I am sending an angel ahead of you to guard you along the way and to bring you to the place I have prepared. Pay attention to him and listen to what he says. Do not rebel against him; he will not forgive your rebellion, since my Name is in him" (Exod. 23:20–21).

The angel of which he speaks, the messenger who bears his name, brought the Israelites out of Egypt, led them through the desert for forty years, and, ultimately, brought them to the place God had prepared. It is important to recognize that God did not say, "Do not rebel against him, I will not forgive your rebellion," but, rather, "he will not forgive your rebellion." The right to forgive the rebelliousness of the Israelites in their trek from Egypt to Canaan was laid squarely upon the Messenger Yahweh.

---

[377] John 8:58.

The biblical text recounts many rebellions on the part of the Israelites that almost led to their destruction. One such example was the golden calf incident.[378] Another example was after the spies returned from exploring the promised land.[379] In each case, the one who spoke to Moses face-to-face, whom we now understand to be the Messenger Yahweh, threatened to annihilate the entire camp and rebuild the nation through Moses. In each case, Moses interceded for the nation, and the people were forgiven. Things did not return to their original state, however. In the golden calf incident, the covenant was renewed, but with Moses as a cosigner.[380] After the refusal of the nation to enter the promised land because of the bad report brought back by the spies, the generation that left Egypt was doomed to die in the desert.[381] Nonetheless, in these cases of rebellion and others, individuals might have suffered the consequences for their sins, but as a nation, they were forgiven. They were forgiven by the messenger who went with them in the pillar of cloud and fire, the messenger who possessed the authority to forgive.

All Authority

The prophet Daniel described to his readers the events of a vision he had during the first year of Belshazzar, king of Babylon. In his vision, he was shown four beasts that symbolized four consecutive world empires. Toward the end of the vision, he was shown two individuals who, interestingly, have a similar relationship to each other that exists between the Creator and his great messenger. Here, they are presented as the Ancient of Days and the Son of Man.

> As I looked,
> thrones were set in place, and the Ancient of Days took
> his seat.

---

[378] Exodus 32:1-35.
[379] Numbers 13:1–14:45.
[380] Exodus 34:27.
[381] Numbers 14:26–35.

His clothing was as white as snow; the hair of his head
was white like wool.
His throne was flaming with fire, and its wheels were
all ablaze.
A river of fire was flowing, coming out from him.
Thousands upon thousands attended him; ten thousand
times ten thousand stood before him.
The court was seated, and the books were opened ...

In my vision at night I looked, and there before me was
one like a son of man, coming with the clouds of heaven.
He approached the Ancient of Days and was led into his
presence. He was given authority, glory and sovereign
power; All peoples, nations and men of every language
worshipped him. His dominion is an everlasting
dominion that will not pass away, and his kingdom is
one that will never be destroyed (Dan. 7:9-10, 13–14).

It is important that we recognize that this is a dream and is stated as such
by Daniel in the very first verse of the chapter. The beasts portrayed in
the dream are not real but representative of world empires. Thus, we
can assume by the context that the visage of the Ancient of Days is also
representative of the creator and not a literal viewing of his personage.
The apostle John's statement that "no one has ever seen God"[382] would
seem to support this understanding.

Nevertheless, the fact that he "took his seat," "thousands upon thousands
attended him," "ten thousand times ten thousand stood before him," and
before him, "court was seated," and "the books were opened" imply that
his seat is one of ultimate authority. The other figure that Daniel saw was
like "a son of man," a term written in Aramaic as בר אנש (bar anash),
corresponding to the Hebraic term בן אדם (ben adam). It literally means
"son of man," but colloquially, it means "the likeness of a man." In other
words, there was an individual in heaven who, unlike all those around
him, looked like us. It would make sense that he would be the perfect

---

[382] John 1:18.

candidate to interface with humanity to represent God. This humanoid had access to the throne[383] and approached the Ancient of Days and was led into his presence. In addition, he was "given authority, glory, and sovereign power" *and* was worshiped by all "peoples, nations and men of every language." This is his position in heaven. When he is sent to earth to do God's bidding as a messenger, he brings with him all the "authority, glory, and sovereign power" that has been delegated to the Son of Man.

He has the authority to commission, forgive sins, and accomplish all the tasks that God has sent him to do.

Illuminated New Testament Passages

Now that we have a deeper understanding of the central figure of the Old Testament, we can use it to illuminate some of the statements made by Jesus in the Gospels. Let us begin with something Jesus said under oath at his trial.

> The high priest said to him, "I charge you under oath by the living God: tell us if you are the Christ, the son of God."
>
> "Yes, it is as you say," Jesus replied. "But I say to all of you: In the future you will see the son of man sitting at the right hand of the mighty one and coming on the clouds of heaven."
>
> Then the high priest tore his clothes and said, "He has spoken blasphemy! Why do we need any more witnesses? Look, now you have heard the blasphemy. What do you think?"
>
> "He is worthy of death," they answered (Matt. 26:63–66).

---

[383] Do you remember the previous discussion about the Talmudic concept of Metatron, "meta" (μετα—"with") and "thronos" (θρονος—"throne")?

This passage contains the intersection of many important theological titles. The charge of the high priest and his subsequent reaction to Jesus's answer is revealing. His charge reveals his understanding that the Messiah (Christ) is of divine origin by associating the title with the phrase "son of God." After Jesus claims the title of "Son of Man" mentioned by the prophet Daniel, the high priest levels a blasphemy charge against him. What the high priest did not do is noteworthy. He did not say, "Why are you changing the subject? I did not ask you if you were the Son of Man. I asked if you were the Messiah." This small detail allows us to conclude that the high priest's theology included the idea that the Messiah (Christ), the Son of God, and the Son of Man figure from Daniel's vision were one and the same person. In the same way, by stating, "Yes, it is as you say" and what followed, Jesus declared forthrightly his role, his origin, and, as the Son of Man, his authority. Just as the prophet Micah stated regarding the one who was to be born in Bethlehem, his "origins are from of old, from ancient times."[384]

Jesus referred to himself often as "the Son of Man." He had made a similar allusion to being the Son of Man of Daniel's vision only hours before his trial, while he was still with his disciples, praying,

> "Father, the time has come. Glorify your Son, that your Son may glorify you. For you granted him authority over all people that he might give eternal life to all those you have given him" (John 17:1–2).

This prayer was being spoken by the Son of Man addressing the Ancient of Days, acknowledging the fact that he had been given "authority, glory, and sovereign power" over "all peoples, nations, and men of every language."[385]

In the same manner, just prior to his ascension, Jesus demonstrated his authority to commission.

---

[384] Micah 5:2.
[385] Daniel 7:14.

"All authority in heaven and on earth has been given to me. Therefore go and make disciples of all nations" (Matt. 28:18–19).

As he had done earlier when he commissioned them to preach the message of an impending kingdom to the nation of Israel,[386] he was now sending them to make disciples of all nations. He was able to send them because he had the authority to commission as he did when he commissioned Moses. In fact, the ability of the disciples to perform miracles and to command evil spirits was derived from the authority that he had delegated to them.

> He called his twelve disciples to him and gave them authority to drive out evil spirits and to heal every disease and sickness (Matt. 10:1).

> Calling the Twelve to him, he sent them out two by two and gave them authority over evil spirits (Mark 6:7).

> When Jesus had called the Twelve together, he gave them power and authority to drive out all demons and to cure diseases, and he sent them out to preach the kingdom of God and to heal the sick (Luke 9:1–2).

> The seventy-two returned with joy and said, "Lord, even the demons submit to us in your name." He replied, "I saw Satan fall like lightning from heaven. I have given you authority to trample on snakes and scorpions and to overcome all the power of the enemy … All things have been committed to me by my Father" (Luke 10:17–22).

Also in the same manner, Jesus demonstrated his authority to forgive sins.

---

[386] Matthew 10:1–16; Mark 6:6–12; Luke 9:1–6, 10:1–24.

A few days later, when Jesus again entered Capernaum, the people heard that he had come home. So many gathered that there was no room left, not even outside the door, and he preached the word to them. Some men came, bringing to him a paralytic, carried by four of them. Since they could not get him to Jesus because of the crowd, they made an opening in the roof above Jesus and, after digging through it, lowered the mat the paralyzed man was lying on. When Jesus saw their faith, he said to the paralytic, "Son, your sins are forgiven." Now some teachers of the law were sitting there, thinking to themselves, "Why does this fellow talk like that? He's blaspheming! Who can forgive sins but God alone?" Immediately Jesus knew in his spirit that this was what they were thinking in their hearts, and he said to them, "Why are you thinking these things? Which is easier: to say to the paralytic, 'Your sins are forgiven,' or to say, 'Get up, take your mat and walk'? But that you may know that the Son of Man has authority on earth to forgive sins ..." He said to the paralytic, "I tell you, get up, take your mat and go home." He got up, took his mat and walked out in full view of them all. This amazed everyone and they praised God, saying, "We have never seen anything like this!" (Mark 2:1–12 [Matt. 9:1–8, Luke 5:17–26])

Matthew's account adds this note.

When the crowd saw this, they were filled with awe; and they praised God, who had given such authority to men (Matt. 9:8).

Jesus used a standard *a fortiori* argument. Which is more difficult, to make the statement "Your sins are forgiven" or to heal someone who is unable to walk. He used his authority to perform the latter in order to confirm his authority to do the former. However, his authority to forgive sins not only helped validate his claim to the title of Son of Man from

Daniel's vision, but it also associated him with the messenger from the Exodus story. It was odd that the teachers of the law asked themselves, "Who can forgive sins but God alone?" For there was someone besides God who could forgive sins. Do you remember previously when we read the passage from Exodus?

> "See, I am sending an angel ahead of you to guard you along the way and to bring you to the place I have prepared. Pay attention to him and listen to what he says. Do not rebel against him; he will not forgive your rebellion, since my Name is in him" (Exod. 23:20–21).

The מלאך (*malakh*)/אלהים (*elohim*) who spoke with Moses and led the Israelites out of Egypt, whom we have come to know as the Messenger Yahweh (מלאך יהוה—*malakh YHWH*), had the authority to forgive sins. The story of Jesus healing the paralytic and forgiving his sins is a critical piece of the puzzle. His claim that "the Son of Man has authority on earth to forgive sins" connects Jesus, the Son of Man, with the Messenger Yahweh, the one person besides God who has authority to forgive sins.

Thus, in light of the previous section entitled "Delegated Authority," Jesus's own words indicate that he was that person referenced in the law and the prophets as having authority, glory and sovereign power, including the authority to commission and the authority to forgive sins.

Finally, in the same manner, Jesus's own words associate him with the Messenger of the Divine Council. You might recall in the previous section entitled "The Divine Messenger," we used our understanding of the words אלהים (*elohim*) and אל (*el*) to illuminate Psalm 82:1.

> אלהים (*elohim*) stand in the council/assembly of אל (*el*);
> In the midst of the אלהים (*elohim*), he judges.

That understanding will prove to be useful as we examine the event that took place during Hanukkah. The verses of interest are toward the end of the passage. All other verses have been included to provide context.

Then came the feast of dedication at Jerusalem. It was winter, and Jesus was in the temple area walking in Solomon's Colonnade. The Jews gathered around him, saying, "How long will you keep us in suspense? If you are the Christ, tell us plainly."

Jesus answered, "I did tell you, but you do not believe. The miracles I do in my father's name speak for me, but you do not believe because you are not my sheep. My sheep listen to my voice; I know them, and they follow me. I give them eternal life, and they shall never perish; no one can snatch them out of my hand. My Father, who has given them to me, is greater than all; no one can snatch them out of my Father's hand. I and the Father are one.

Again the Jews picked up stones to stone him, but Jesus said to them, "I have shown you many great miracles from the Father. For which of these do you stone me?"

"We are not stoning you for any of these," replied the Jews, "but for blasphemy, because you, a mere man, claim to be God [θεος—*theos*]."

Jesus answered them, "Is it not written in your Law, 'I have said you are gods [plural of θεος—*theos*]'? If he called them 'gods,' to whom the word of God came - and the scripture cannot be broken - what about the one whom the Father set apart as his very own and sent into the world? Why then do you accuse me of blasphemy because I said 'I am God's [ο θεος—*ho theos*] Son'?" (John 10:22–36, *parenthetical gloss added*).

We must recognize that Jesus and the Jews in this story were not speaking Greek to each other. What they said in Hebrew, or possibly Aramaic, was translated into Greek by the apostle John for the benefit of his

Greek-speaking readers. However, the argument about to be presented works in either language.

The key to understanding this verbal exchange is to notice John's use of the word "the" when speaking of God(s)/god(s). Unfortunately, it is left untranslated by the English translators. The word "the," or the definite article, is used to point out particular identity, or specificity. Without it, a word like ανθρωπος (*anthropos*) would be translated "man" or "a man," whereas ο ανθρωπος (*ho anthropos*) would be translated as "the man." [387] Consequently, John is making a distinction between the words θεος and ο θεος in this passage.[388] The Jews were not accusing Jesus of claiming "to be God" because he said, "I am God's Son." They were accusing him of claiming to be θεος because he said he was the son of ο θεος, *the* God.

It would be helpful if we understood θεος, as it is used in this passage, in the same way we understand אלהים (*elohim*), in the general sense, referring to a class of heavenly beings. That is exactly how it is used in Psalm 82:1, and in the verse Jesus quotes in his reply.

> "I said, 'You are gods [אלהים]; you are all sons of the Most High [עליון]'" (Ps. 82:6, *Hebrew text added*).

In verses 1–5 of this Psalm, אל (*el*) is chastising some of the אלהים (*elohim*) because of their failures. God is speaking to the members of his Divine Council.

Suddenly, the accusation of the Jews against Jesus seems much more logical. His claim of being the Son of God was equivalent to claiming to be the son "of the Most High (עליון)" and of אל (*el*), "the" God (ο θεος—*ho theos*) who presides over the Divine Council. Thus, he also must be θεος (*theos*)/אלהים (*elohim*) as they are. Nonetheless, there is

---

[387] In this particular case and inflection, the word for "the" is simply the Greek letter omicron, or "o." When it is used as the definite article in front of another word, it is pronounced like the "ho" in "hot."

[388] As he also does in John 1:1–2.

something unique about his origins, for John clearly stated earlier in his Gospel that Jesus was the uniquely begotten θεος/אלהים, or μονογενης θεος (*monogenes theos*).[389] His accusers understood that Jesus's claim implied that he was more than just a human being and that he had heavenly origins.

There was something more in Jesus's response, however, that often goes undetected. To understand it, we must remind ourselves of the definition of αγγελος (*aggelos*) and מלאך (*malakh*), found at the beginning of this chapter. The best translation for these would be "messenger"—a person who has been sent by someone else.

> "Is it not written in your Law, 'I have said you are gods [אלהים]? If he called them 'gods' [plural of θεος—*theos*] to whom the word of God came—and the scripture cannot be broken—what about the one whom the Father set apart as his very own and sent into the world?" (John 10:34–36, *parenthetical gloss added*).

When Jesus said that, he was making a claim that went well beyond his heavenly origins and being the "uniquely begotten" Son of God. His Father, who is ο θεος (*ho theos*), the אל (*el*)/עליון(*elyon*) who stands in the midst of the divine council of אלהים (*elohim*), set him apart and sent him into the world. The fact that the Father "set him apart" (ο πατηρ ηγιασεν)[390] makes him "the Holy One." The fact that the Father, the leader of the אלהים (*elohim*) of his council, commissioned him to be their spokesperson makes Jesus the Messenger of the Great Council. Do you remember how the writers of the Greek Septuagint translated their Hebrew copy of Isaiah 9:6?

---

[389] John 1:18.

[390] The root of ηγιασεν is αγιαζω, which means "to dedicate, sanctify, make holy." The adjectival form is αγιος and was used as a title for Jesus in John 6:69, Mark 1:24, and Luke 4:34 by both disciples and demons when they called him "the Holy One of God" (ο αγιος του θεου).

Unto us a child is born, and a son is given, the government is upon his shoulders, and his name is called the Messenger of the Great Council.

All these titles lead back to one person.

מלאך (malakh)/אלהים (elohim), or divine messenger
Messenger Yahweh (מלאך יהוה—malakh YHWH)
Messenger of the Great Council
The one set apart by God and sent into the world
Son of the Most High, עליון (elyon)
Son of God, אל (el)
Son of "the" God, ο θεος (ho theos)
Son of Man
The Holy One
The uniquely begotten God, or μονογενης θεος (monogenes theos)
"I AM (אהיה, or ehyeh)
The One who has the authority to commission and forgive sins

In his final hours with his disciples, just before his arrest, Jesus prayed to his Father. Now that we understand who he is and his role in God's plan for humankind, one line of his prayer takes on new meaning. I suggest you read it slowly.

"I will remain in the world no longer, but they are still in the world, and I am coming to you. Holy Father, protect them by the power of your name—*the name you gave me*—so that they may be one as we are one." (John 17:11, *italics added*)

Before that day, many years earlier, when a maiden and a young carpenter were told to name him Jesus,[391] he already had another name. He and

---

[391] Matthew 1:21; Luke 1:31.

the name he bore were part of a divine story and party to numerous covenants in ages past. His "origins are from of old, from ancient times.[392]

Final Thought

Jesus is and has always been the mediator between God and man.[393] From the garden of Eden to the patriarchs, to Moses, the judges, the prophets, and the New Covenant,[394] when the ancients interacted with God, they were interacting with his messenger, set apart and sent into the world. The messenger's name was YHWH (יהוה), like that of his Father who sent him. Consequently, he not only is the mediator between God and man, he is also the mediator of the covenants.[395] As Moses represented the Israelites in the covenant process, the Messenger Yahweh represented the Creator and the council who sent him. Without a doubt, Moses knew very well who was speaking to him.

> "If you believed Moses, you would believe me, for he wrote about me" (John 5:46).

---

[392] Micah 5:2.

[393] 1 Timothy 2:5.

[394] Hebrew 8:6, 9:15, 12:24.

[395] When referring to John the Baptist, Jesus quoted part of Malachi 3:1 "See, I will send my messenger, who will prepare the way before me" (Matt 11:10; Luke 7:27). The rest of Malachi 3:1 speaks of Jesus, the Messiah, specifically as "the Lord you are seeking" and "the messenger of the covenant" (מאלך הברית—*malakh habrit*).

A LIGHT FOR
THE GENTILES

When Jesus, the מלאך (*malakh*)/אלהים (*elohim*), was sent by his father to be born into Adam's race, he was given a two-part mission. As Israel's king, he would first address the needs of his own people. On one occasion, he stated, "I was sent only to the lost sheep of Israel."[396] When sending his disciples to spread the message—"Repent, for the kingdom of heaven is near"—he gave them explicit instructions.

> "Do not go among the Gentiles or enter any town of the Samaritans. Go rather to the lost sheep of Israel" (Matt. 10:5–6).

The first part of his mission was to seek and to save what was lost,[397] specifically, those lost sheep of Israel who were his. The process of gathering his sheep is relatively simple to understand. Jesus used the metaphor of shepherding to explain it.

> "The man who enters by the gate is the shepherd of his sheep. The watchman opens the gate for him, and the sheep listen to his voice. He calls his own sheep by name and leads them out. When he has brought out all of his own, he goes on ahead of them, and his sheep follow him because they know his voice. But they will never follow a stranger; In fact, they will run away from him because they do not recognize a stranger's voice" (John 10:2–5).

---

[396] Matthew 15:24.
[397] Luke 19:10.

Those who followed him did so because they recognized his voice.[398] His message and his teachings were somehow familiar to them. In this passage, he probably had the "lost sheep of Israel" in mind. And thus, they probably recognized his voice because they were very familiar with what he had said through Moses and the prophets without the added burden of some of the traditions.

The second part of his mission is revealed in a subsequent statement.

> "I have other sheep that are not of this sheep pen. I must bring them also. They too will listen to my voice, and there shall be one flock and one shepherd" (John 10:16).

These "other sheep" were the non-Jewish flock. He seemed to indicate that these sheep were already his; he simply needed to gather them. Ultimately, the two flocks would be united. The gathering of the "other sheep" harkens back to God's statement to Abraham when he told him, "And all peoples on earth will be blessed through you."[399] God had already planned to bless the nations, those under the Noahic covenant who had rebelled against him at Babel, through Abraham's descendants, and those under the Abrahamic and Sinaitic Covenants. The obedience and sacrifice of one particular descendant[400] would be the key component of this plan.

The People of the Light

The Hebrew scriptures, or the Old Testament, are replete with prophetic utterances related to the Gentiles and their place in God's divine plan. Both as people groups and as nations, they are mentioned as beneficiaries of God's benevolence, as observers of God's handiwork regarding Israel,

---

[398] It is interesting how, later in the chapter, Jesus uses this metaphor to explain to his opponents the real reason they don't believe him, "You don't believe me because you are not my sheep" (John 10:26).
[399] Genesis 12:3.
[400] Galatians 3:16; Genesis 12:7, 13:15, 24:7.

and as participants in God's final kingdom age. In a previous chapter entitled "The Covenant with Abraham," specifically in the sections called "The Judgment of the Nations" and "The Divine Appointments Over the Nations," we saw that the nations of the world rejected God. Consequentially, they were, in a sense, exiled from God and placed under the oversight of subordinate heavenly beings known as the "the sons of God," (בני אלים—*bnei elim*).[401] Even though they suffered the judgment of God for their rebellious acts during the incident at Babel, there still was an everlasting covenant (ברית עולם—*brit olam*) in place—the Noahide Laws and the promise to never again be destroyed by a flood. As with God's covenant with Israel, the permanency of these binding relationships indicates that God was actively preserving both groups and intended for both to be recipients of his grace. His attention to both groups is rooted not only in their respective covenants but also in the fact that there is a remnant of the faithful in both groups. Regarding Israel, God awaits a future faithful generation of Israelites to ratify the final renewal of the covenant as a nation. However, there have always been individuals throughout its history who have internalized his laws. Sometimes God specifically addressed them through prophecy.

"Hear me, you who know what is right, you people who have my law[402] in your hearts" (Isa. 51:7).

Likewise, regarding the Gentiles, the apostle Paul states,

Indeed, when Gentiles who do not have the law, do by nature things required by the law, they are a law for themselves, even though they do not have the law, since they show that the requirements of the law are written on their hearts, their conscience is also bearing witness, and their thoughts now accusing, now even defending them (Rom. 2:14–15).

---

[401] Deuteronomy 32:8, variant reading from Dead Sea Scrolls, LXX, and other texts.
[402] Lit. "my Torah."

Nonetheless, the nations of the world as a whole remained estranged from God. If they were to return to their creator and submit to his appointed ruler, someone needed to show them the way home. Someone needed to bring to them the message of reconciliation. Someone needed to carry the light to a lost world.

Let us examine some of God's statements about the nations since that fateful day at Babel.

The Gentiles as beneficiaries of God's benevolence

About three hundred years after the Tower of Babel incident, God chose Abraham to be the conduit through whom he would restore his relationship with a fallen world.

> "Leave your country, your people and your father's household and go to the land I will show you.
> I will make you into a great nation
> and I will bless you;
> I will make your name great,
> and you will be a blessing.
> I will bless those who bless you,
> and whoever curses you I will curse;
> and all peoples of the earth
> will be blessed through you" (Gen. 12:1–3).

Later, when Abraham was walking with the person whom we now understand to be the Messenger Yahweh (מלאך יהוה—*malakh YHWH*), we read something similar.

> Then the LORD said, "Shall I hide from Abraham what I am about to do? Abraham will surely become a great and powerful nation, and all the nations on earth will be blessed through him. For I have chosen him, so that he will direct his children and his household after him to keep the way of the LORD by doing what is right and

just, so that the LORD will bring about for Abraham what he has promised him" (Gen. 18:17–19).

It is clear in both iterations of the promise that God had chosen Abraham and his descendants for a purpose, that the nations of the earth would be blessed.[403] These were the very nations that had rejected him hundreds of years earlier. If Abraham and his descendants kept "the way of the LORD by doing what is right and just," they would be illuminating the way back to God by demonstrating their faith in action. In essence, God's intention was to use them as the first flicker of light to the Gentiles.

Advancing to the end times, specifically the Messianic age, we again see God's benevolence to the Gentile nations in the form of peace, justice, and instruction.

> In the last days the mountain of the LORD's temple will be established as chief among the mountains; it will be raised above the hills and all nations will stream to it. Many peoples will come and say, "Come, let us go up to the mountain of the Lord, to the house of the God of Jacob. He will teach us his ways, so that we may walk in his paths." The law will go out from Zion, the word of the LORD from Jerusalem. He will judge between the nations and will settle disputes for many peoples. They will beat their swords into plowshares and their spears into pruning hooks. Nation will not take up sword against nation, nor will they train for war anymore (Isa. 2:2–4 [Mic. 4:1–3]).

This indeed speaks of a time when the estrangement between God and the nations will be in the past. They will seek his instruction and his counsel and experience a time of unprecedented peace.

---

[403] In Galatians 3:8, Paul refers to this promise as the time when God "announced the Gospel in advance."

The Gentiles as observers of God's handiwork regarding Israel

God brought the Israelites out of bondage in Egypt to fulfill a promise he had made to Abraham over four hundred years earlier. However, the manner in which he rescued them, using signs and wonders and defeating the Egyptian army, demonstrated that he was targeting a much larger audience. Egypt was a world empire. The emigration of 2 million people and a major blow to its military strength would send repercussions throughout the world. God's long-range goals were made clear when he told Pharaoh,

> Let my people go, so that they may worship me, or this time I will send the full force of my plagues against you and against your officials and your people, *so you may know that there is no one like me in all the earth*. For by now I could have stretched out my hand and struck you and your people with the plague that would have wiped you off the earth. But I have raised you up for this very purpose, *that I might show you my power and that my name might be proclaimed in all the earth* (Exod. 9:13–16, *italics added*).

The events of the Exodus were a proclamation to the nations. To this day, the story serves as evidence of God's power and who he is. It illuminated a dark world that had rejected him, reminding it that he had not gone quietly into the night, that he was a force to behold, and that he protected his own. Henceforth, he would continue to shine a light, revealing himself indirectly to the outside world by way of his relationship with his chosen nation.

Later, in his final words to the Israelites, Moses made it very clear that what God had done for them was not done in isolation. Even in giving the Israelites his Torah, God had a broader audience in mind. Regarding God's laws, he said,

Observe them carefully, for this will show your wisdom and understanding to the nations, who will hear about all these decrees and say, "Surely this great nation is a wise and understanding people." What other nation is so great as to have their gods near them the way the LORD our God is near us whenever we pray to him? And what other nation is so great as to have such righteous decrees and laws as this body of laws I am setting before you today? (Deut. 4:6–8).

If they had followed Moses's directive, the Israelites would have caught the attention of the Gentiles. Their wisdom and understanding would have been traced back to their laws. Their laws would have been traced back to the God who spoke to them at Mount Sinai. Their obedience to God's laws would have made them a beacon in the darkness with Jerusalem as its apex.[404]

Solomon perpetuated this idea during the dedication of Israel's first temple, in both his prayer to God and his subsequent blessing of the assembly.

As for the foreigner who does not belong to your people Israel but has come from a distant land because of your name–for men will hear of your great name and your mighty hand and your outstretched arm— when he comes and prays toward this temple, then hear from heaven, your dwelling place, and do whatever the foreigner asks of you, *so that all the peoples of the earth may know your name and fear you*, as do your own people Israel, and may know that this house I have built bears your name (1 Kings 8:41–43, *italics added*).

---

[404] This is why Jesus, when preparing his Jewish disciples to spread his message of an impending kingdom to the lost sheep of Israel, said, "You are the light of the world. A city on a hill cannot be hidden" (Matt. 5:14).

> May the LORD our God be with us ... May he turn our
> hearts to him ... may these words of mine ... be near to
> the LORD our God ... *so that all the peoples of the earth
> may know that the LORD is God and that there is no other"*
> (1 Kings 8:57–60, *italics added*).

However, it is interesting that the opposite response from the Israelites
would serve the same purpose. Moses anticipated their disobedience
and the many calamities that would befall them as a result. In response
to God's judgment upon his rebellious nation:

> All the nations will ask: "Why has the LORD done this
> to this land? Why this fierce, burning anger?" And the
> answer will be: "It is because this people abandoned
> the covenant of the LORD, the God of their fathers, the
> covenant he made with them when he brought them out
> of Egypt. They went off and worshipped other gods and
> bowed down to them, gods they did not know, gods he
> had not given them. Therefore the LORD's anger burned
> against this land, so that he brought on it all the curses
> written in this book (Deut. 29:24–27).

Even in their disobedience, the judgment and character of the God of
Israel would be acknowledged among the nations.

The Gentiles as participants in God's final kingdom age

It should be stated clearly that God's sovereignty over the nations of the
world was not relinquished when he delegated their oversight after the
Tower of Babel incident. He remains "Ruler of the Nations."[405] His reign
is on both a personal and a political level. He is attentive to the individual
and to the nation. Even on a national level, he adjusts his rulings with
respect to the recipient nation's repentance or rebelliousness.

---

[405] Psalm 22:27–28, 47:7–9.

"If at any time I announce that a nation or kingdom is to be uprooted, torn down and destroyed, and if that nation I warned repents of its evil, then I will relent and not inflict on it the disaster I had planned. And if at another time I announced that a nation or kingdom is to be built up and planted, and if it does evil in my sight and does not obey me, then I will reconsider the good I had intended to do for it" (Jer. 18:7–10).

Currently, there are righteous and unrighteous people in the world as well as righteous and unrighteous nations. Those individuals who are alive when the Son of Man appears at the end of this age will experience a purging. The unrighteous, or "weeds/tares" will be removed and the righteous, or "wheat," will remain to experience the literal earthly reign of David's descendant, Messiah Jesus.[406] Likewise, the nations at that time will experience a purging that will determine whether or not they will continue during the kingdom of God.

"When the Son of Man comes in his glory, and all the angels with him, he will sit on his throne in heavenly glory. All the nations will be gathered before him, and he will separate the people[407] one from another as a shepherd separates the sheep from the goats. He will put the sheep on his right and the goats on his left" (Matt. 25:31–33).

The remaining verses in Matthew 25 describe how the King, the Son of Man, will judge these two groups based on how they treated "my brothers." Truly, this will be an awesome day of reckoning on a political level. For those of us who might have forgotten, Jesus is Jewish. At that time, as the Son of Man, he will have come on the clouds of heaven, as the Son of David, he will have taken his rightful place on the throne,

---

[406] Matt. 13:24–30, 36–43, 24:36–51.
[407] The word "people" is not in the original Hebrew Matthew text, nor is it in the Greek translation. In each case, the word that is used should have been translated as "them," referring to the nations.

and now, as Ruler of the Nations, he is essentially saying to them, "Let's discuss how you have treated the Jewish people."

> "In those days and at that time, when I restore the fortunes of Judah and Jerusalem, I will gather all nations and bring them down to the valley of Jehoshaphat. There I will enter into judgment against them concerning my inheritance, my people Israel, for they scattered my people among the nations and divided up my land" (Joel 3:1–2).

The manner in which the various nations interacted with Israel and how they treated the Jews of the diaspora living in their midst will determine their participation in his kingdom. To one he will say, "Depart from me" and to the other "Come, you who are blessed by my Father; take your inheritance, the kingdom prepared for you since the creation of the world."[408]

The Person of the Light

The prophet Isaiah reveals to us that this "Light for the Gentiles (Nations)" will culminate in a person whom the Lord calls "my servant."[409] The "light" metaphor is used to represent many facets of his servant's

---

[408] We must understand this on a geopolitical level. Whether or not a specific nation continues to exist in the kingdom of God is not relevant to individual citizens of that nation. If the individual is righteous, albeit "wheat" and not "weed/tare," they will enter the kingdom of God regardless of God's decision about their nation. We can assume that those who are righteous but whose nation is not will become citizens of some nation that will be part of the kingdom of God.

[409] God uses the title "my servant" to refer to various people in the writings of Isaiah (i.e., to Isaiah 20:3, to Eliakim 22:20, to David 37:35, and to Jacob/Israel 41:8–9, 44:1–2, 44:21, 45:4). The other references (42:1, 42:19, 43:10, 49:6, 52:13) require the reader to use the context to discern the servant's identity. Even in Isaiah 49:3, where "my servant, Israel" is stated, the context (Isa. 49:5–7) clearly shows the servant working on behalf of Israel and therefore must be referring to someone acting as a representative for Israel.

influence. It refers to his laws and the justice he will bring to the nations. It refers to the justification and forgiveness he brings to those who accept his divinely appointed kingship. It refers to the enlightenment all this provides to those who were blind and captive without it and to their ultimate deliverance from darkness. He is identified earlier by Isaiah as "a great light," one born as a child and bearing the government on his shoulders, a descendant of David, "establishing and upholding it with justice and righteousness."[410] Later, he identifies him as "a shoot … from the stump of Jesse," indicating his right to the throne of David, and that he will judge the earth with justice and righteousness. Under his reign, even the animal kingdom will be at peace.[411]

The first reference in the book of Isaiah that identifies this servant figure as "a light for the Gentiles" is found in chapter 42. The structure of Isaiah 42:1–7 is interesting. In verses 1–4, God speaks "of" his servant, whereas in verses 5–7, he speaks "to" his servant.

> "Here is my servant, whom I uphold, my chosen one in whom I delight; I will put my spirit on him and he will bring justice to the nations. He will not shout or cry out, or raise his voice in the streets. A bruised reed he will not break, and a smoldering wick he will not snuff out. In faithfulness he will bring forth justice; he will not falter or be discouraged till he establishes justice on earth. In his law the islands will put their hope" (Isa. 42:1–4).

> This is what God the LORD says—he who created the heavens and stretched them out, who spread out the earth and all that comes out of it, who gives breath to its people, and life to those who walk on it:

> "I, the Lord, have called you in righteousness; I will take hold of your hand. I will keep you and will make you to be *a covenant for the people* and *a light for the Gentiles*, to

---

[410] Isaiah 9:2, 9:6–7.
[411] Isaiah 11:1–9.

open eyes that are blind, to free captives from prison and
to release from the dungeon those who sit in darkness"
(Isa. 42:5–7, *italics added*).

The second reference in the book of Isaiah states:

"It is too small a thing for you to be my servant to restore
the tribes of Jacob and bring back those of Israel I have
kept. I will also make you a *light for the Gentiles*, that you
may bring my salvation to the ends of the earth" (Isa.
49:6, *italics added*).

Paired with a subsequent verse, the titles are identical to what we read
in chapter 42.

I will keep you and make you to be *a covenant for the
people*, to restore the land and to reassign its desolate
inheritances (Isa. 49:8, *italics added*).

It is evident that this "servant" has a dual role: to bring justice and
salvation to the world at large and to uphold the covenant with Israel
regarding the land and the tribal inheritances.[412]

The servant has a special relationship with the God who is sending
him. He is favored ("in whom I delight"). He is hand-picked for the

---

[412] It is precisely this dual role that helps to resolve a dilemma in Isaiah 49. The
"servant" figure is not specifically identified in chapters 42 and 52–53 as he is in
other passages. This, of course, leads to speculation by scholars and laymen alike.
The usual candidates are Isaiah himself, Israel, or the Messiah. Here, in chapter 49,
the Isaiah option is unlikely since he did not "restore the tribes of Israel" or "bring
salvation to the ends of the earth." Oddly, the name "Israel" is actually stated in
Isaiah 49:3. However, it is illogical that the exiled nation of Israel will be used to
restore itself and the land to itself (Isa. 49:5–6, 49:8). It would appear that the title
"Israel" is being applied to an individual who represents the ideals of the nation,
who then, as the representative of the fallen, exiled nation will fulfill God's intended
role for them as a light for the Gentiles *and* to restore them to the promised land and
to reassign the tribal inheritances. Consequently, the better interpretation would
be to understand Isaiah 49 as being messianic.

task ("my chosen one"). He bears the very seal of authenticity as God's representative ("I put my spirit on him"). He was summoned for the listed purposes ("I ... called you"). He will be guided by God until the mission has been completed ("I will take hold of your hand. I will keep you ..."). His mission is directed at two particular groups: Israel and the Gentiles (nations). He will mediate the final renewal of God's covenant with Israel.[413] He will rule over the nations and implement his justice worldwide. With such a mission and such a calling, the servant could be none other than the mediator of the covenants himself, the divine messenger (מלאך—*malakh*)/אלהים—*elohim*), the Messenger Yahweh (מלאך יהוה—*malakh YHWH*). The Gospel writer Matthew quoted Isaiah 42:1–4, applying its early stages to the ministry of Jesus.[414]

The Gospel writer Luke recounted the story of Joseph and Mary's encounter with a man named Simeon. The story begins with the circumcision of Jesus. In observation of the Abrahamic Covenant,[415] it happened on the eighth day of his birth, at which time his parents gave him the Hebrew name Yeshua (ישוע), as the angel had instructed them.[416] Then, after completing the thirty-three-day process of purification, Mary proceeded to Jerusalem to make her post-childbirth offerings.[417]

> Now there was a man in Jerusalem called Simeon, who was righteous and devout. He was waiting for the consolation of Israel, and the Holy Spirit was upon him. It had been revealed to him by the Holy Spirit that he would not die before he had seen the Lord's Christ. Moved by the Holy Spirit, he went into the temple courts. When the parents brought in the child Jesus to do for him what the custom of the Law required, Simeon took him in his arms and praised God, saying:

[413] The phrase in Isaiah 42:6, "a covenant for the people" (לברית עם), is literally translated "a covenant of people" or "a covenant of a people," inferring a covenant with one people group in particular. This could only refer to Israel.
[414] Matthew 12:18–21.
[415] Genesis 17:12.
[416] Luke 2:21; Matthew 1:21; Luke 1:31.
[417] Leviticus 12:1–8; Luke 2:22–24.

"Sovereign Lord, as you have promised, you now dismiss your servant in peace. For my eyes have seen your salvation, which you have prepared in the sight of all people, a light for revelation to the Gentiles and for glory to your people Israel" (Luke 2:25–32).

Simeon's words, "a light for revelation to the Gentiles and for glory to your people Israel" harken back to the prophecies of Isaiah about "a light for the Gentiles" and "a covenant for the people." The Holy Spirit had made it clear to Simeon that he would live to see the person who would fill this role in God's plan for Israel and for the nations. That day in the temple courts, Simeon held the person that God, through Isaiah, had called "my servant."

Before leaving the Simeon story, we should take note of another part of his statement, "For my eyes have seen your salvation." Although Luke recorded his Gospel in Greek, Simeon most likely made his statement in Hebrew: "ראו עיני ישועתך" or "my eyes have seen your *yeshuah* (ישועה)." *Yeshua* (ישוע), or Jesus, and *yeshuah* (ישועה), or salvation, are simply the masculine and feminine forms of the same word. Is it more than coincidence that he is speaking of seeing the Lord's salvation while holding a child that bears that name? As Joseph was told in a dream, "You are to give him the name Jesus (ישוע—*yeshua*), because he will save (יושיע—*yoshea*) his people from their sins."[418]

The apostle John noted Jesus's use of the light metaphor when speaking of himself and his mission. Thus, John began his gospel by describing Jesus in this manner.

In him was life, and that life was the light of men. The light shines in the darkness, but the darkness has not understood it. There came a man who was sent from God; His name was John. He came as a witness to testify concerning that light, so that through him all men might

---

[418] Matthew 1:21. See George Howard, *Hebrew Gospel of Mathew* (Macon: Mercer University Press, 1995), 5.

believe. He himself was not the light; he came only as a witness to the light. The true light that gives light to every man was coming into the world (John 1:4–9).

In subsequent chapters, he documented Jesus's own words on the subject.

I am the light of the world. Whoever follows me will never walk in darkness, but will have the light of life (John 8:12).

While I am in the world, I am the light of the world (John 9:5).

You are going to have the light just a little while longer. Walk while you have the light, before darkness overtakes you. The man who walks in the dark does not know where he is going. Put your trust in the light while you have it, so that you may become sons of the light (John 12:35–36).

"When a man believes in me, he does not believe in me only, but in the one who sent me. When he looks at me, he sees the one who sent me. I have come into the world as a light, so that no one who believes in me should stay in darkness" (John 12:44–46).

God's light was intended for the whole world. Because of his relationship with the patriarchs and with Israel by way of their respective covenants, he would bring the light first to the Jewish people and then through the Jewish people. For now, Israel as a nation would not be the conduit for the light for the Gentiles. At least, not the Israel of the first century. As was discussed previously, that would have to wait for a future generation. However, as individuals, Jewish believers continued the work.

The Messengers of the Light

The New Covenant, or God's renewed covenant with Israel, was not ratified by the nation in the first century. As a nation, Israel did not accept Jesus as its Messiah. Even after his death and resurrection, the option remained viable as indicated by Peter.

> "Therefore let all Israel be assured of this: God has made this Jesus, whom you crucified, both Lord and Christ."
>
> When the people heard this, they were cut to the heart and said to Peter and the other apostles, "Brothers, what shall we do?"
>
> Peter replied, "Repent and be baptized, every one of you, in the name of Jesus Christ for the forgiveness of your sins. And you will receive the gift of the Holy Spirit. The promise is for you and your children and for all who are far off - for all whom the Lord our God will call" (Acts 2:36–39).
>
> "Now, brothers, I know that you acted in ignorance, as did your leaders. But this is how God fulfilled what he had foretold through the prophets, saying that his Christ would suffer. Repent, then, and turn to God, so that your sins may be wiped out, that times of refreshing may come from the Lord, that he may send the Christ, who has been appointed for you—even Jesus. He must remain in heaven until the time comes for God to restore everything, as he promised long ago through his prophets" (Acts 3:17–20).

The door of opportunity eventually closed for that generation. In 70 CE, the Romans destroyed both Jerusalem and the temple. Nonetheless, those in Israel who followed Jesus had become participants of the New Covenant as individuals. The Torah was written on their hearts, and they recognized God's appointed King and Messiah. Henceforth, as

Jewish believers in Jesus, they went forth to spread the message of their Lord as "ministers of a new covenant."[419] They were not bringing the New Covenant to the Gentiles as if to convert them to Judaism and its covenant. Rather, as ambassadors of their covenant (Sinaitic) with God, they would bring the truth of Jesus's death and resurrection, and consequently the forgiveness of sins, to the world at large, which was under its own covenant (Noahic) with God. Essentially, they would be ministers of one covenant bringing a "message of reconciliation" to a group of people under a different covenant. This is one of the many reasons our study of everlasting covenants is so important. The covenants are permanent, and they are applicable to particular groups of people.

Church history teaches that most of the apostles and disciples brought the Gospel to foreign lands. However, the most prominent one in the New Testament, having written much of it, is the apostle Paul. Bible students are familiar with the story of Saul, a student of the great Rabban Gamaliel I,[420] and a man with great religious zeal who received authorization to pursue and arrest those in Israel who believed in Jesus. One day, while on his way to Damascus to arrest the followers of Jesus, he encountered the risen Jesus. He was blinded by a flash of light and was subsequently given instructions to continue on to the city. Once in the city, he could do nothing but wait, unable to do anything without someone leading him by the hand. However, there was a follower of Jesus in Damascus called Ananias. The Lord spoke to him in a vision:

> "Go to the house of Judas on Straight Street and ask for a man from Tarsus named Saul, for he is praying. In a vision he has seen a man named Ananias come and place his hands on him to restore his sight." "Lord," Ananias answered, "I have heard many reports about this man and all the harm he has done to your saints in Jerusalem. And he has come here with authority from the chief

---

[419] 2 Corinthians 3:6.
[420] Acts 5:34, 22:3. See also Wikipedia, s.v. Gamaliel, en.wikipedia.org/wiki/Gamaliel.

priests to arrest all who call on your name." But the Lord said to Ananias, "Go! This man is my chosen instrument to carry my name before the Gentiles and their kings and before the people of Israel. I will show him how much he must suffer for my name" (Acts 9:11–16).

Saul was chosen specifically to carry the message of Jesus to the Gentile world and the Jewish people of the diaspora. As he went on his various missionary journeys, he always went to the synagogues first.[421] There, he reasoned with the Jews and the God-fearing Gentiles. At other times, he spoke to people who had little knowledge of the One True God. As the other ministers of the New Covenant undoubtedly had to do, he had to tailor the message to accommodate the understanding of his listeners.[422]

The Message of the Light

For their Jewish listeners, the message was simple. As Peter stated, "Repent and be baptized in the name of Jesus Christ," or Messiah Yeshua, and "repent and turn to God." Essentially, it was a call to accept God's appointed leader and to internalize the transgenerational covenant that God had made with their fathers at Sinai. Christian Bible students often overlook the fact that the Jewish followers of Jesus in the first century were zealous for the Torah.[423]

---

[421] Acts 13:5, 13:14–16, 13:26, 14:1, 17:2, 17:4, 17:10–12, 17:16–17, 18:4, 18:19, 19:8, 19:10.

[422] There are many stories, even from modern times, about missionaries having encountered a cultural element or a tradition among unreached peoples that served as a starting point for the Gospel. The missionaries were able to use these elements much in the same way the apostle Paul used the story of the "unknown god" when speaking to the Athenians (Acts 17:22–23). Sometimes the folklore of certain groups within the culture seemed to indicate previous direct involvement by God, to prepare them for the arrival of the missionaries. The books of Don Richardson are excellent sources for such encounters, specifically *Peace Child*, *Lords of the Earth*, and *Eternity in Their Hearts*.

[423] Acts 21:20. It is often overlooked that, in this section of Acts 21, Paul is taking part in a purification rite associated with a Nazirite vow (Num. 6:18; Acts 18:18,

For their Gentile listeners, they preached a somewhat similar "message of reconciliation." As Paul told his Corinthian readers,

> All this is from God, who reconciled us [Jewish believers] to himself through Christ and gave us the *ministry of reconciliation*: that God was reconciling the world to himself in Christ, not counting men sins against them. He has committed to us [Jewish believers] the *message of reconciliation*. We are therefore Christ's ambassadors [to the Gentiles], as though God were making his appeal through us. We implore you [Gentiles] on Christ behalf: Be reconciled to God. God made him who knew no sin to be sin for us [all of us], so that in him we might become the righteousness of God (2 Cor. 5:18–21, *italics and parenthetical gloss added*).

In order to understand this "message of reconciliation" to the Gentile world, we will begin by seeing how it applied to a special group of Gentiles, known in Judaism as "God-fearers." This group of people already believed in the God of Israel. They were not converts. They were not circumcised nor did they adhere to the whole law of Moses. They understood, via Genesis 9:1–17 and the Jewish tradition,[424] that they were obligated to keep the Noahide Laws. One such person lived in Caesarea—a Roman centurion named Cornelius.

> He and all his family were devout and God fearing; He gave generously to those in need and prayed to God regularly (Acts 10:2).

Acts 10 relates the story of how he was visited by an angel and told to summon the apostle Peter. Peter arrived in Caesarea four days later. Cornelius had invited many relatives and friends just to hear what Peter

---

21:24). This process would culminate with Paul making a sin offering, burnt offering, and fellowship offering (Num. 6:16–17) and placing the hair he grew during the time of the vow upon the fire of the altar.
[424] Tosefta Abodah Zarah 8:4; Talmud Sanhedrin 56a.

would tell them. Peter began his discourse by telling them things about Jesus that were already well-known.[425] Then he mentioned how he and others were witnesses to both his death and resurrection. But when he relayed the message that Jesus commanded him to preach, something happened.

> "He commanded us to preach to the people and to testify that he is the one whom God appointed as judge of the living and the dead. All the prophets testify about him that everyone who believes in him receives forgiveness of sins through his name" (Acts 10:42–43).

At that moment, the Holy Spirit came upon all who heard the message. Peter would later associate this event with what happened to the Jewish believers on the Day of Pentecost years earlier.[426] These believers at Cornelius's house simply needed the knowledge of who Jesus was. His death and resurrection qualified him to have the Messianic appointment "judge of the living and the dead." The evidence of the Holy Spirit at this event confirmed their reception of the message and their acceptance by God.

It may be noted that there is no mention of "Repent, for the kingdom of heaven it near."[427] Some might argue that the message of an impending kingdom had dissipated along with the hope of that generation of Israelites repenting as a nation. Also, this group of God-fearing Gentiles did not need to repent. That was done when they became "God-fearing." They simply needed the information about Jesus. This would be the case with many of the Gentiles encountered by the apostle Paul in his journeys. Upon entering a city, he would preach in the synagogues first. In most cases, there were God-fearing Gentiles in attendance.

The message of reconciliation to the non-God-fearing Gentiles would require repentance. With the average Gentile not being familiar with the

---

[425] Acts 10:34–38.

[426] Acts 15:8.

[427] Matthew 3:2, 4:17, 10:7; Mark 1:15.

Jewish scriptures, it would also require more background information. Such was the case with the apostle Paul when speaking to the Athenians. Upon his arrival in Athens, he followed his custom of attending the local synagogue and reasoned with the Jews and the God-fearing Greeks. He also spoke in the marketplace to anyone who happened to be there. Because his words upset some of the people there, he was brought to the local governing body, known as the Areopagus, to explain himself. There, he presented his message to a completely Gentile audience, one that was unfamiliar with the God of the Bible.

> The God who made the world and everything in it is the Lord of heaven and earth and does not live in temples built by hands. And he is not served by human hands, as if he needed anything, because he himself gives all men life and breath and everything else. From one man he made every nation of men, that they should inhabit the whole earth; and he determined the times set for them and the exact places where they should live. God did this so that men would seek him and perhaps reach out for him and find him, though he is not far from each one of us. "For in him we live and move and have our being." As some of your poets have said, "We are his offspring."
>
> Therefore since we are God's offspring, we should not think that the divine being is like gold or silver or stone - an image made by man's design and skill. In the past God overlooked such ignorance, but now he commands all people everywhere to repent. For he has set a day when he will judge the world with justice by the man he has appointed. He has given proof of this to all men by raising him from the dead (Acts 17:24–31).

Paul needed to clarify the God about whom he was speaking, namely the Creator. He even quoted Greek literature to facilitate their understanding.

Whether God-fearing or not, Paul knew the back story of his Gentile audience. He knew how the nations had abandoned God at the Tower of Babel incident and how they had drifted into idolatry. He knew how God had worked with Abraham to create his own nation through whom "all peoples on the earth would be blessed." But now the atonement needed to provide forgiveness had been made through the death of Jesus. His resurrection from the dead solidified his position as judge of the living and the dead. The existence of God-fearing Gentiles demonstrated that there already were Gentile believers throughout the world. However, the time for reconciliation between God and the nations had arrived. Having overlooked the ignorance of the past, "now he commands all people everywhere to repent."

The Mystery

We cannot leave the subject of a light for the gentiles without discussing a closely related topic—a topic that is identified by the apostle Paul as "the mystery." The Bible is clear that during the Messianic age, on a national or political level, the nation of Israel will have supremacy on the world stage. This is evident by many biblical passages such as the following:

> In the last days the mountain of the Lord's temple will be established as chief among the mountains it will be raised above the hills and all nations will stream to it (Isa. 2:2).

However, some Jewish traditions leading up to the first century CE taught Jewish superiority on an ethnic level, leading to the idea that Gentiles were somehow "unclean." This is not a concept taught by the Torah. In fact, just prior to the conquest of Canaan, Moses warned the Israelites about having an attitude of self-righteousness regarding their success over the current inhabitants.

After the Lord your God has driven them out before you, do not say to yourself, "The Lord has brought me here to take possession of this land *because of my righteousness.* "No, it is on account of the wickedness of these nations that the Lord is going to drive them out before you. *It is not because of your righteousness or your integrity* that you are going in to take possession of their land; But on account of the wickedness of these nations, the Lord your God will drive them out before you, to accomplish what he swore to your fathers, to Abraham, Isaac and Jacob. Understand, then that *it is not because of your righteousness* that the Lord your God is giving you this good land to possess, for *you are a stiff-necked people* (Deut. 9:4–6, *italics added*).

Nonetheless, this idea of Jewish ethnic superiority was present in the first century, and God needed to address it in order to advance the Gospel worldwide. This was important since his plan required the individual participants of the New Covenant, the Jewish followers of Jesus, to bring the light to the Gentiles. One very prominent person in this plan, the Apostle Peter, needed to "see the light" in this matter.

Fifty days after the resurrection of Jesus, on the anniversary of the giving of the Torah on Mount Sinai, the Holy Spirit descended on Jesus's followers in Jerusalem. Peter would be the one that day to explain to the crowds what had happened.[428] Sometime later, Philip[429] brought the message of Jesus to the Samaritans. However, they did not immediately receive the Holy Spirit. It was important that God's work with this unique group of people be associated with the work he had done in Jerusalem on Pentecost, and that it be placed under the leadership of the apostles. Consequently:

When the apostles in Jerusalem heard that Samaria had accepted the word of God, they sent Peter and John to

---

[428] Acts 2:14–41.
[429] Not the apostle Philip but, rather, the Grecian Jew (Acts 6:5).

them. When they arrived, they prayed for them that they might receive the Holy Spirit, because the Holy Spirit had not yet come upon any of them; they had simply been baptized into the name of the Lord Jesus. Then Peter and John placed their hands on them, and they received the Holy Spirit (Acts 8:14–17).

We can see a pattern developing here. In order to inhibit the interpretation that this was a separate religious movement, the presence of Peter and John helped to link this outpouring of the Holy Spirit with the first one. Consequently, the same thing must happen when the same Spirit would come upon the first group of Gentile believers. Before that could be done, the messenger of choice needed to understand that the intended recipients were not unclean in God's eyes.

Bible students are familiar with the story of the apostle Peter's dream in Acts 10. Around noon, while waiting for the meal to be prepared, Peter fell into a trance.

He saw heaven opened and something like a large sheet being let down to earth by its four corners. It contained all kinds of four-footed animals, as well as reptiles of the earth and birds of the air. Then a voice told him, "Get up, Peter. Kill and eat."

"Surely not, Lord!" Peter replied. "I have never eaten anything impure or unclean."

The voice spoke to him a second time, "Do not call anything impure that God has made clean" (Acts 10:11–15).

The vision occurred a total of three times. Immediately afterward, three men came to his door seeking an audience with him. They had been sent by a God-fearing man, a Roman soldier, requesting that Peter come and deliver God's message to them. Peter left with them the very next day. At some point between receiving the vision from God and his arrival at the home of this centurion named Cornelius, Peter realized that the vision had nothing to do with the Jewish dietary laws but, rather, with his traditional understanding that Gentiles were unclean. He mentioned this realization once after arriving and again during his speech to Cornelius and his guests.

> "You are well aware that it is against our law[430] for a Jew to associate with a Gentile or visit him. But God has shown me that I should not call any man impure or unclean" (Acts 10:28).

> "I now realize how true it is that God does not show favoritism but accepts men from every nation who fear him and do what is right" (Acts 10:34–35).

His speech that day did not include a call to repentance. There was no need, his Gentile listeners were already God-fearers. They simply needed to hear the rest of the story. For when Peter spoke of Jesus— "All the prophets testify about him that everyone who believes in him receives forgiveness of sins through his name"[431]—the Holy Spirit came upon all who heard the message. Apparently, they had believed. Just as apparent, some of the Jews who accompanied Peter had also maintained his previously held views about Gentiles.

> The circumcised believers who had come with Peter were astonished that the gift of the Holy Spirit had been poured out even on Gentiles (Acts 10:45).

It seemed that a mystery was being revealed to the Jewish believers of that day. Certainly, on a national level, Israel would always be preferred by God. The very first lines of the Sinai Covenant state:

---

[430] Peter is using the term "law" very generically here to include Jewish tradition and Rabbinic directives. The Torah does not specify such restrictions.
[431] Acts 10:43.

Now if you obey me fully and keep my covenant, then out of all *nations* you will be my treasured possession. Although the whole earth is mine, you will be for me a *kingdom* of priests and a holy *nation* (Exod. 19:5–6, *italics added*).

However, as individuals, believers everywhere would have equal status before God. The Old Testament, for the most part, contains the history of God's interactions with his chosen nation. The work of God in individuals worldwide was not given the same detail. This is why the apostle Paul states:

Surely you have heard about the administration of God's grace that was given to me for you, that is, *the mystery* made known to me by revelation, as I have already written briefly. In reading this, then, you will be able to understand my insight into *the mystery* of Christ, which was not made known to men in other generations as it has now been revealed by the Spirit to God's holy apostles and prophets. *This mystery* is that through the gospel *the Gentiles are heirs together with Israel, members together of one body, and sharers together in the promise in Christ Jesus* (Eph. 3:2–6, *italics added*).

I have become its servant by the commission God gave me to present to you the word of God in its fullness— *the mystery* that has been kept hidden for ages and generations but is now disclosed to the saints. To them God has chosen to make known among the Gentiles the glorious riches of *this mystery*, which is Christ in you, the hope of glory (Col. 1:25–27, *italics added*).

When Gentiles repent and believe in Jesus, they are willfully submitting to God's appointed leader, the divine messenger or מלאך (*malakh*)/אלהים (*elohim*), the Messenger Yahweh (מלאך יהוה—*malakh YHWH*). It should not be understood as something new or of recent origin. The ancient people of Israel, those who were circumcised in heart, followed the earthly Yahweh out of respect for the Creator Yahweh who sent him.[432] The same practice continues now that he has entered Adam's race and been given the name Jesus/Yeshua. Thus, believing Gentiles, having received "the light," are simply being brought into an existing program, a program with the same divinely appointed leader and a program with the same mediator between God and the individual. With this in mind, Paul warns the Gentile component of the church at Rome. Using the metaphor of believing Israel as an olive tree and the Gentiles as grafted branches, he says,

> If some of the branches have been broken off, and you, though a wild olive shoot, have been grafted in among the others and now share in the nourishing sap from the olive root, do not boast over those branches. If you do, consider this: You do not support the root, but the root supports you (Rom. 11:17–18).

Paul understood that his "ministry of reconciliation" contained within it a message of inclusion. Israel is God's chosen nation, but not all who are descendants of Jacob are part of God's Israel.[433] Only those who are circumcised in heart are considered his people.[434] In the same manner, all who believe in his Messiah, Jew and Gentile, would be included in his flock. Paul expounds upon this message of inclusion.

> In him we were also chosen, having been predestined according to the plan of him who works out everything in conformity the purpose of his will, in order that we, who were the first to hope in Christ [the Jewish believers], might be for the praise of his glory. And you [the Gentile believers] also were included in Christ when you heard the word of truth, the gospel of your salvation. Having believed, you were marked in him with a seal,

---

[432] This very idea is expressed by Jesus in John 5:19–30, especially v. 23.
[433] Romans 9:6–7.
[434] Romans 2:25–29.

the promised Holy Spirit, who is a deposit guaranteeing our inheritance until the redemption of those who are God's possession—to the praise of his glory (Eph. 1:11–14, *italics and parenthetical gloss added*).

Therefore, remember that formerly, you who are Gentiles by birth and called "uncircumcised" by those who call themselves "the circumcision" (that done in the body by the hands of men) – remember that at that time you *were separate from Christ, excluded* from citizenship in Israel and foreigners to the covenants of the promise, without hope and without God in the world. But now in Christ Jesus, you who once were far away *have been brought near through the blood of Christ* (Eph. 2:11–13, *italics added*).

Consequently, you are no longer foreigners and aliens, but fellow citizens with God's people and members of God's household (Eph. 2:19).

Although it was a mystery and not well documented in the Old Testament, the inclusion of the nations as people of God did not go unmentioned, for Zechariah tells us:

"Shout and be glad, O Daughter of Zion. I am coming, and I will live among you," declares the LORD. "*Many nations will be joined with the* LORD *in that day and will become my people*. I will live among you and you will know that the LORD Almighty has sent me to you. The LORD will inherit Judah and his portion in the Holy Land and will again choose Jerusalem. Be still before the LORD, all mankind, because he has roused himself from his holy dwelling" (Zech. 2:10–13 *italics added*).

Covenantal Responsibilities

The giving of the Holy Spirit to the different groups attests to the inclusiveness of the Gospel message. As individual believers in the sight of God, there is neither Jew nor Gentile, slave nor freeman, male nor female, we are all one in the Messiah.[435] However, all believers in general are under the everlasting covenant (ברית עולם—*brit olam*) of Noah and the Jewish believers, in particular, are under the everlasting covenant (ברית עולם—*brit olam*) of Sinai. Since much of the Sinai Covenant is applicable to the land of Israel and also dependent upon a functioning temple, the adherence to certain statutes is limited for those Jews living among the diaspora and those living before the erection of the third and final temple. Nonetheless, each covenant participant has his or her instructions for righteous living.

It would be advantageous for the reader to review the chapter entitled "The Covenant with Noah," specifically the section entitled "The Jerusalem Council." You might recall that the topic revolves around the responsibilities of the new Gentile believers. There was never any question or discussion about Jewish responsibilities. The Jewish believers were still under the Sinai Covenant. However, some claimed that the Gentile believers needed to convert, to be circumcised, and to follow the Law of Moses.[436] In the end, after Peter's testimony about the events at the house of Cornelius, the council concluded that the Gentile believers did not have to convert but would simply continue observing the Noahide laws.[437]

---

[435] Galatians 3:28; Colossians 3:11.
[436] Acts 15:5.
[437] Acts 15:19–31, 16:4, 21:20, 21:25.

QUESTIONS AND ANSWERS

Did Jesus offer the New Covenant to Israel?

As was discussed in the chapter entitled "The Covenant with Israel: In the Future," the New Covenant is simply the final renewal of the covenant that already existed between God and Israel. The Sinaitic Covenant is everlasting (עולם ברית—*brit olam*). The New Covenant mentioned by the prophet Jeremiah[438] should not be understood to be a replacement of the existing covenant but, rather, the internalization of that covenant by the "house of Judah" and the "house of Israel" as one nation. It was Moses's hope that Israel would one day "circumcise their hearts."[439] With that in mind, there was no need for Jesus to offer a replacement. He simply needed to call them to repentance and to teach them to internalize the existing covenant. His message to Israel during the time of his ministry was "Repent, for the kingdom of heaven is near." His Torah instruction during the so-called Sermon on the Mount was replete with the phrase "You have heard it said ... but I say to you," intended to make the ordinances of God the law within the hearts of his Jewish listeners. Had Israel at that time repented as a nation and internalized the Torah as taught by Jesus, their hearts would have been circumcised and the New Covenant would have been ratified.

Did Jesus institute/inaugurate the New Covenant?

This question is usually asked in reference to the following verses:

> This is my blood of the covenant, which is poured out for many for the forgiveness of sins (Matt. 26:28).

---

438 Jeremiah 31:31-34.
439 Deuteronomy 10:16, 30:6.

"This is my blood of the covenant, which is poured out for many," he said to them (Mark 14:24).

In the same way, after the supper he took the cup, saying, "This cup is the new covenant in my blood, which is poured out for you" (Luke 22:20).

In the same way, after supper he took the cup, saying, "This cup is the new covenant in my blood; do this, whenever you drink it, in remembrance of me" (1 Cor. 11:25).

The references, of course, are from a statement made by Jesus during the Last Supper where he used a cup of wine to explain the events that would occur over the next twenty-four hours, specifically his death by crucifixion. In each example, there is mention of a covenant and blood. We have seen in previous chapters that a blood sacrifice is often part of a covenant ceremony, even with a covenant renewal.[440] Whether the "forgiveness of sins" is actually stated, or the text simply says, "which is poured out for you (many)," forgiveness of sins is understood to be the goal. But it is the combination of "forgiveness of sins" and the topic of covenant that ties it back to the prophecy of Jeremiah.

"The time is coming," declares the LORD, "when I will make a new covenant with the house of Israel and the house of Judah ... For I will forgive their wickedness and remember their sins no more" (Jer. 31:31, 31:34).

It is imperative that we do not read two thousand years of church history back into the statements of Jesus. He was not talking about the church at this point in time. The church is a mixed group of people, Jew and Gentile, having the same Lord but each associated with their own covenants. As we seek to understand this intimate moment between Jesus and his disciples, we must be aware of the context, which was simple. A Jewish rabbi was speaking to his Jewish followers about Jewish things. The

---

[440] Joshua 8:30–35.

understanding of his words must be observed from a Jewish perspective. We must understand Jesus's words as they related to his mission to the nation of Israel. His mission was to call them to repentance because the kingdom of heaven was near. The opportunity to do so continued even after his death and persisted by way of the apostle's preaching.[441]

God fulfilled his promise to the nation to forgive their sins through the suffering of his servant.

> Surely he took up our pain and bore our suffering,
> yet we considered him punished by God, stricken by him, and afflicted.
> But he was pierced for our transgressions, he was crushed for our iniquities;
> the punishment that brought us peace was on him, and by his wounds we are healed.
> We all, like sheep, have gone astray, each of us has turned to our own way;
> and the Lord has laid on him the iniquity of us all (Isa. 53:4–6).

Jesus's suffering on the cross paid for the sins of the nation's past. God had fulfilled his promise through Jeremiah regarding the New Covenant and the forgiveness of their wickedness and sins. The slate was clean. The statement "This is the new covenant in my blood" essentially meant that his death would be the provision for the renewed ancient covenant between God and the nation. The resulting atonement meant there was/ is only one thing left to do: both parties must ratify the agreement, the covenant. God ratified it by offering it in the first place at Sinai and by sending the provision for the New Covenant in the form of his son. The only thing Israel needed to do to ratify it was to repent, as a nation.

Unfortunately, as in the past when the Israelites stood at the southern border of the promised land and were told to enter, they refused to do so. That generation was ultimately destroyed over a forty-year period,

---

[441] Acts 2:37–39, 3:17–20.

and the promise was left to a subsequent believing generation. Likewise, about forty years after Jesus made the provision for the covenant renewal through the sacrifice of his own body, the generation of his day passed away, as did the offer for that generation. Eventually, the Romans came and destroyed Jerusalem.

How did the decision of the Jerusalem Council relate to the preceding covenants?

Let's review the chapter entitled, "The Covenant with Noah," specifically the sections called "The Noahide Laws" and "The Jerusalem Council." The primary contention at the Council in Acts 15 was the issue of Gentile believers and their practices. Many Gentiles were coming to faith in Jesus due to the missionary work of people like the apostle Paul. One faction at the council believed that these God-fearers needed to convert to Judaism, to be circumcised and to follow the law of Moses. The other faction held to a view, which is documented in Talmud, that God-fearing Gentiles are only responsible for observing the Noahide Laws. The events at the home of Cornelius, as iterated by Peter during the exchange, helped to convince the majority that God had indeed accepted the Gentile believers in their current state. The decision of the council was documented and contained the rules of conduct that many understand to be derived from the Noahide Laws. In doing so, they recognized that Gentile and Jewish believers are followers of the same Lord and Messiah and, at the same time, respected the fact that one group is under the more general covenant and the other is under a more specific one.

To be clear, the entire world is under the Noahic Covenant. The Sinai Covenant came later but incorporated everything from the previous covenant. The former is generic to the whole world and the latter is specific to a nation.[442] This might be the reason for the comment made

---

[442] Some rabbinic sources have shown how the Torah can be used to further delineate the Noahide Laws. See WikiNoah, s.v., Subdividing the Seven

by James at the council. After listing the laws for the Gentile believers, he stated,

> For Moses has been preached in every city from the earliest times and is read in the synagogues on every Sabbath (Acts 15:21).

There were synagogues in much of the eastern hemisphere at that time. Apparently, he was suggesting that if the Gentile believers wanted the details, they could consult with the local Jewish community.

What did Paul mean when referring to people like himself as ministers of a new covenant and having a message of reconciliation?

The message of Jesus, to repent for the kingdom of heaven was near, went unheeded by the nation of Israel as a whole. Consequently, the offer would pass to a future generation who would repent and acknowledge his Messiahship. However, those in Israel who followed Jesus had become participants of the New Covenant as individuals. The Torah was written on their hearts, and they recognized God's appointed King and Messiah. Henceforth, as Jewish believers in Jesus, they went forth to spread the message of their Lord as "ministers of a new covenant."[443] They were not bringing the New Covenant to the Gentiles as if to convert them to Judaism and its covenant. Rather, as ambassadors of their covenant (Sinaitic) with God, they would bring the truth of Jesus's death and resurrection, and consequently the forgiveness of sins, to the world at large that was under its own covenant (Noahic) with God. Essentially, they would be ministers of one covenant bringing a "message of reconciliation"[444] to a group of people under a different covenant. The need for reconciliation harkens back to the event at the Tower of Babel.

Commandments, http://www.wikinoah.org/en/index.php/Subdividing_the_Seven_Commandments.
[443] 2 Corinthians 3:6.
[444] 2 Corinthians 5:18–21.

There, the people of that day, who would eventually become the nations of the world after the confusion of the languages, rebelled against God and were subsequently judged and alienated from him. The promise to Abraham that through him all the nations of the earth would be blessed[445] was really a preview of what would ultimately be the "message of reconciliation." In other words, it was the message that atonement for their sins had been made and that they should repent and return to their Creator by accepting his appointed ruler: Jesus.

What did Paul mean when he used the term "old covenant"?

The entire *third chapter of 2 Corinthians* is key to understanding the context of Paul's use of the term "old covenant" in 2 Corinthians 3:14. It begins with Paul defending his ministry by suggesting that the changed lives he left at Corinth were sufficient evidence of the authenticity of his office and his message. In verse 6, he identifies himself as a minister of a new covenant. As mentioned in previous questions and in previous chapters, we understand the New Covenant to be a renewal of the Sinai Covenant at a time when the nation of Israel will finally circumcise their hearts, internalize the Torah, and recognize Jesus/Yeshua as the Messiah and rightful heir to the Davidic throne. So to understand this chapter of 2 Corinthians, we must be aware that the term "old covenant" in verse 14 and the term "new covenant" in verse 6 are referring to the same covenant. The difference between the two is about where they are written. One is engraved only in stone, and the other is written on the heart. The first one is now considered "old" because the second one has been introduced.

> By calling this covenant "new," he has made the first one obsolete; And what is obsolete and aging will soon disappear (Heb. 8:13).

---

[445] Genesis 12:3.

Since the contents of the covenants are the same and one is the final renewal of the other, what really is "obsolete and aging" is the medium upon which they are written. Ultimately:

> "I will put my law in their minds and write it on their hearts. I will be their God, and they will be my people. No longer will a man teach his neighbor, or a man his brother, saying, 'Know the LORD,' because they will all know me, from the least of them to the greatest," declares the LORD (Jer. 31:33–34).

Consequently, the "old covenant" is simply noninternalized Torah.

What does the term "better covenant" mean?

The phrase "better covenant" is found in Hebrews 7:22. It is part of a long discourse that spans Hebrews 4:14–10:18, which ties together the topics of the Melchizedekian priesthood of Jesus, the New Covenant, and the specific duties of the high priest on the Day of Atonement.

Jesus's priesthood is superior to that of the Levitical priesthood. The primary argument revolves around the frequency of the atonement ritual for each. For the Levitical High Priest, he entered the Holy of Holies once a year.[446] The author concludes that this demonstrated that the atonement was not only temporary but was unable to "clear the conscience of the worshiper."[447] Regarding the priesthood of Jesus, he entered the heavenly sanctuary with his own blood once and for all.[448] Because he "lives forever, he has a permanent priesthood. Therefore he is able to save those who come to God through him, because he always lives to intercede for them."[449]

---

[446] Hebrews 9:7; Leviticus 16:34.
[447] Hebrews 9:8–10.
[448] Hebrews 9:24–26.
[449] Hebrews 7:24–25.

This permanent priest who serves in the heavenly sanctuary is the mediator of the New Covenant.[450] This covenant, which is the final renewal of the Sinai Covenant, is for the united houses of Israel and Judah,[451] for that day when God will write his law upon their hearts.[452]

Even though this high priest and mediator of the New Covenant has provided the means for the forgiveness of Israel's[453] sins in anticipation of that time, the fact remains that his priesthood is in the order of Melchizedek.[454] This means that his priesthood, unlike Aaron's, is not limited to the Jewish people or the nation of Israel. Jesus's priesthood is all-encompassing, affecting Jew and Gentile, because the Melchizedekian priesthood predates the Abrahamic, Sinaitic, Davidic, and Levitic covenants.[455] The writer of Hebrews also provides his own reasoning regarding the superiority of Melchizedek's priesthood over that of Aaron's.[456]

The permanency of Jesus's priesthood due to his resurrection, the superiority of his priesthood due to its Melchizedekian nature, and the efficacy of his atonement upon all peoples of the world is the reason that the renewed Sinai Covenant (New Covenant) with which it is associated is said to be "better."

> But the ministry Jesus has received is superior to theirs
> as the covenant of which he is mediator is superior to the
> old one, and it is founded on better promises (Heb. 8:6).

It should be noted that the superiority of Jesus's priesthood does not imply the eradication of the Aaronic priesthood any more than the covenant with which it is associated implies the eradication of the everlasting covenant (ברית עולם—*brit olam*) of Sinai. During the reign

---

[450] Hebrews 9:15.
[451] Hebrews 8:8; Jeremiah 31:31.
[452] Hebrews 8:10; Jeremiah 31:33.
[453] Jeremiah 31:34.
[454] Hebrews 5:6–10, 6:20, 7:11, 7:15, 7:17; Psalm 110:4.
[455] Genesis 14:18–20.
[456] Hebrews 7:4–10.

of the Messiah on the earth in the final age, both will be preserved. In a subsequent question, we will demonstrate how the Jewish followers of Jesus during the first century were zealous for the Torah and participated in the sacrificial system during the years after Jesus's resurrection and up to the destruction of the temple in 70 CE.

If "it is impossible for the blood of bulls and goats to take away sins," why were they required?

During the long discourse on the Melchizedekian priesthood of Jesus, the New Covenant, and the specific duties of the high priest on the Day of Atonement, the writer of Hebrews makes an interesting comment.

> The law is only a shadow of good things that are coming - not the realities themselves. For this reason it can never, by the same sacrifices repeated endlessly year after year, make perfect those who draw near to worship. If it could, would they not have stopped being offered? For the worshippers would have been cleansed once for all, and would no longer have felt guilty for their sins. But those sacrifices are an annual reminder of sins, because it is impossible for the blood of bulls and goats to take away sins (Heb. 10:1–4).

The context of the preceding chapters in Hebrews and the terms "year-to-year" and "annual" in the text above indicate that the author has the Day of Atonement in mind. However, the last clause about the blood of bulls and goats has general application. If these sacrifices, the Yom Kippur/Day of Atonement offering and the general sin offering,[457] do not take away sins, then why were they required?

The Day of Atonement was an annual opportunity for the Israelites to reset their relationship with God. The atonement one received was not for sins committed against another human being. This day was

---

[457] Leviticus 4:1–5:13.

set aside to specifically address one's sins against God.[458] Note that the sacrifice of the goat in the temple that day was not sufficient to take away sins without the conscious participation of the penitent Israelite. Those who participated were required to fast and to rest.[459] Without these two actions, the Yom Kippur sacrifice did not provide atonement for nonparticipants. The abstinence of food and work on the part of the participants demonstrated to God that they were cognizant of their sinful state and their need for forgiveness from a merciful God. The atonement was acquired by the intermediary function of the priesthood and the humble and obedient response of the repentant sinner.

Likewise, the sin offering did not bring atonement automatically. It must be clarified that this offering was applicable to individuals who had sinned unintentionally.[460] Those who sinned intentionally were subject to prosecution. This clarification is important because it is one of the many ways in which God has incorporated into his law the recognition of "mens rea,"[461] or the absence thereof. The point of this is that a sin offering made by a person who intentionally did what God had forbidden would not receive atonement. Therefore, it is obvious that the sacrificed bull, goat, lamb, or bird did not have the ability to "take away sins." As above, the atonement was acquired by the intermediary function of the priesthood and the humble and obedient response of the repentant sinner. Once the offender became aware of his sin, he faced his responsibilities to the offended party and subsequently confessed/addressed his sin before God by presenting a sin offering.

This brings us to an important observation. There were occasions when sin offerings were required, but the person offering it had not sinned. Two such examples can be found in the ordination ceremony of the priests and the ceremony following the completion of a Nazirite vow. In each example, there were three offerings: the sin offering, the burnt

---

[458] Mishnah Yoma 8:9.

[459] Leviticus 23:27–28, 23:32.

[460] Leviticus 4:2, 4:13, 4:22, 4:27, 5:2–4.

[461] Latin for "guilty mind." This is a legal principle whereby the state of mind of the accused party is considered when determining culpability.

offering, and the fellowship offering. They were to be presented in that order.[462] The sin offering was for atonement. The burnt offering was for dedication. The fellowship offering was communal: parts were burned at the altar, other parts were given to the officiating priest, and the reminder was eaten by the person who offered it and his invited guests. The reason for the order of the offerings on these occasions becomes obvious. Before one can fellowship with God's people unhindered, he needs to submit himself wholly to God. Before one can submit or dedicate himself to God, he needs to recognize his sinfulness. In these two examples, the people involved had not committed some specific unintentional sin that would require a sin offering. One group was actually preparing for ordination and a life of service to God. The other had just completed an avowed period of service to God. Nonetheless, a sin offering was a required part of the process. If "it is impossible for the blood of bulls and goats to take away sins," as the writer of Hebrews states, then apparently these sin offerings were required to facilitate a person's need to acknowledge a previously unknown sin or to simply confess/acknowledge one's general sinfulness before a merciful God.

Did Paul offer sacrifices in the temple?

Yes. He offered sin offerings, burnt offerings, and fellowship offerings. He was Jewish. He was under the Law/Torah. And, like most of the Jews of his day who were followers of Jesus, he was zealous for the laws that had been given to his people by God.[463]

After Paul left Corinth for the final time, he stopped at Cenchrea … for a haircut.[464] This is notable because it was during one of his missionary journeys and, most importantly, it was "because of a vow he had taken." Most likely, this was his practice after all his missionary trips. Also, before going home to Syria, he wanted to stop in Jerusalem. Why? There

---

[462] Exodus 29:10–34; Leviticus 8:14–36; Numbers 6:16–17 (also note the order of the sin and burnt offering in Num. 6:11).
[463] Acts 21:20.
[464] Acts 18:18.

were probably two reasons. As an observant Jew, he was required to make a pilgrimage to Jerusalem three times a year.[465] Because of the distance between the Holy City and Philippi, he had been unable to go there during the Feast of Unleavened Bread.[466] Now he was hoping to make it there by Pentecost.[467] But he was not going to Jerusalem simply for the required pilgrimage. He needed to go there to complete his vow, bringing his trimmed hair with him. Before moving on, let us review the vow that Paul had taken that required him to cut his hair and bring it to Jerusalem.

The Nazirite vow is explained in Numbers chapter 6. It begins this way.

> The LORD said to Moses, "Speak to the Israelites and say to them: 'If a man or woman wants to make a special vow, a vow of separation to the LORD as a Nazarite, he must abstain from wine and other fermented drink and must not drink vinegar made from wine or from other fermented drink. He must not drink grape juice or eat grapes or raisins. As long as he is a Nazarite he must not eat anything that comes from the grapevine, not even the seeds or the skin.

> During the entire period of his vow of separation *no razor may be used on his head.* He must be holy until the period of his separation to the LORD is over; *He must let the hair of his head grow long.* Throughout the period of his separation to the LORD he must not go near a dead body. Even if his own father or mother or brother or sister dies, he must not make himself ceremonially unclean on account of them, because the symbol of his separation to God is on his head. Throughout the period of his separation he is consecrated to the LORD'" (Num. 6:1–8, *italics added*).

---

[465] Exodus 23:14–17, 34:22–24.
[466] Acts 20:6.
[467] Acts 20:16.

When the Bible records the individuals who were Nazirites, the writer might use the actual term, or simply say that "no razor will touch his head," or "he is to never take wine or other fermented drink."[468] The prophet Samuel, Samson, and John the Baptist were separated for God's service from the womb and considered Nazirites from birth. Everyone else would simply make a Nazarite vow for a designated length of time (i.e., the time it would take to spread the Gospel to the Gentiles during a missionary journey). In such cases, there was a closing ceremony.

> Now this is the law for the Nazarite when the period of his separation is over. He is to be brought to the entrance of the tent of meeting. There he is to present his offerings to the LORD: a year old male lamb without defect for a burnt offering, a year old ewe lamb without defect for a sin offering, a ram without defects for a fellowship offering, together with their grain offerings and drink offerings, in a basket of bread made without yeast - cakes made of fine flour mixed with oil, and wafers spread with oil.

> The priest is to present them before the LORD and make the sin offering and the burnt offering. He is to present the basket of unleavened bread and is to sacrifice the ram as a fellowship offering to the LORD, together with its grain offering and drink offering.

> Then at the entrance to the tent of meeting, the Nazarite must shave off the hair that he dedicated. He is to take the hair and put it in the fire that is under the sacrifice of the fellowship offering (Num. 6:13-18).

The period of one's separation from God by way of a Nazirite vow concludes with three offerings; sin, burnt, and fellowship. This unique ceremony concludes with the very hair grown during the time of separation being placed on the fire of the altar. It could be concluded

---

[468] Judges 13:5; 1 Samuel 1:11; Luke 1:15.

that the time spent in separation and service to God, as represented by the Nazirite's hair, is the primary offering in view here since it is the last item to be placed in the fire.

The apostle Paul concluded such a vow upon his arrival in Jerusalem. There he joined four other men who had taken a similar vow.[469] This was done specifically to demonstrate by example to onlookers that there was no truth to the rumor that he had been turning Jews away from Judaism[470] and that he himself was, in fact, Torah-observant.[471]

> The next day Paul took the men and purified himself along with them. And he went to the temple to give notice of the date when the days purification would end and the offerings would be made for each of them (Acts 21:26).

The offerings mentioned in this passage refer to the ones required to conclude the Nazirite vow. Even during his trial before the governor Felix, Paul stated that he had returned to Jerusalem to present offerings.[472] And thus, Paul did participate in the sacrificial system mandated by God for the Jewish people by way of an everlasting covenant (ברית עולם—*brit olam*).

Was Paul "under the law"?

Yes. Paul was Jewish and was therefore under the everlasting covenant (ברית עולם—*brit olam*) established at Sinai for the nation of Israel and the Jewish people. As an individual, he participated in the New (Renewed) Covenant because of his faith in Jesus as Israel's Messiah.[473]

---

[469] Acts 21:23–24.

[470] Acts 21:21.

[471] Acts 21:24.

[472] Acts 24:17.

[473] At first glance, 1 Corinthians 9:20 seems to contradict this, where Paul supposedly states, "though I myself am not under the law". This phrase is not found in numerous manuscripts. In light of the fact that Paul was proud of his Jewish

The phrase "under the law" has come to mean something in Christian theology—that is, different from its use in the apostolic writings or so-called New Testament. In most cases, the phrase "the law" means the Torah, which in turn means the Sinai Covenant. Moses equated the terms "covenant" and "Ten Commandments."[474] He even called the tablets upon which the commandments were written "the tablets of the covenant."[475] The phrase "under the law" should not be understood by Christians as referring to their state of existence prior to believing in Jesus. If someone is Jewish or a convert to Judaism, they are under the law, the Torah, the Sinai Covenant. Everyone else is under the Noahic Covenant and is subject to the Noahide laws.

What did Jesus mean when he spoke about abolishing/fulfilling the law?

(The following is taken almost verbatim from my book *The Mountain Yeshiva*.)[476]

This question originates from the following statement made by Jesus:

> Do not think that I have come to abolish the law or the prophets. I have not come to abolish these things but to fulfill them (Matt. 5:17, NET).

Let us begin with a general understanding of the Sinai Covenant. After the Exodus, the Israelites traveled to Mount Sinai, where Moses ascended to meet with the Lord. The Lord said to him,

---

heritage, boasted about being a student of Gamaliel the Elder, made the required pilgrimages to Jerusalem, made a Nazarite vow and presented the associated sin/burnt/fellowship offerings, it is more conceivable that this phrase was not written by Paul but introduced later.

[474] Deuteronomy 4:13.

[475] Deuteronomy 9:11.

[476] James R. Ward, *The Mountain Yeshiva* (Maitland: Xulon Press, 2020), 17–20.

"Thus you will tell the house of Jacob, and declare to the people of Israel: 'You yourselves have seen what I did to Egypt and how I lifted you on eagles' wings and brought you to myself. And now, if you will diligently listen to me and keep my covenant, then you will be my special possession out of all the nations, for all the earth is mine, and you will be to me a kingdom of priests and a holy nation.' These are the words that you will speak to the Israelites" (Exod. 19:3–6, NET).

There was a deal on the table. If they obeyed his commands (that is the meaning of "keep my covenant"), they would be his treasured possession over all the other nations. They consented.[477] God provided them with the initial terms of the covenant.[478] That is why this section is subsequently called, "The Book of the Covenant."[479] After Moses recounted the terms of the covenant, the people consented again,[480] essentially ratifying it. This would be done again forty years later on the Plains of Moab when the commands in Deuteronomy 12:26 were added and then ratified by the next generation.[481] The Ten Commandments, written on the tablets, became the primary document of the covenant between God and Israel.[482]

Now let us consider God's statement late in the book of Leviticus.

If, however, you do not obey me and keep all these commandments—If you reject my statutes and abhor my regulations so that you do not keep all my commandments and you break my covenant—I for my part will do this to you: I will" (Lev. 26:14–16, NET).

---

[477] Exodus 19:7–8.
[478] Exodus 20:1–23:33.
[479] Exodus 24:4, 24:7.
[480] Exodus 24:3, 24:7.
[481] Deuteronomy 26:16-19, 29:1.
[482] Deuteronomy 4:13.

In spite of this, however, when they are in the land of their enemies, I will not reject them and abhor them to make a complete end of them, to break my covenant with them, for I am the Lord their God. I will remember for them the covenant with their ancestors whom I brought out from the land of Egypt in the sight of the nations to be their God. I am the Lord (Lev. 26:44–45, NET).

Notice God's usage of the phrase "break my covenant." For the Jews, this meant to disobey, reject, and abhor his statutes and regulations. The Jewish people have a covenant relationship with God. Breaking a commandment is not simply a sin or a crime. It is a violation of an agreement. This is why there are so many references in the Torah, where certain violations resulted in an individual being "cut off" from their people. Their choice of behavior could cause them as individuals to be viewed by God as being outside the covenant group.[483]

After all the disciplinary action listed in Leviticus 26:16–43, God stated in verses 44 and 45, "I will not reject them and abhor them to make a complete end of them, to break my covenant with them." The apostle Paul no doubt had this in mind when he wrote the following:

In regard to the gospel they are enemies for your sake, but in regard to election they are dearly loved for the sake of the fathers. For the gifts and the call of God are irrevocable (Rom. 11:28–29, NET).

So how does this relate to Jesus's statement in Matthew 5:17? The passages above from Leviticus 26, specifically verses 15 and 44 contain the phrase "break my convent." In each case, the word used in the Hebrew text is פרר (parar). This word is usually used regarding agreements. It is generally not used for the "breaking" of a commandment. When someone under the Sinai Covenant does not observe these specific commands, it is an affront against the unique relationship that God has with his covenant

---

[483] Romans 2:25–29, 11:17–24.

nation. Therefore, this specific kind of disobedience is understood to be "breaking the covenant."

This information becomes relevant when we read Matthew 5:17 from the original Hebrew.[484] Remember to read from right to left.

תורה	להפר	שבאתי	תחשבו	אל
Torah	break-to	came-I-that	think	not

The word that Jesus used for "break" is הפר, which is the infinitive form of פרר (*parar*). It is the same word used in the passages we studied in Leviticus 26. Just as the Messenger Yahweh (מלאך יהוה—*malakh YHWH*) told Moses, "I will not reject them and abhor them to make a complete end of them, to break my covenant with them," so now the one person who is simultaneously understood to be

- the earthly LORD (Gen. 19:24) who sent fire and brimstone from the LORD in heaven,
- the messenger of the LORD who spoke with Moses from the bush (Exod. 3:2) and delivered the Torah,
- the physical being seen by Moses and the elders (Exod. 24:9–11),
- the individual who spoke with Moses face-to-face (Exod. 33:11, Num. 12:8),
- the only person ever to be seen as the physical representative of God (John 1:18), and
- the Son of Man (Dan. 7:13)

is now, once again, on a mountain with his disciples, confirming to them that he has not come to break the Torah, the covenant, but, rather, to uphold or to make good on it. Making good on his covenant, God will either reward the nation of Israel with blessings for obedience or punishment for disobedience just as he described in Leviticus 26.

---

[484] George Howard, *Hebrew Gospel of Mathew* (Macon: Mercer University Press, 1995), 17.

Jesus's message was, "Repent, for the kingdom of heaven is near." The time had come for Israel to circumcise their hearts. He would not break his covenant with them by "rejecting them and abhorring them to make a complete end of them."[485] Rather, he would uphold the covenant by sending them blessings or curses depending on their response to his call to repent.

What does Paul mean when he said, "Christ is the end of the law"?

This phrase is found at the end of the following passage.

> Brothers, my heart's desire and prayer to God for the Israelites is that they may be saved. For I can testify about them that they are zealous for God, but their zeal is not based on knowledge. Since they did not know the righteousness that comes from God and sought to establish their own, they did not submit to God's righteousness. Christ is the end of the law so that there may be righteousness for everyone who believes (Rom. 10:1–4).

The manner in which this phrase, "end of the law," is regularly translated causes the reader to falsely conclude that the Law, or Torah or Sinai Covenant, has ended. Throughout this book, we have carefully covered the Bible's use of the phrase, "everlasting covenant" (עולם ברית—*brit olam*). It is assumed that the reader comprehends the meaning of the word "everlasting." Thus, the discerning Bible student will interpret a passage like Romans 10:4 in context with the whole Bible. The idea of the law, or the Torah, or the Sinai Covenant, terminating in the context of God's covenants being everlasting is untenable. Consequently, we are forced to examine the translation.

---

[485] Leviticus 26:44.

The phrase "Christ is the end of the law" (τελος γαρ νομου χριστος) contains the word τελος (*telos*). This word can certainly mean "end" or "termination" depending on the context. However, consider its use in the following verses.

> You have heard of Job's perseverance and have seen what the Lord finally brought about [το τελος κυριου—lit. "the end/goal of the Lord"] (Jas. 5:11, *Greek and literal translation added*).

> The goal [τελος] of this command is love, which comes from a pure heart and a good conscience and a sincere faith (1 Tim. 1:5, *Greek translation added*).

> For you are receiving the goal [τελος] of your faith, the salvation of your souls (1 Pet. 1:9, *Greek translation added*).

The word τελος (*telos*) carries with it the additional meaning of "goal" or "purpose." This is documented in the Greek/English lexicons. Thus, the decision by the translators to use the phrase "Christ is the end of the law" instead of the more accurate "Christ is the goal/purpose of the law" demonstrates theological bias. Since the covenants are everlasting, the law/Torah has not ended but, rather, its goal/purpose was to point to the Messiah.

Will the sacrificial system be revived with the New Covenant and Third Temple?

The way in which one answers this question will be determined by their understanding of the word "everlasting," as in everlasting covenant (עולם ברית—*brit olam*), and their particular hermeneutical discipline. In other words, do you understand God's covenants to be permanent, and what is your method of interpreting scripture (literal vs. nonliteral). These appear to be the deciding factors in both Christianity and Judaism. I understand the Bible literally, except where there is an obvious use of symbols, metaphors, parables, or similes and the interpretation of such things is provided in the text. Thus, when the New Covenant is finally ratified by Israel as a nation and the final temple has been constructed, I expect the sacrificial system to resume.

The concept of Jewish followers of Jesus participating in a fully functional temple, bringing the prescribed offerings, in a post-crucifixion and post-resurrection era is a fact of history. As was discussed in a previous question, Paul returned to Jerusalem after his last missionary journey for two reasons: He wanted to fulfill a Torah requirement to be there on Pentecost[486] and to complete his Nazirite vow by making the corresponding offerings and placing his recently cut hair on the fire of the altar.[487]

> The next day Paul and the rest of us went to see James, and all the elders were present. Paul greeted them and reported in detail what God had done among the gentiles through his ministry. When they heard, this they praised God. Then they said to call: "You see, brother, how many thousands of Jews have believed, and all of them are zealous for the law" (Acts 21:18–20).

These thousands of Jews who followed Jesus had not stopped practicing Judaism. Rather, they had become even more Torah-observant. As the story continues in Acts 21, they encouraged Paul to join four other men who were about to complete their Nazirite vows, by participating in the purification process and making the prescribed offerings. Consequently, if this is the way the Messianic community exercised their faith after the death and resurrection of Jesus, it is not difficult to imagine these practices resuming in the kingdom age after the final temple is constructed.

The prophet Ezekiel had much to say about the third and final temple. In chapters 40–48 of his book, the prophet was taken by God by way

---

486 Acts 20:16; Exodus 23:14–17.
487 Acts 18:18; Numbers 6:18.

of a vision to Jerusalem, to the time of the final temple. He saw the various walls, gates, rooms, and even the altar. He was accompanied the whole time by a man with a measuring rod who gave him very precise measurements of everything he saw. Later, he was also given the details of the new land allotments for each tribe. In the midst of these chapters are details of the rooms where the priests are to prepare the animals for sacrifice,[488] where they are to consume the priestly portion of the offerings,[489] the required sacrifices to consecrate the newly built altar,[490] and other details regarding the sacrifices and holy days.[491] These details help to demonstrate that the future temple will be fully functional, complete with an Aaronic priesthood (specifically the descendants of Zadok) and burnt, sin, and fellowship offerings.

Finally, there is one Jewish holiday that will be celebrated by all the nations during the time of God's kingdom on earth. The prophet Zachariah tells us:

> Then the survivors from all the nations that have attacked Jerusalem will go up year after year to worship the King, the LORD Almighty, and to celebrate the Feast of Tabernacles. If any of the peoples of the earth do not go up to Jerusalem to worship the King, the LORD Almighty, they will have no rain. The LORD will bring on them the plague he inflicts on the nations that do not go up to celebrate the Feast of Tabernacles. This will be the punishment of Egypt and the punishment of all nations that do not go up to celebrate the Feast of Tabernacles (Zech. 14:16–19).

During the Feast of Tabernacles, seventy bulls in addition to numerous other animals were sacrificed over an eight-day period.[492] Some

---

[488] Ezekiel 40:38–43.
[489] Ezekiel 42:13.
[490] Ezekiel 43:13–27.
[491] Ezekiel 45:13–46:24.
[492] Numbers 29:12–40.

understand the seventy bulls to correspond to the seventy nations depicted in the table of nations in Genesis 10. If this is true, the prophetic importance of worldwide participation in this holiday would be greatly diminished if it were not for a functioning temple and priesthood.

BIBLIOGRAPHY

Banks, Todd S. Beall and William A. *Old Testament Parsing Guide.* Nashville, TN: Broadman and Holman Publishers, 2000.

Barker, Margaret. *The Great Angel: A Study of Israel's Second God.* Louisville: Westminster/John Knox Press, 1992.

Benner, Jeff A. *The Ancient Hebrew Language And Alphabet.* College Station, TX: Virtualbookworm.com Publishing Inc., 2004.

Biblia Hebraica Stuttgardensia. Germany, Stuttgard: German Bible Society, 1997.

Charles, R. H. *The Apocrypha and Pseudepigrapha of the Old Testament.* Oxford: Clarendon Press, 1913.

Etheridge, J. W. *The Targums of Onkelos and Jonathan Ben Uzziel.* 1862. http://www.targum.info/pj/psjon.htm.

Francis Brown, S. R. Driver, and Charles Briggs. *The Brown-Driver-Briggs Hebrew and English Lexicon.* Peabody, MA: Hendrickson Publishers, Inc., 2001.

Heiser, Michael S. *The Unseen Realm: Recovering the Supernatural Worldview of the Bible.* Bellingham, WA: Lexham Press, 2015.

Hirsch, Rav Samson Raphael. *The Hirsch Chumash: Sefer Bemidbar.* New York: Feldheim Publishers, 2007.

—. *The Hirsch Chumash: Sefer Shemos.* New York: Feldheim Publishers, 2005.

—. *The Hirsch Chumash: Sefer Vayikra.* New York: Feldheim Publishers, 2000.

Horton, Michael. *Introducting Covenant Theology.* Grand Rapids, MI: Baker Books, 2006.

Howard, George. *Hebrew Gospel of Matthew.* Macon: Mercer University Press, 1995.

Josephus, Flavius. *The Works of Josephus.* Translated by William Whiston. Peabody, MA: Hendrickson Publishers, 1987.

Judeus, Philo. *The Works of Philo.* Translated by C. D. Yonge. Peabody, MA: Hendrickson Publishers, 2006.

Kasdan, Rabbi Dr. Barney. *Matthew Presents Yeshua, King Messiah - A Messianic Commentary.* Clarksville, MD: Lederer Books, 2011.

Merkle, Benjamin L. *Discontinuity to Continuity: A Survey of Dispensational and Covenantal Theologies.* Bellingham, WA: Lexham Press, 2020.

Midrash Rabbah Volume I. Translated by Rabbi Dr. H. Freedman and Maurice Simon. London: The Soncino Press, 1961.

Novum Testamentum Graece. Germany, Stuttgard: German Bible Society, 2001.

Proclamation 5956—Education Day, U.S.A., 1989 and 1990.. n.d. https://www.presidency.ucsb.edu/documents/proclamation-5956-education-day-usa-1989-and-1990 (accessed 2022).

Robertson, O. Palmer. *The Christ of the Covenants.* Phillipsburg, NJ: Presbyterian and Reformed Publising Co., 1980.

Rydelnik, Michael, and Edwin Blum,. *The Moody Handbook of Messianic Prophecy.* Chicago: Moody Publishers, 2019.

Ryrie, Charles C. *Dispensationalism.* Chicago, IL: Moody Publishers, 2007.

Sarna, Nahum M. *The JPS Torah Commentary: Genesis.* Philadelphia: The Jewish Publication Society, 1989.

Segal, Alan F. *Two Powers in Heaven.* Brill, Leiden, The Netherlands: Brill Acedemic Publishers Inc., 2012.

Septuaginta. Germany: Stuttgard: German Bible Society, 1979.

Stern, David H. *Jewish New Testament Commentary.* Clarksville, Maryland: Jewish New Testament Publications, Inc., 1992.

The Holy Bible, New International Version. Colorado Springs, CO: International Bible Society, 1984.

The Jewish Encyclopedia. n.d. www.jewishencyclopedia.com (accessed 2022).

The Sefaria Library. n.d. www.sefaria.org/Book_of_Jubilees?tab=contents (accessed 2022).

The Sefaria Library. n.d. www.sefaria.org/Mishneh_Torah,_Foundations_ of_the_Torah. (accessed 2022).

The Sefaria Library. n.d. www.sefaria.org/Targum_Jonathon_on_ Genesis (accessed 2022).

The Sefaria Library. n.d. www.sefaria.org/The_Testaments_of_the_ Twelve_Patriarchs (accessed 2022).

The Tosefta Volume Two. Translated by Jacob Neusner. Peabody, Massachusetts: Hendrickson Publishers, 2002.

Ward, James R. *The Mountain Yeshiva.* Maitlan, FL: Xulon Press, 2020.

Zahavy, Tzvee. *Halakhah.com (based on the classic Soncino translation).* n.d. https://www.halakhah.com. (accessed 2022).

BIBLICAL AND
EXTRABIBLICAL INDEX

1

1 Chronicles
1:43-50 .90
2:13-14 109
3:17-19 116
6:1-3 130
10:1-7 .109
11:1-3 .109
17:10-14 110
17:24 110
23:28-32 132
24:1-19 132
25:1-31 132
26:1-19 132
26:20-32 132
28:2-3, 5-6 110
28:4 118
28:9 111
29:23 107
1 Corinthians
8:1-13 17
9:20 234
10:14-33 17
11:25 222
15:24 . . . . .29, 166
1 Enoch
20:1-8 .168
68:1 119
82:1 119
108:1 119
1 Kings
8:41-43 197
8:57-60 198
11:11 133
11:11-13 113

11:26 108
11:29-39 108
15:3-4 .114
16:2 108
1 Peter
1:9 240
1 Samuel
1:11 233
8:7-9 107
8:10-18 107
9:15-17 107
10:20-24 107
11:14-15 107
13:13 108
13:14 109
16:6-12 109
16:12 109
16:14-23 109
18:5 109
24:1-22 110
26:1-25 110
28:13-15 155
31:1-6 .109
1 Timothy
1:5 240
2:5 190

2

2 Chronicles
6:15-16 112
7:12, 17-18 112
13:5 138
16:9 . . . . .26, 154
18:18 153
21:6-7 .114

2 Corinthians
  3:6 .207, 225
  3:14 226
  5:18-21 .225
  5:18-21a 209
2 Kings
  8:18-19 .114
  9:1-13 108
  17:15 133
  23:32, 37 115
  24:8-17 .150
  24:9 115
  24:10-11, 15 115
  24:17-18 116
  25:2 150
  25:27-30 116
2 Samuel
  2:1-7 109
  4:1-12 109
  5:1-5 109
  7:11-13, 15-16 110
  7:16 110
  7:26 110
  23:5 111

A

Acts
  2:14-41 .213
  2:37-39 .223
  2:38-39 .206
  3:17-20 . . . . .206, 223
  5:34 207
  6:5 213
  8:14-17 .214
  9:11-16 .208
  10:2 209
  10:11-15 214
  10:28 215
  10:34-35 215
  10:34-38 210
  10:42-43 210
  10:43 215
  10:45 215
  13:5, 14-16, 26 208

  14:1 208
  15:1 14
  15:2 14
  15:5 . . . . .14, 219
  15:7 15
  15:7-11 15
  15:8 210
  15:16-18 .15
  15:19 15
  15:19-31 219
  15:20 16
  15:21 225
  16:4 219
  17:2, 4, 10-12, 16-17 208
  17:22-23 208
  17:24-31 211
  18:4, 19 .208
  18:18 . . . . 208, 231, 241
  19:8, 10 .208
  20:6 232
  20:16 . . . . .232, 241
  21:18-20 241
  21:20 . . . . .208, 231
  21:20, 25 219
  21:21 234
  21:23-24a 234
  21:24 209
  21:24b 234
  21:26 234
  22:3 207
  24:17 234
Amos
  3:2 59
  9:11-12 15

C

Colossians
  1:15-16 .174
  1:25-27 .216
  2:10 .29, 166
  3:11 219

D

Daniel
  7:9-10, 13-14 180
  7:13 238
  9:21 169
Deuteronomy
  1:2 76
  2:14-15 79
  4:6-8 197
  4:12, 15 .153
  4:13 . . . . 64, 235, 236
  4:13-14 64
  4:15-16 .175
  6:4-5 80
  6:6-9 144
  7:1-6 86
  9:4-6 213
  9:9, 11 64
  9:11 235
  10:4 64
  10:16 . . . . 80, 144, 221
  11:1 . . . . .35, 64
  12:1 . . . . 9, 68, 88, 133
  12:1-26:19 141
  13:1-18 65
  15:1-6 68
  15:12-18 .68
  15:19-20 .68
  16:18-20 .68
  17:2-7 65
  17:12 68
  17:14-20 106
  19:15-21 .65
  19:16-21 .68
  21:18-21 .65
  22:1-4 68
  23:19-20 .68
  24:7 65
  24:10-13 .68
  24:17-18 .68
  24:19-22 103
  25:5-10 97
  26:1-17 68
  26:16-19 . . . . 9, 85, 141, 236

  27:1-8 86
  27:1-26 32
  27:6-7 10
  29:1 . . . . 79, 122, 141, 236
  29:2-15 9
  29:2-30:20 141
  29:9-15 . . . . .86, 141
  29:14 .21, 62
  29:16-28 141
  29:24-27 198
  30:1 .80, 141
  30:1-10 .143
  30:2, 6, 10 80
  30:6 . . . . 80, 144, 221
  30:14 80
  31:9-13 . . . . .122, 144
  31:19-22 .27
  31:24 80
  31:24-25 122
  31:25-26 .80
  31:28 80
  32:7-9 27
  32:8b 32, 193
  32:9 28

E

Ephesians
  1:11-14 .218
  1:21 166
  1:21, 6:12 29
  2:11-13 .218
  2:19 218
  3:2-6 216
  6:12 166
Exodus
  1:8-9 53
  1:11-14 54
  2:11-15 59
  2:15-16 40
  2:23-24 60
  3:1 40
  3:1-6 158
  3:2 .165, 238
  3:6 . . . . .60, 177

3:7 177
3:7-8 60
3:15 52
3:17 52
4:16 155
6:2-5 61
6:4, 8 52
6:6-8 61
6:14-20 57
7:7 . . . . .56, 59
9:13-16 196
12:37 60
12:40 . . . . .53, 57, 58
14:19 162
14:19, 24 165
19:1 . . . . .20, 37, 61
19:1-6 9
19:3-6 . . . . 62, 85, 236
19:5 71
19:5-6 216
19:7-8 .9, 236
19:8 . . . . .69, 74
19:11, 16 63
19:22, 24 128
20:1-23:33 .236
20:3 65
20:3-17 64
20:4-6 65
20:7 65
20:8-11 .65, 71
20:12 65
20:13 65
20:14 65
20:15 65
20:16 65
20:17 65
21:1 65
21:1 22:20 65
21:2 66
21:2-11 65
21:12 . . . . .65, 66
21:12-13 4
21:12-36 . . . . .66, 67
21:15,17 65
21:16 65

21:28 66
21:28-32 4
22:1-17 67
22:18-20 67
22:21-22 68
22:21-23:19 68
22:25-27 68
22:28 .68, 155
22:29a 68
22:29b-30 .68
23:1-3 68
23:4-5 68
23:6-9 68
23:14-17 . . . . 68, 232, 241
23:20-21 178
23:20-33 . . . . .68, 75
23:21 177
23:23-33 86
24:1 170
24:3 9
24:3, 7 . . . . 69, 74, 236
24:3-8 .19, 21
24:4-6 9
24:4, 7 . . . . 64, 80, 129, 236
24:4-8 86
24:7 9
24:9-11 . . . . .175, 238
24:12 129
25:1-31:18 129
27:21 134
28:1 128
28:30 . . . . .107, 153
28:43 134
29:4-9 . . . . .126, 129
29:9 136
29:10-34 231
29:28 135
29:45 155
30:20-21 136
31:12-17 . . . . .7, 70
31:14 65
32:1-34:35 140
32:1-35 179
32:7-10 74
32:9-10 140

32:11-14 .75
32:26-29 125
33:11 238
34:1, 28 75
34:10-16 .75
34:18-26 .75
34:22-24 232
34:27 . . . . 75, 140, 179
34:28 64
35:2 65
40:12-15 132

Ezekiel
1:2 150
16:44-58 149
16:59-63 149
20:10-12 .70
20:12 7
20:20 70
34:22-31 148
37:21-28 149
40:38-43 242
42:13 242
43:13-27 242
45:13-46:24 242

Ezra
3:2 116

G

Galatians
2:9 13
3:8 195
3:16 .46, 192
3:28 219
5:3 14

Genesis
1:1 155
1:28 2
1:29 2
1:30 2
4:10-11 18
5:21-24 .119
6:2 28
6:2, 4 154
6:11 4

6:17 1
6:18 1
8:14 . . . . .1, 19
8:15-19 10
8:20 . . . . .19, 86
8:20-22 . . . . .10, 20, 21
9:1 2
9:1-7 .11, 21
9:1, 7 26
9:1-17 10
9:2-4 2
9:4 . . . . .12, 18
9:5 66
9:6 66
9:6a 3
9:7 2
9:8 20
9:8-11 6
9:8-17 .5, 86
9:12 . . . . .20, 38
9:12-13 6
9:14-16 7
9:16 . . . . .11, 18, 29
9:17 8
9:20 10
9:26 35
10:8-10 25
10:10-11 .25
10:22 96
10:25 23
11:1 27
11:2, 8 25
11:3-4 25
11:5 26
11:31-12:3 50
12:1-3 . . . . .31, 194
12:2 . . . . .34, 40, 75
12:2-3 87
12:3 . . . . 30, 152, 192, 226
12:7 . . . . 32, 87, 192
13:6 34
13:14-17 . . . . .33, 35
13:15 192
13:16 159
14:18-20 228

14:19-20 34
15:1-9 37
15:5 . . . . 35, 159
15:9-10, 17-19 86
15:13 . . . . .21, 57, 58
15:13-16 36
15:16 . . . . 54, 57, 130
15:18 36
16:4 90
16:7-14 .159
17:1 41
17:1-27 7
17:6 89
17:12 203
17:18, 20-21, 24-25 40
17:21 47
17:23-27 .43
18:1-2 153
18:3-8 153
18:14 41
18:16-33 100
18:17-19 195
18:20-21 26
19:21-22 100
19:24 . . . . .170, 238
19:36-38 102
21:2 90
21:5 41
22:1 44
22:2, 15-18 19
22:7 45
22:11-18 161
22:17 159
22:18 30
24:7 192
24:62 48
25:1-2 90
25:1-4 40
25:12-18 .40
25:20 48
25:22 48
25:23 48
25:26 55
25:26b 48
25:27-34 .49

25:29-34 .90
26:5 . . . . .35, 64
27:1-29 .90
27:41 49
27:41-28:2 122
28:12-13 153
28:16-19 51
28:20-21 50
28:20-22 . . . . .90, 125
28:21-22 128
31:3 50
31:3, 13 .122
32:1, 3 . . . . .26, 154
32:29 . . . . .165, 177
32:30 165
33:18 93
33:18-19 123
34:5 123
34:6-23 .124
35:1 93
35:3, 7 51
35:8 93
35:11 90
35:27 128
36:31-43 90
38:7 96
38:9 97
38:11 97
38:12 97
38:26 98
41:32 33
41:46 56
47:9 56
47:9, 28 .55
47:28 56
48:15-16 165
49:1 91
49:8, 10 . . . . .91, 94
49:10 105
50:4-14 .53
50:26 56

H

Haggai
2:23 116
Hebrews
4:14-5:10 34
5:6-10 228
6:20 228
7:1-9:28 34
7:4-10 228
7:11, 15, 17 228
7:22 227
7:24-25 227
8:6 . . . . 190, 228
8:8 228
8:10 228
8:13 226
9:7 227
9:8-10 227
9:15 . . . . 190, 228
9:24-26 227
10:1-4 229
12:24 190
Hosea
2:18-23 146
3:4-5 118
8:4 108
13:11 107

I

Isaiah
2:2 212
2:2-4 195
2:13 155
4:2 117
6:1 153
9:2, 6-7 201
9:6 . . . . 167, 188
11:1-9 201
11:6-9 147
20:3 200
22:20 200
37:35 200
41:8-9 200
42:1-4 . . . . 201, 203
42:1, 19 200
42:5-7 202
42:6 . . . . 145, 203
43:10 200
44:1-2, 21 200
45:4 200
49:3 . . . . 200, 202
49:5-6, 8 202
49:6 . . . . 200, 202
49:8 202
49:8-9 145
51:7 193
52:13 200
53:4-6 223
54:9-10 142
55:3b 146

J

James
5:11 240
Jasher
16:11 34
Jeremiah
18:7-10 199
22:24 116
23:5-6 117
29:1-23 150
30:22 155
31:31 228
31:31-32 151
31:31-34 221
31:31, 34 222
31:33 228
31:33-34 . . . . 152, 227
31:34 228
32:1 117
33:14-21 117
33:14-22 138
33:15 117
33:25 134
Job
1:6 154
1:6, 2:1 . . . . 26, 28
1:6-11 44

2:1	154	8:10-11	24
2:1-5	44	8:12	24
Joel		9:1	24
3:1-2	200	10:21, 27	25
John		10:29	24
1:1	176	10:34	24
1:1-2	187	11:13-12:15	30
1:4-9	205	11:17-23	30
1:18	153, 176, 180, 188, 238	12:19-21	31
5:19-30	217	12:22	31
5:46	190	12:25	120
6:69	188	12:26-27	121
8:12	205	14:1-9	37
8:58	178	14:10	37
9:5	205	14:19	86
10:2-5	191	15:1	44, 57, 58
10:16	192	16:13	37
10:22-36	186	17:15	44
10:26	192	17:15-16	44
10:33	176	19:15-30	49
10:34-36	188	21:10	121
12:35-36	205	21:23-25	48
12:44-46	205	30:2	123
17:11	189	30:5-6	124
Josephus	26, 174	31:3-5	94
Joshua		31:12	94
2:2-3	100	31:13-15	127
2:4-7	100	31:18-19	124
2:8-11	101	31:18-20	94, 105
2:12-14	101	31:26-30	93
2:17-21	101	31:27	127
3:1	79	31:31	105
6:22-25	101	32:1	125
6:25	101	32:2-10	128
8:30-31	10	32:4	51
8:30-35	21, 32, 87, 222	32:5	51
13:1-24:33	88	45:13	56
24:20	88	45:15-16	122
24:25	88	46:7	53
Jubilees		46:8	53, 56
6:1	1, 20	46:8-11	46
6:11	20	46:9	54, 56
6:18	20	46:9, 11	53
7:20-39	120	47:1	56
8:10	25	47:1, 2	54

48:1 .57, 58
Judges
1:1-3:6 .88
1:19, 21, 27-35. 88
2:1-5 161
6:11-24 163
13:5 233
13:15-23 165
13:17-18 177

L

Leviticus
4:1-5:13 229
4:2, 13, 22, 27. 230
5:2-4 230
6:18 135
7:34 135
7:36 135
8:5-13 .126
8:6-9, 13 129
8:14-36 231
10:1-5 .132
10:9 136
10:11 122
10:15 135
12:1-8 .203
16:34 227
17:11, 14. 3
18:16 97
19:9-10 103
20:10 65
23:14, 21, 41. 68
23:22 103
23:27b-28, 32. 230
24:3 134
24:8 73
24:8-9 .136
25:25-55 104
26:3-8 .147
26:12 155
26:14-16 236
26:16-43 237
26:27,33 150
26:44 239

26:44-45 . . . . .142, 237
Luke
1:15 233
1:31 . . . . .189, 203
2:21 203
2:22-24 203
2:25-32 204
3:21-22 157
3:23-38 116
4:34 188
5:17-26 184
7:27 190
9:1-2 183
9:1-6 183
9:32 156
10:1-24 183
10:17-22 183
19:10 191
22:20 222

M

Malachi
2:4-5, 8 133
3:1 190
Mark
1:10-11 157
1:15 210
1:24 188
2:1-12 .184
6:6-12 .183
9:6 156
14:24 222
Matthew
1:3-6 102
1:11-12 116
1:12 116
1:21 . . . . 189, 203, 204
3:2 210
3:16-17 157
4:17 210
5:14 197
5:17 . . . . .235, 237
9:1-8 184
10:1-16 183

10:5-6	191
10:7	210
11:10	190
12:18-21	203
13:24-30, 36-43	199
15:24	191
17:5-6	156
24:36-51	199
25:31-33	199
26:28	221
26:63-66	181

Micah

4:1-3	195
5:2	182, 190

Mishnah

Bava Kamma 8:1	66
Sanhedrin 4:5	18
Yoma 8:9	230

N

Numbers

1:2-16	100
1:3	60
2:32-33	60
6:1-8	232
6:1-21	164
6:11	231
6:13-18	233
6:16-17	231
6:18	208, 241
9:13	74
10:8	137
12:6	153
12:8	153, 238
13:1-14:45	179
13:4-16	100
14:26-35	179
16:1-11	128
18:1-7	125, 137
18:19	135, 138
18:22-23	137
20:16	162
22:1	79
23:19	151

25:1-3	130
25:4-5	131
25:6-9	131
25:10-13	132
26:1-4	77
29:12-40	242
31:8	90
31:16	130
35:9-28	4
35:27	18

P

Philippians

3:5	14
Philo	173

Proverbs

15:3	26, 154

Psalms

22:27-28	198
47:7-9	198
50:16	133
82:1	155, 166, 185, 187
82:1-7	29
82:6	187
89:19-37	112
105:8-11	72
110:4	34, 228
132:11-12	113

R

Revelation

4:5, 5:6	26

Romans

2:14-15	193
2:25-29	144, 217, 237
9:6-7a	217
10:1-4	239
11:1, 29	72
11:17-18	217
11:17-24	237
11:28-29	237

Ruth

1:16-17	103
2:11-12	104

4:18-22 98
4:21-22 104

T

Talmud
  Nedarim 32b 34
  Sanhedrin 38b 171
  Sanhedrin 56a 12, 209
  Sanhedrin 56b 17
Targum Jonathon
  Gen 3:8 .172
  Gen 18:17 172
Testaments of the Twelve Patriarchs
  Benjamin 9:1 122
  Dan 5:6 .122
  Judah 10:1 96
  Judah 10:1-7 95
  Judah 10:6 97
  Judah 11:1-5 96
  Judah 17:5-6 93
  Judah 22:1-3 92
  Judah 22:2-3 105
  Levi 1:3-5 123
  Levi 4:2- 5:2 124

Levi 5:3 .124
Levi 6:10 124
Levi 8:2-18 126
Levi 9:1-2 126
Levi 9:3-4 127
Levi 9:5 .128
Levi 9:6-8 128
Levi 10:5, 14:1 122
Levi 12:5 123
Naphtali 4:1 122
Simeon 5:4 122
Zebulon 3:4 122
Tosefta
  Abodah Zarah 8:4 . . . . .12, 209
  Abodah Zarah 8:6 12

Z

Zechariah
  2:10-13 .218
  3:8 117
  4:10 26
  6:12 117
  14:16-19 242

Printed in the United States
by Baker & Taylor Publisher Services